The Rights of the Child

Stockholm Studies in Child Law and Children's Rights

VOLUME 7

The titles published in this series are listed at *brill.com/sscl*

The Rights of the Child

Legal, Political and Ethical Challenges

Edited by

Rebecca Adami, Anna Kaldal and Margareta Aspán

BRILL | NIJHOFF

LEIDEN | BOSTON

The Library of Congress Cataloging-in-Publication Data is available online at https://catalog.loc.gov
LC record available at https://lccn.loc.gov/2023005449

Typeface for the Latin, Greek, and Cyrillic scripts: "Brill". See and download: brill.com/brill-typeface.

ISSN 2405-8343
ISBN 978-90-04-51115-6 (hardback)
ISBN 978-90-04-51116-3 (e-book)

This book is printed on acid-free paper and produced in a sustainable manner.

Contents

Preface – Contrasting Perspectives on Child Rights

Rebecca Adami

The tensions dealt with in this volume between legal, political, and ethical perspectives on children's rights foreground limited notions of justice, equality, and non-discrimination of children. The purpose is to set several perspectives in conversation with each other, both in terms of how national law relates to the Convention on the Rights of the Child, CRC, and how children's rights can be developed and understood from a philosophical standpoint. This book is dedicated to students, researchers, and professionals working with children's rights. The chapters, each of which concludes with a cross-disciplinary response, can be read separately or as a whole, starting with either the contributions from Legal scholarship (Part 1) or the more philosophical discussions on children's rights and justice (Part 2), depending on one's field of interest.

This volume addresses legal gaps in the codified ethics of children's rights, and discusses several of the principles of the CRC that require political policy developments on a societal level. The *first part* of the volume addresses the complexity, critique, and ambiguity of how to interpret and understand children's rights and the four core principles of the CRC,[1] on different topics and from various angles. Chapter 1 explores ways in which we can understand the right to have rights for Swedish children abroad, prevented from returning to Sweden, and how children's right to agency and residence, recognized in Swedish law as well as in international human rights, is implemented. Chapter 2 furthers the notion of welfare rights for children in Sweden; legal challenges are analyzed in how underlying assumptions and conditions limit the fulfilment of the right to an adequate standard of living for the most economically vulnerable children. According to the CRC, children have participation rights and Chapter 3 discusses limitations of such rights in proceedings in custody cases and child abuse cases in Sweden due to the questioning of children's competence and credibility. The assumption that children in conflict with the law are treated unbiased in Sweden is problematised through two legal case studies in Chapter 4. Lastly, in terms of children's right to quality healthcare,

1 The four principles are the right to participation, the best interests of the child, the right to life and development, and the principle of non-discrimination and equality.

Chapter 5 discusses the vulnerable conditions of children as developing to be taken seriously in treatment advancements in paediatric care.

The *second part* of the volume addresses how we can understand the notions of justice, equality, and non-discrimination when it comes to children, and the role that ethical judgements play in theoretical and methodological studies on children's human rights. Chapter 6 develops theoretical tools to analyse intersecting prejudice against children including age-based forms of discrimination; Chapter 7 concerns new ways of conceptualizing participation; Chapter 8 seeks to develop a more justice-oriented understanding of children's human rights during childhood; Chapter 9 adds the problematization of what epistemic justice could mean in terms of children's right to culture and the arts; and finally, Chapter 10 raises critical reflections on the methodological and ethical considerations in ethnographic research dealing with children in vulnerable situations.

Many of the examples touched upon in the chapters deal with the situation in Sweden, discussing Swedish law and court cases. Sweden can be seen in an international perspective as an interesting case of a welfare democracy in which the social and economic structure is supposed to create a safety net for children in vulnerable situations. Sweden ratified the CRC in 1990 without any reservations, and in January 2020 the convention was incorporated into Swedish law. What this will mean more concretely remains to be seen. Even though Sweden is often described as one of the world's most child-friendly countries, the challenges when it comes to fulfilling and realizing children's rights are many. This volume deals with some of them. Although the focus to a large extent is on Sweden, the discussions and findings in this book are of broader interest as the realization of children's rights entails inherent challenges in any legal system.

This work would not have been possible without the close editorial collaboration that merged different fields of research on children's rights including law, child and youth studies, and education. We would like to thank two foundation bases in Stockholm – *Justitierådet Edvard Cassels stiftelse* and *Stiftelsen Juridisk Fakultetslitteratur*, as well as the Vice Chancellor at Stockholm University for funding workshops and open access costs. Further, we want to extend our thanks to all the contributors in the volume and to language reviewer Peggy Oskarsson. We want to extend a special thanks to Pernilla Leviner, Professor in Public Law and Director of the Stockholm Centre for the Rights of the Child, Faculty of Law, Stockholm University, in her role as General Editor for the *Stockholm Studies in Child Law and Children's Rights* for her valuable comments on the manuscript, together with Johanna Schiratzki, Guest Professor in Family Law at Stockholm University. Last, but not least, we wish to extend our thanks to Laura Lundy, Professor of International Children's Rights at the School of Education at the Queen's University of Belfast, and Noam Peleg, Senior Lecturer at the Faculty of Law and Justice, University of New South Wales, for their invaluable international lenses on this work.

Abbreviations

CEDAW	Convention on the Elimination of All Forms of Discrimination against Women
CERD	International Convention on the Elimination of All Forms of Racial Discrimination
CFR	Charter of Fundamental Rights of the European Union
CRC	United Nations Convention on the Rights of the Child
CRPD	Convention on the Rights of Persons with Disabilities
ECHR	Convention for the Protection of Human Rights and Fundamental Freedoms/ European Convention on Human Rights
ECOSOC	United Nations Economic and Social Council
EU	European Union
HCCH	Convention of 19 October 1996 on Jurisdiction, Applicable Law, Recognition, Enforcement and Co-operation in respect of Parental Responsibility and Measures for the Protection of Children/ the Hague Convention 1996
HFD	Högsta förvaltningsdomstolen (the Supreme Administrative Court in Sweden)
ICCPR	International Covenant on Civil and Political Rights
ICESCR	International Covenant on Economic, Social and Cultural Rights
NJA	Nytt juridiskt arkiv (Periodical publishing of Swedish Supreme Court rulings)
UDHR	Universal Declaration of Human Rights
UN	United Nations

Notes on Contributors

Rebecca Adami
is Associate Professor at the Department of Education, Stockholm University. Adami specializes in human rights studies on women and UN history, cosmopolitanism and ethics, and children's rights.

Margareta Aspán
is Senior Lecturer at the Department of Child and Youth Studies at Stockholm university. Her research focuses on children's participation, both formal and informal, in school settings and is based in social studies of childhood and ethical theories.

Tim Holappa
is PhD candidate of Public Law at the Faculty of Law, Stockholm University. His research interests lie in social welfare law, social rights and children's rights. His PhD project concerns the realization of the right to housing in Sweden with a focus on families with children.

Anna Kaldal
is Professor of Procedural Law at the Faculty of Law, Stockholm University. Kaldal's research interest is children as victims or witnesses of violence and sexual abuse, their participation in legal proceedings and evaluation of evidence. Kaldal's research therefore also involves criminal law, family (custody) law and child protection law.

Sandra Karlsson
is Senior Lecturer at the Department of Special Education, Stockholm University. Her doctoral thesis is on asylum seeking children's lived rights and everyday politics. Karlsson's research interest lies in methodology with children and of exploring how children negotiate social and spatial power relations.

Katrin Lainpelto
is Associate Professor of Procedural Law, at the Faculty of Law, Stockholm University. Her research focus on criminal procedural and evidentiary issues conducted within the framework of interdisciplinary collaborations, including methodological issues.

Pernilla Leviner
is Professor of Public Law at the Faculty of Law, Stockholm University. She is the Director of the Stockholm Centre for the Rights of the Child, Stockholm University, a research centre dealing with child law with a strong focus on interdisciplinary perspectives. Leviner's research interests lie across the fields of public and family law – more specifically child law and welfare law.

Lars Lindblom
is Associate Professor at the Department of Culture and Society, Linköping University. He is Director of the Centre for Applied Ethics at Linköping University. His areas of specialization are political philosophy and applied ethics.

Linde Lindkvist
is Associate Professor of human rights studies at the School of Human Rights, University College Stockholm, and Senior Advisor at the Swedish Institute for Human Rights. He specializes in questions of human rights history, the right to religious freedom and children's rights.

Laura Lundy
is Co-Director of the Centre for Children's Rights, Professor of Children's Rights at Queen's University, Belfast and Professor of Law at University College Cork. She is Joint Editor in Chief of the *International Journal of Children's Rights* and a qualified barrister at law. Her expertise is on international children's rights with a particular focus on the implementation of the UN Convention on the Rights of the Child in law and policy, education rights and children's right to participate in decision-making.

Noam Peleg
is Senior Lecturer at the Faculty of Law and Justice, University of New South Wales. His work focuses on international children's rights law and its intersection with human rights law, childhood studies, and family law. He has published widely in leading journals and edited books, and his book *The Child's Right to Development* was published by Cambridge University Press in 2019.

Johanna Schiratzki
is Guest Professor of Family Law at the Faculty of Law, Stockholm University and Visiting Researcher, Department of Sociology, Stockholm University. Her research concerns legal aspects of the principle of the best interests of the child, and covers numerous issues of child, family and welfare law.

Kavot Zillén
is Associate Professor of Public Law at the Faculty of Law, Stockholm University. She is the deputy director of the Stockholm Centre for the Rights of the Child, Stockholm University. Zillén's research interests lie primarily in Medical law and human rights in health care settings, in particular the right to health, freedom of religion and protection against discrimination.

Introduction

Children's Rights from an International Perspective

Laura Lundy

I welcome and commend this important edited collection on the legal and ethical aspects of children's rights, which brings together scholars from diverse disciplinary backgrounds who have applied their expertise and distinct perspectives to reflect on significant children's rights issues in Sweden and beyond. Whatever the disciplinary perspective, whatever the children's rights principles involved, and whichever children are the focus of the analysis, it is always useful in any study of children's rights to step back and reflect on what makes children's rights distinctive. Why do or should children have bespoke versions of human rights, and how, if at all, do these rights differ from those of adults?

Children are, of course, humans; at least in theory, children have all the rights that adults enjoy in a range of human rights treaties. From the Universal Declaration on Human Rights (UDHR) to the twin covenants, children fall not only within the definition of 'human' or 'everyone' but also have additional human rights due to their status as children. Until 1989, these additions were very limited. For example, the UDHR mentions children only briefly, and in each instance pairs them and their entitlements with the adults in their lives: first their mothers (along with whom they are entitled to special care) and then both parents, who are afforded the right to choose an education for their child. The UN Covenant on Economic, Social, and Cultural Rights (CESCR) continues in this vein while adding a bundle of extra protections from economic and social exploitation (e.g. 'Their employment in work harmful to their morals or health or dangerous to life or likely to hamper their normal development should be punishable by law', Article 10). In contrast, the UN Covenant on Civil and Political Rights (CCPR) barely mentions children other than to provide for their right to a name, nationality, and birth registration.

The adoption of UN Convention on the Rights of the Child (1989) (the 'CRC' or 'Convention') provided global recognition that children would require many more 'special protections' if their human rights were to be realized. When I am introducing my masters' students to children's rights, I begin with this question: what actually makes children different from adults? Take a minute, I ask, and think about your instinctive reaction to that question. Most people respond by suggesting that children are more vulnerable to harm or are dependent on adults. For the most part, adults define children in terms of a deficit – children lack what adults have. It is important to understand these typical conceptions of children, as they are often the very same as those held by the

DOI:10.1163/9789004511163_002

adults who drafted the Convention. The content of the CRC reflects this fact; a huge portion of this convention is dedicated either to protecting children from harm or securing their development.

The preamble of the CRC, although not legally binding, provides an initial insight into the assumptions that underpin the drafters' rationale and conceptualization of children. The text is overtly paternalistic, asserting for example that childhood is entitled to 'special care and assistance', and reiterating the statement of the 1929 Declaration of the Rights of the Child: 'the child, by reason of his physical and mental immaturity, needs special safeguards and care, including appropriate legal protection, before as well as after birth'. However, while the preamble emphasizes protection and care, the content of the CRC is much more comprehensive, capturing not only a wide range of new protections from harm but also a largely untouched set of civil and political rights, including the right to freedom of expression, privacy, association, and assembly. I say largely untouched, but there is a significant omission – the right to participate in political life, including the right to vote, is omitted – and this issue is now receiving much attention. That said, the inclusion of all the other civil and political rights underscores the fact that children are also entitled to these rights, a fact that is often misunderstood or misrepresented in practice, with child activists and human rights defenders experiencing a range of restrictions that would not be imposed on adults.

The CRC has received much criticism, and rightly so. Looking at the Convention through the lenses of feminism or post-colonialism, for example, will expose some of its flaws. However, it has also been accused of being 'adultist' – a criticism that one might not expect about a treaty designed to enhance human rights protections for children. One example of this is the fact that Article 2, the CRC's comprehensive discrimination provision, does not include 'age' as a protected category. Many of us who work in the field of children's rights are fully aware of the justified criticisms of this politically negotiated compromise, yet we continue to promote its implementation. Why? For others in the field and for me, the CRC affords children all (or at least nearly all) of the human rights given to adults, but children also receive additional protections that recognize their lived realities: they are all still developing; some may be more vulnerable to harm; and crucially, all will be living in contexts (families) where others will and indeed often must make decisions for them. All of these factors mean that for children to enjoy the fundamentals of human rights (dignity, equality, and respect for their worth as a human being), they need bespoke versions of human rights. These are not different rights but articulations of the same human rights for the distinctive social context of childhood.

Article 12, which provides for the child's right to have their views sought and given due weight in accordance with their age and maturity, is an interesting case in point. Some have argued that it detracts from children's human rights, limiting their right to freedom of expression through the emphasis on their age and maturity. I, on the other hand, struggle to see how that is possible when Article 13 means that children continue to have the same right to freedom of expression as adults. For me, Article 12 gives an additional entitlement that recognizes the reality – that many decisions are made about and for children, and that this places an onus on those tasked with making those decisions to ensure that children's views are sought and taken seriously. Adults have no equivalent right because there is an assumption (probably also partially erroneous) that adults always get to make decisions for themselves.

I asked you to think about what makes children different from adults. When we ask children the same question, as I have done many times, their answers are usually very different. They see adults as having a deficit as well: adults have no time to play, have too much responsibility, are too worried or serious. This difference in perception is also important, as there is no doubting the irony of children having a treaty written for them and not together with them, and there is also no doubt that the CRC might have been different (although not perhaps as much as is sometimes suggested) had children been involved in drafting it. Would children have been less paternalistic? Probably not. Would they have added civil and political rights? Probably yes in respect of the right to vote. However, the reality is not that children do not enjoy the 'participatory' civil and political rights of adults but that the additional 'protection' rights afforded to children are sometimes used by adults to limit children's autonomy, and often in ways that are not necessary or proportionate. This is not a failure of the Convention but of public understanding and implementation – a reality that makes the study of children's rights on which you are about to embark so crucial.

When I asked you to think about how children differ from adults, what child did you have in mind? What age, gender, ethnicity? Clearly a baby differs significantly from an adult compared to a 17-year-old. Understanding and implementing children's rights is always child-, decision-, and context-specific. A litmus test for me in terms of how we treat children is always to ask: would we do this to an adult? If we would not, the next question is always to probe why we are prepared to treat a child that way, and whether such treatment can be justified within the overall human rights ambition of respecting the child's dignity, affording equality, and ensuring respect for the worth of the individual human being. That can rarely be achieved without seeking the views of children themselves.

A Children's Rights Dilemma – Paternalism versus Autonomy

Noam Peleg

The questions of paternalism and autonomy, and the challenges of balancing the two when it comes to children and their opportunities to exercise their rights, are two of the main questions that underpin this book.

Paternalism is invoked regularly in children's rights scholarship, explicitly but more often inexplicitly.[1] However, paternalism has different meanings that should be carefully unpacked before analysing how this phenomenon operates with, for, and mainly against children. One definition, which is used in non-children (rights)-specific literature, suggests that paternalism is an act of limiting one's general autonomy and agency to make decisions as a means to promote one's welfare.[2] A different definition indicates that paternalism is an act of overriding one's decision in the name of their safety, wellbeing, or other similar harm prevention objectives.[3] Both definitions portray paternalism as a harm prevention measure, based on the underpinning logic that one's autonomy should be limited in the name of protection. The first definition is broader, as it justifies overriding one's agency and autonomy to make decisions altogether, rather than nullifying a specific decision that can result in harm, as the second definition seems to suggest. Nonetheless, these definitions both work in the same way – they override individual autonomy based on an abstract risk-assessment exercise, which can be (and often is) a euphemism for the subjective, value-driven assessment of one's general capacity to make, or to be entitled to make, a decision about one's own life or to exercise one's agency.

One of the key arguments against paternalism is the liberal claim that individuals are in the best position to judge their own interests and values through their personal process of reasoning, and therefore they should have the freedom to decide and face the consequences of their choices. This approach

1 Freeman, M., *Magna Carta for Children: Rethinking Children's Rights* (Cambridge: Cambridge University Press, 2020): 31–45.

2 Düber, D., 'The Concept of Paternalism'. In Schramme, T. (Ed.) *New Perspectives on Paternalism and Health Care* (Berlin: Springer Verlag, 2015): 31–45.

3 Shiffrin, S.V., 'Paternalism, Unconscionability Doctrine, and Accommodation', *Philosophy & Public Affairs* 29, no. 3 (2000): 205–250, 205, 213.

values the authority of a hypothetical 'competent adult' over a paternalistic prioritization of assumed wellbeing. However, for children, this line of reasoning requires some modifications, irrespective of the rights theory that we prefer, as neither the will theory nor the interests theory sufficiently account for children's vulnerability.[4]

Vulnerability is often used as a justification for paternalism in general, and this is certainly true for children, as one of the traditional justifications for protecting children's rights is due to their 'inherent' vulnerability. Moreover, according to the UN Committee on the Rights of the Child, some children are even 'more vulnerable' than others: 'An important element to consider is the child's situation of vulnerability, such as disability, belonging to a minority group, being a refugee or asylum seeker, victim of abuse, living in a street situation, etc'.[5] In General Comment 13, the Committee lists additional situations of enhanced or increased vulnerability, including indigeneity, sexual orientation or gender identity, chronic illness, low socioeconomic status, and children affected by conflicts or natural disasters, among other characteristics.[6]

When it comes to international children's rights law, Article 5 of the 1989 UN Convention on the Rights of the Child ('the Convention' or 'CRC') coins the Evolving Capacities principle, which accords children the space to exercise their autonomy and rights based on their evolving capacities, as assessed and determined by adults.[7] As such, the CRC seems to be an embodiment of the second definition of paternalism. The story that the Convention tells about children's autonomy and capacities is more complex however, as will be discussed below.

Back in the 1970s, the child liberationist argued that there is no justification for paternalistic approaches towards children. People like Richard Farson (1974) and John Holt (1974) argued that the law should not differentiate between children and adults, and that all human beings, irrespective of age, are best positioned to make decisions about their own lives.[8] According to these views,

---

4 Tobin, J., 'Justifying Children's Rights', *International Journal of Children's Rights* 21 (2013): 395–441.

5 United Nations Committee on the Rights of the Child. *General Comment No. 14 (2013) on the Right of the Child to Have His or Her Best Interests Taken as a Primary Consideration* (Art. 3, para. 1). CRC/C/GC/14 (29 May 2013), para. 75.

6 United Nations Committee on the Rights of the Child. *General Comment No. 13 (2011) The Right of the Child to Freedom from All Forms of Violence*. CRC/C/GC/13 (18 April 2011), para. 72(g).

7 Daly, A., 'Assessing Children's Capacities', *International Journal of Children's Rights* 28 (2020): 471–499.

8 Farson, R., *Birthright* (New York: Macmillan Publishing, 1974); Holt, J., *Escape from Childhood* (London: Penguin Books, 1974).

paternalistic laws directed at children, allegedly put in place to protect them from themselves (and often from their parents), should be abolished in favour of full liberation and full respect for children's autonomy. This approach did not leave a mark in the literature and gained little traction in practice. Joel Feinberg wrote in opposition to this trend and, having tried to square the circle, suggested that children's autonomy should not be overridden unless there is an immediate and concrete threat to their physical safety or overall well-being. In addition, if the child's autonomy is restricted or fully ignored due to these considerations, then it should not be seen as a permanent state of affairs but as a temporary measure that aims to ensure long-term ability to exercise autonomy.[9]

In other words, Feinberg's paternalism is not based on one's permanent character, but rather on the paternalists' ability and duty when it comes to the parent-child relationship, as a means to prevent concrete harm from taking place. Freeman suggests that this approach, which he refers to as 'limited paternalism', permits interference with a child's autonomy where the child's decision would result in death and would thus deny her any future.[10] The weight of this argument depends in turn on what the paternalist considers as 'harm'. Another possible point of view is to ask: what room for mistakes do adults provide for children? An example here would be when a child makes a decision that will not necessarily result in immediate pain or death, but about which an adult – usually a parent – will be displeased.

The tension between children's rights as an emancipatory project and the child, whose image – including under the Convention – is of a human being lacking capacity, or as someone who gradually acquires capacities over the course of childhood, is apparent. Article 12 of the Convention is the embodiment of this tension and the best example of the Convention's attempt to reconcile it. On the one hand, Article 12 respects the child's right to participate in decisions concerning her life, and it is often celebrated as one of the biggest achievements of the Convention in moving children's social and legal positionalities from subject to object. But on the other hand, Article 12 gives adults the power to decide whether and how children will participate, and how much weight a child's voice should be given, by enabling adults to qualify children as immature and consequently silencing them. Thus, this requires adults who

9 Feinberg, J., 'The Child's Right to an Open Future'. In Aiken, W., and LaFollette, H. (Eds.), *Whose Child?* (New Jersey: Rowman and Littlefield, 1980): 124–153.

10 Freeman, M., (2020), 202.

are willing to create a structure that enables children to participate to begin with.[11] In that sense, even the seemingly liberating Article 12 leaves adults in charge and in control of children's lives. Moreover, it leaves adults in charge of children's opportunity to express their opinion, which is not a harmful exercise as such, as paternalism is often invoked against the imaginary or concrete fear of physical harm. It is true that for some children, even the exercise of participation can be triggering or harmful; in these cases, the participation method should be carefully designed to prevent or minimize this harm. Still, Article 12 gives adults much more power than this.

Article 5 and the Evolving Capacities principle, which was mentioned earlier, also condition children's autonomy to their capacities, as assessed by adults. Reading Article 5 in this way raises a question about the image and positionality of babies and toddlers as rights holders under the Convention, as they are seen as lacking (in capacities). John Eekelaar accepts the latter description, suggesting that children's rights aim 'to bring the child to the threshold of adulthood with the maximum opportunities to form and pursue life-goals which reflect as closely as possible an autonomous choice'.[12]

The Convention's story is more complicated, however, as Article 6(2) establishes the right of the child to develop. This right includes the development of capabilities that seem to be prerequisites for exercising rights. However, this reading of the Convention is premised on a model of deficiency, in which children are seen as 'not-adults' and therefore are lacking in the assumed ability to exercise autonomy. However, looking at Article 6 as an opportunity to remedy or counter the paternalistic work of the Convention and how such work can be mitigated can lead to an alternative interpretation, where the right to development is understood as an emancipatory right.[13]

The 'best interest of the child' is probably the main area in which paternalism is most prominent, especially in situations of enhanced vulnerability. In these cases, it is the duty bearers' task to determine the best interest of the child, who is the rights holder. However, as the Committee clarifies in General Comment 14, a best-interests analysis must incorporate the child's own voice.[14] Nonetheless, in some circumstances, the Committee authorizes states to ignore

---

11 Lundy, L., '"Voice" is Not Enough: Conceptualising Article 12 of the United Nations Convention on the Rights of the Child', *British Educational Research Journal* 33 (2007): 927–942.

12 Eekelaar, J., 'The Interests of the Child and the Child's Wishes: The Role of Dynamic Self Determinism', *International Journal of Law, Policy and the Family* 8 (1994): 42–61.

13 Peleg, N., *The child's right to development* (Cambridge: Cambridge University Press, 2019).

14 United Nations Committee on the Rights of the Child. *General Comment No. 14* (2013).

the child's personal will when scientific arguments can be made, for example regarding brain development and its impact on cognitive capabilities.[15] The best-interests principle is also open to abuse and misuse, usually in the name of protecting children from their parents, and as several chapters in the book demonstrate, it can also be used as a euphemism for racial biases against children from racialized minorities.

In a sense, the effect of vulnerability is the reduction of rights holders to a position of victimhood from which it is almost impossible to escape, not least due to institutional constraints that exclude the victims' voices and conceptual biases that favour a top-down approach, from which victims need to be saved by human rights norms and institutions. This, in turn, quashes the utility of the emancipatory element of the Convention, namely Article 12; it also ignores Articles 5 and 6, and repositions children as the subject of adults' paternalistic control.

Can children escape this inherent positionality of inferiority? One way to address these challenges and to make rights a living reality for children can be found in this book. Interdisciplinary research that looks at children's lives from a range of perspectives and points of view, where children share their own experiences and operation of the law is studied both theoretically and in light of its practical operation, can move the discussion forward and contribute to shifting the balance away from paternalism towards an emancipatory practice of children's rights.

References

Daly, Aoife. 2020. "Assessing Children's Capacities", *International Journal of Children's Rights* 28: 471–499.

Düber, Dominik. 2015. "The Concept of Paternalism", in Thomas Schramme (Ed.), *New Perspectives on Paternalism and Health Care,* 31–45. Berlin: Springer Verlag.

Eekelaar, John. 1994. "The Interests of the Child and the Child's Wishes: The Role of Dynamic Self Determinism", *International Journal of Law, Policy and the Family* 8: 42–61.

Farson, Richard. 1974. *Birthrights.* New York: Macmillan Publishing.

Feinberg, Joel. 1980. "The Child's Right to an Open Future", in William Aiken and Hugh LaFollette (Eds.), *Whose Child?,* 124–153. New Jersey: Rowman and Littlefield.

15 United Nations Committee on the Rights of the Child. *General Comment No. 24 on Children's Rights in the Child Justice System.* CRC/C/GC/24 (18 September 2019) para. 22.

Freeman, Michael. 2020. *Magna Carta for Children: Rethinking Children's Rights.* Cambridge: Cambridge University Press.

Holt, John. 1974. *Escape from Childhood.* London: Penguin Books.

Lundy, Laura. 2007. "'Voice' is Not Enough: Conceptualising Article 12 of the United Nations Convention on the Rights of the Child", *British Educational Research Journal* 33: 927–942.

Peleg, Noam. 2019. *The child's right to development.* Cambridge: Cambridge University Press.

Shiffrin, Seana Valentine. 2000. "Paternalism, Unconscionability Doctrine, and Accommodation", *Philosophy & Public Affairs* 29(3): 205–250.

Tobin, John. 2013. "Justifying Children's Rights", *International Journal of Children's Rights* 21: 395–441.

United Nations Committee on the Rights of the Child. *General Comment No. 13 (2011) The Right of the Child to Freedom from All Forms of Violence.* CRC/C/GC/13 (18 April 2011).

United Nations Committee on the Rights of the Child. *General Comment No. 14 (2013) on the Right of the Child to Have His or Her Best Interests Taken as a Primary Consideration.* CRC/C/GC/14 (29 May 2013).

United Nations Committee on the Rights of the Child. *General Comment No. 24 on Children's Rights in the Child Justice System.* CRC/C/GC/24 (18 September 2019).

PART 1

Legal Challenges Regarding the Rights of the Child

CHAPTER 1

Children's Right to Have Rights – on the Importance of Statutory Rights for Swedish Children Living outside the Country

Johanna Schiratzki

1 Introduction: Whose Rights Are Protected, and by Whom?

Some 80 years ago, in 1941, Hannah Arendt fled Paris, where in addition to being an academic, writer, and political theorist, she had worked as an activist and social worker with children escaping the ongoing Nazi annihilation. Ten years later, in her book *The Origins of Totalitarianism*, she asks her now well-known question: 'Who has the right to have rights?'. Her answer is that the concept of global human rights is a paradox because these rights depend on national states' protection of a person who wants to benefit from these supposedly supra-national human rights. This paradox has been interpreted to reveal two often understated premises for enjoying rights: 'the right for one's presence and the right for one's agency to be qualified or officially recognised'.[1] States are largely at liberty to decide whom they want to protect, and to whom they want to deny rights through statutory rights.[2] If a person does not enjoy the protection of a state, human rights are difficult to enforce.[3]

This chapter explores how the right to residence and to have one's agency recognized applies for children in the detention camps in northeast Syria for former IS members. The very difficult political and legal processes of bringing home Swedish subjects from these detention camps is examined. In 2019, 70 children who were either born in Sweden or having Swedish mothers were reported to be in detention. In the following years, 18 of these children were

1 Field, S., 'Law of Peace and Children's Right to have Rights', *The International Journal of Children's Rights* 27, no. 3 (2019): 425–454.

2 Faghfouri Azar, L., 'Hannah Arendt: The Right to Have Rights'. Key concepts. *Critical Legal Thinking* (2019). https://criticallegalthinking.com/2019/07/12/hannah-arendt-right-to-have-rights. Accessed 19 August 2021.

3 Bhabha, J., 'Arendt's Children: Do Today's Migrant Children Have a Right to Have Rights?', *Human Rights Quarterly* 31, no. 2 (2009): 410–451; Brittle, R., and Desmet, E., 'Thirty Years of Research on Children's Rights in the Context of Migration', *The International Journal of Children's Rights* 28, no. 1 (2020): 36–65.

reported to have left the camps and arrived in Sweden through the help of relatives.[4] In mid-2022, between eight and 30 Swedish children are reported to be still imprisoned in the Roj camp and a few in the Al-Hol camp.[5]

The Swedish position on these children's 'right to have rights' when residing outside Sweden's national jurisdiction corresponds to the approach of other Western democratic states. European states have treated the rights of their underaged citizens in the detention camps in slightly different ways, i.e. in regard to whether children should be evacuated at all, and if so, with their mothers or alone?[6] A common feature, however, is the hesitance to bring these children back to European states, and the uncertainty about the extent to which the children have agency independently of their parents. Another striking feature are the different positions on children's rights taken by supranational organisations such as the United Nations (UN) compared to European states, exemplified by the communications to France from the UN Committee on the Rights of the Child.[7]

In this chapter, the Swedish approach is analysed in relation to the impact of statutory rights for Swedish children inside and outside the country. The chapter first offers a brief introduction to the Swedish legal system in general terms, and continues with a discussion of human rights for children whose statutory rights are not fully recognized in terms of what is labeled here as 'a ladder to inclusion' in national jurisdiction. The contradicting views on the rights for children expressed by the United Nations and the Swedish government are then analyzed, followed by a concluding discussion on children's right to abode and to recognition of their agency.

4 Sundén, J. 'Därför kommer inte IS-barnen hem', *Svenska Dagbladet* (Stockholm, Sweden), 13 April 2021, www.svd.se/darfor-kommer-inte-is-barnen-hem. Accessed 9 August 2022.

5 Harris, G., *'Rädda barnen larmar: Barnens situation i al-Hol ohållbar', Dagens Nyheter* (Stockholm, Sweden), 25 Mai 2022. Accessed 28 June 2022.

6 https://www.euractiv.com/section/politics/short_news/denmark-to-bring-isis-children-home-but-not-mothers/ https://yle.fi/news/3-12024840 https://www.spiegel.de/politik/deutschland/geheim-operation-aussenministerium-holt-zehn-deutsche-is-anhaengerinnen-aus-syrien-a-21bb4119-ccaf-476f-aefe-e573b295af07 https://www.nrk.no/nyheter/fn-ekspert-ber-norge-hente-is-barn-1.15839263 https://www.savethechildren.org.uk/news/media-centre/press-releases/statement-call-for-British-children-to-recover-in-UK.

7 Decision adopted by the Committee under the *Optional Protocol to the Convention on the Rights of the Child on a communications procedure, concerning communications No. 79/2019* and *No. 109/2019*, (CRC/C/85/D/79/2019), (CRC/C/85/D/109/2019), 2 November 2020 (see also observations 4 February 2021 and 23 February 2022).

2 Statutory Rights of Children in Sweden Related to International Law

During the 70 years since the publication of Arendt's ground-breaking work,[8] 'rights' have developed in number as well as depth – as human rights with an aim towards global recognition and as national statutes. Three human-rights instruments with a strong bearing on the statutory rights of children are the Charter of Fundamental Rights of the European Union (CFR), the European Convention on the Fundamental Human Rights and Freedoms (ECHR), and the United Nations Convention on the Rights of the Child (CRC).[9] The CRC was adopted and opened for signature, ratification, and accession by General Assembly Resolution 44/25 of 20 November 1989 and entered into force on 2 September 1990.

Sweden is a member of the United Nations, European Union, and the European Council. European law has increasing importance in several areas, including human rights and free movement. Preparatory work plays an important role in the interpretation of legal acts passed by the Swedish Parliament. The central preparatory works are the Government Legislative Bills and Government inquiries published as the Government Official Report Series. The latter are the results of lengthy investigations, often produced through collective work involving experts and civil servants. A Government Legislative Bill summarizes one or several Governmental Official Reports as well as the responses of a referral process among authorities and stakeholders. Substantial changes may be made in relation to the Governmental Official Report's proposal, depending on the government's political agenda or other considerations. Government Legislative Proposals are frequently used when analysing the aim and possible interpretations of a legal act.

Another feature of the Swedish legal system is the dichotomy of the court system, which consists of two main branches: general courts and general administrative courts. In contrast to neighbouring Denmark and Norway, Sweden has two general courts that issue precedents: the Supreme Court (*Högsta domstolen*), for the general courts, and the Supreme Administrative Court (*Högsta förvaltningsdomstolen*), for the general administrative courts.

Sweden ratified the CRC in 1990. This meant that although the rights of the child according to the CRC could be argued in court or administrative

8 Arendt, H., *The Origins of Totalitarianism* (New York: Harcourt Inc., 1973).

9 Dane, L., 'Europadomstolen och barnets bästa', *Förvaltningsrättslig tidskrift, no.* 2 (2015): 193–224; Grahn-Farley, M., 'Högsta domstolens rättighetspraxis från 2003 till 2015: utmaningar och möjligheter med en inkorporering av Barnkonventionen', *Europarättslig tidskrift*, no. 3 (2017): 651–669.

procedures, the CRC was arguably not applicable in court or administrative procedures with the same standing as statutes issued by the Parliament. According to the understanding of Swedish NGOs, these statutes took precedence over the CRC.

Regardless of this assertion, the Supreme Court and the Administrative Supreme Court have passed judgements based on the CRC, both before and after the incorporation of the Convention.[10] Rights and concepts originating from human rights have thus found their way into national statutory rules as well. Principles that originate from the human rights sphere – mostly from the CRC – are transformed into Swedish statutory rights. This transformation started in 1997, well before the CRC was incorporated into Swedish law in 2020. However, as pointed out by Hoffman and Thorburn Stern, neither transformation nor incorporation offer a guarantee for the enforceability of children's rights.[11]

In 1997, Sweden's Aliens Act (*utlänningslag*) and Social Services Act (*socialtjänstlag*) were amended to include Articles 3 and 12 of the CRC; this was followed in 1998 with amendments in the Parental Code (*föräldrabalken*) Chapter 6 on custody, residence, and contact. The principle of the best interests of the child in relation to compulsory care was introduced in 2003 in the Care of Young Persons Act (*lag med särskilda bestämmelser om barn och unga*). In 2009 and 2010, Articles 3 and 12 were implemented in the Health and Medical Services Act (*hälso- och sjukvårdslagen*), the Patient Act (*patientlagen*), and the Support and Service for Persons with Certain Functional Impairments Act (*lag med stöd och service till vissa funktionshindrade*). In 2011, the constitution was amended to include a specific provision for children. Chapter 1 Section 2.5 of the Instrument of Government (*regeringsformen*) now reads:[12]

10 E.g. in case NJA 2020 p. 761, the Supreme Court assessed that the best interests of the child should be investigated and assessed in extradition for (alleged) commission of a crime; the Migration Court of Appeal considered the CRC in relation to family reunification in cases MIG 2018:20 13, November 2018 and MIG 2012:3, 21 February 2012. The Supreme Court considered the CRC in case NJA 2014 p. 307 on transfer of parental responsibility to foster parents according to Chapter 6, Section 8 of the Parental Code; in case NJA 2013 p. 1143 on the Hague Convention on child abduction; in case NJA 2013 C 41 on execution of the family home; in case NJA 2006 p. 505 on adoption. The Administrative Supreme Court considered the CRC in cases HFD 2011 ref 13 and HFD 2008 ref 55 according to the Care of Young Persons Act. For approval to include court cases: Ethical Review Board (Stockholm) no. 2018/704-31/5.

11 Hoffman, S., and Stern, R. T., 'Incorporation of the UN Convention on the Rights of the Child in National Law', *The International Journal of Children's Rights* 28, no. 1 (2020): 133–156.

12 Legislative Bill 2009/10:80 *En reformerad grundlag.*

> The public institutions shall promote the opportunity for all to attain participation and equality in society and for the rights of the child to be safeguarded.

This provision is not enforceable; rather, it is part of the general aims and ambitions for the governance of children in Sweden.[13] In 2011, the principle of best interests was implemented in the Educational Act (*skollagen*). CRC Article 3 is further implemented in the Detention Act (*fängelselagen*), the Prisons Act (*fängelselagen*), the Act on a Special Representative for Children (*lag om särskild företrädare för barn*), the Act on International Child Adoption (*lag om internationella adoptioner*), and the Act on Dental Care (*tandvård*). The principle of best interests of the child was included in 2018 in the Parental Code's Chapter 5 on adoption.[14]

Thus, the rights of children in Sweden are found in a plurality of norms, such as statutes passed by the Parliament, EU regulations, and international law as well as decrees, guidelines, and other sources of law. As Bhabha notes, fundamental rights under international law to protection, family life, education, and healthcare have been recognized in statutory law.[15] Generally, children are specified by age, and the statutory rights aim towards achieving child protection rather than participation.[16] However, a key question remains: *which* children are entitled to enjoy protection from Swedish statutory rights originating from the human-rights obligation of the Swedish state?[17]

3 Children's Right to Equal Treatment and the Right to Life

The two CRC articles most frequently transformed into Swedish law are, as indicated above, Article 3 on the best interests of the child and Article 12 on the rights of the child to have his or her views taken into account. These are two of the four so-called general principles of the CRC. The other two general principles of the CRC – children's right to equal treatment (Article 2) and the

13 Schiratzki, J., 'Children's Right to Family Life and the Swedish Constitution'. In Haugli, T. et al., (Eds.) *Children's Constitutional rights in the Nordic Countries* (Koninklijke: Brill NV, 2020): 357–373.

14 Schiratzki, J., 'The Elusive Best Interests of the Child and the Swedish Constitution'. In Haugli, T. et al. (Eds.), *Children's Constitutional rights in the Nordic Countries* (Koninklijke: Brill NV 2020): 185–198.

15 Bhabha, J. (2009).

16 See Adami, R., Chapter 6 in this volume.

17 Moyn, S., *Human Rights and the Uses of History* (Brooklyn: Verso, 2014).

right to life (Article 6) – are seldom transformed; the reasons for this are not spelled out in the legal history.[18]

One explanation, however, is that right to equal treatment is covered by other legal instruments, i.e. ECHR Article 14, the EU Charter Article 21, the Instrument of Government (Chapter 2 Sections 12–13), and other statutes, notably the Discrimination Act. The right to life is protected by the Charter Article 2, and in its negative by ECHR Article 2 and the Swedish constitution (the Instrument of Government Chapter 2 Section 4), in that the death penalty is forbidden.[19] Children's rights are covered by Charter Articles 24, 14, and 32.

With regard to children, the protection provided by CRC Articles 2 and 6 is stronger in its wording than the protection offered in the Charter, the ECHR, and the Swedish constitution. Article 2 CRC includes several grounds for protection that are not covered by the Charter, the Swedish constitution, or the ECHR, for example discrimination relating to the origin, beliefs, or status of the child's parent:

1. States Parties shall respect and ensure the rights set forth in the present Convention to each child within their jurisdiction without discrimination of any kind, irrespective of the child's or his or her parent's or legal guardian's race, colour, sex, language, religion, political or other opinion, national, ethnic or social origin, property, disability, birth or other status.
2. States Parties shall take all appropriate measures to ensure that the child is protected against all forms of discrimination or punishment on the basis of the status, activities, expressed opinions, or beliefs of the child's parents, legal guardians, or family members.

Article 6 CRC goes beyond the protection of the right to life provided in the Charter, the Constitution, and the ECHR, in that the CRC obligates the states parties to the ensure the survival and development of children.

18 Legislative Bill 2017/18:186 *Inkorporering av FN:s konvention om barnets rättigheter*. Swedish Government Official Reports 2016:19 *Barnkonventionen blir svensk lag*; Hanson, K. and Lundy, L., 'Does Exactly What It Says on the Tin? A Critical Analysis and Alternative Conceptualisation of the So-called 'General Principles' of the Convention on the Rights of the Child', *International Journal of Children's Rights* 25, no. 2 (2017): 285–306. See also Schiratzki, J., 'Clarification of Concepts – The Four General Principles of the CRC'. In Harvind, H., Schultz T., and Pedersen, A.M., (Eds)., *Children's Rights – an anthology about the impact of the Convention on the Rights of the Child in Danish law* (Copenhagen: DJOF Forlag, 2020): 59–71.

19 The right to life is protected by other international instruments ratified by Sweden. See International Covenant on Civil and Political Rights (ICCPR) Article 6.

1. States Parties recognize that every child has the inherent right to life.
2. States Parties shall ensure to the maximum extent possible the survival and development of the child.

As for children's right to protection against discrimination and right to life, an important consequence of the 2020 incorporation of the CRC is that these fundamental rights are now Swedish law.

The children who have most to gain from the CRC becoming statutory rights of children are those who are at risk or suffering from discrimination, or whose lives are in jeopardy. Who are these children? They are the ones whose presence and agency are questioned – or, in the words of Article 2 CRC, they are children who differ from the majority owing to their own or their parents', guardians', or families' race, colour, sex, language, religion, political or other opinion, national, ethnic, or social origin, property, disability, birth, or other status. Among these children are also those without a residence permit or what is otherwise labelled as a 'weak connection' to Swedish jurisdiction.

4 Children Considered to Have 'Weak' Connections to Swedish Jurisdiction

To understand the implications of a weak connection to Swedish jurisdiction for children's enjoyment of statutory rights under Swedish law, it is important to remember that 'jurisdiction' is a legal term with, at least two meanings.

Firstly, jurisdiction relates to a court's lawful power to adjudicate specific cases based on personal jurisdiction. For a court to have jurisdiction over someone, this person should, as a main rule, reside in that court's district.[20] Under *criminal law*, however, the main principle is that the court in a district where a suspected crime was committed has jurisdiction, irrespective of where the accused resides.[21] For other legal matters, such as family law, when an adult or child has connections to several countries, the matter of which country has jurisdiction is dealt with under *international private law*. Sweden has ratified a number of international conventions regulating jurisdictional matters,

20 Or having agreed to a proceeding in the specific court, see www.law.cornell.edu/wex/jurisdiction. Accessed 28 June 2022.

21 In certain situations, Swedish courts may adjudicate crimes related to terrorism and crimes against humanity committed abroad; see Chapter 2 of the Penal Code.

relating for example to adoption, paternity, parental responsibility, and child protection.[22]

Secondly, the term jurisdiction describes the *territory* over which a government or a court may lawfully exercise power. This means, for example, that a court may not execute an order for child protection in another state's territory.[23] Territorial jurisdiction has been considered by the Committee on the Rights of the Child in communications concerning the repatriation of French children held in the detention camps in the Syrian Arab Republic.[24]

As to children's statutory rights under Swedish law, a long-standing concern regards the rights of children who are present in Sweden without having a legal right to be in the country, e.g. undocumented migrants and EU migrants.[25] Over time, the implementation of the CRC led to children without relevant documents becoming entitled to benefit from a number of positive rights.[26] Thus, asylum-seeking and undocumented children were treated more favourably than an undocumented person who had turned 18, but less favourably than a child with a residence permit. In the wake of the 2015 migration and a changing political landscape, however, resources have generally become limited.

22 Foremost Council Regulation (EC) No 2201/2003 of 27 November 2003 concerning jurisdiction and the recognition and enforcement of judgments in matrimonial matters and the matters of parental responsibility, repealing Regulation (EC) No 1347/2000, and from 1 August 2022 Council Regulation (EU) 2019/1111 of 25 June 2019 on jurisdiction, the recognition and enforcement of decisions in matrimonial matters and the matters of parental responsibility, and on international child abduction (recast); hereinafter the Brussels II; the 1996 Hague Convention of 19 October 1996 on Jurisdiction, Applicable Law, Recognition, Enforcement and Co-operation in Respect of Parental Responsibility and Measures for the Protection of Children; hereinafter the 1996 Hague Convention.

23 A possible alternative is to ask the competent authorities in that country for assistance. The Brussels II; The 1996 Hague Convention.

24 L.H. et al v France CRC/C/85/D/79/2019, CRC/C/85/109/2019. Decision on 2 November 2020.

25 See Hermansson, L. Lundberg, A., Gruber, S., Jolly, A., Lind, A., Righard, E., Scott, H., 'Firewalls; A necessary tool to enable social rights for undocumented migrants in social work', *International Social Work* 00, no. 0 (2020): 1–15; Elsrud, T., Gruber, S. Lundberg, A., *Rättssäkerheten och solidariteten – vad hände?: en antologi om mottagande av människor på flykt* (Linköping University Electronic Press, 2021); Zillén, K., *Barn i välfärdsstatens utkant, Om rätten till sjukvård för barn som är unionsmedborgare och som lever i ekonomisk utsatthet i Sverige* (Uppsala: Iustus, 2019).

26 Referring to Act on the Reception of Asylum Seekers and Others.

5 Ladder to Inclusion

For an immigrant, the association to Swedish jurisdiction can be described in a simplified manner as a ladder. The first rung represents an asylum-seeker with a right to be in the country until a decision under the Aliens Act is taken; the second rung is reached when a residence permit is granted, and the asylum-seeker is considered domiciled;[27] the third step is to become a Swedish citizen, for which the person may apply after three to five years of residence.

From rung two, when a residence permit is granted, the migrant is considered to have a legal connection with Sweden. From rung three, as a Swedish citizen, the subject is in principle fully protected by the constitution.

However, to fit the experiences of many migrants and in the light of recent legal developments, more rungs should be added to the theoretical three-step ladder. Firstly, rung one is to be preceded by a 'rung zero' to illustrate a procedure in which an application is rejected, but for subjective or objective reasons, the migrant is unable to leave the country; such migrants find themselves staying on without recognized connections to Swedish jurisdiction. If they remain in Sweden they may, after a fixed period of time, apply again and return to rung one – i.e. lawful presence in the country but not domiciled in the eyes of the law (although this may differ depending on the legal issue). A fourth rung can be added to distinguish between those with dual citizenship and those with only Swedish citizenship. This distinction may have bearing on children's right to protection in cross-border child-abduction cases, as two states may lawfully regard the child as a subject.

For Swedish subjects – children and adults alike – their rights are protected by the constitution. The constitutional rights of a citizen include the right to return to Sweden. For a Swedish subject abroad, the constitutionally protected right does not cease at the country's border, but it cannot be automatically used to 'get home'.[28] Whether or not a citizen should, in line with the views of the UN Committee for the Rights of the Child,[29] receive diplomatic or financial assistance to return is at the discretion of the Government. It is tempting to suggest that the decisions are influenced by the strength of the subject's legal association with Sweden compared to connections with other states.

---

27 In part, this development was preceded by 1970s integration policy, in which the importance of citizenship was downplayed as the importance of domicile was emphasized (Legislative Bill 1975:26). See also Schiratzki, J., *Föräldraansvar i välfärdsrätten* (Stockholm: Norstedts Juridik, 2013).

28 See www.swedenabroad.se. Accessed 4 April 2022.

29 CRC/C/85/D/79/2019, CRC/C/85/D/109/2019.

6 Swedish Children in Detention Camps in Northeast Syria

As mentioned above, in 2019, 70 Swedish children, either orphaned or with their mothers, were reported to be in held in detention camps for former members of Daesh from outside the region and who were suspected of serious crimes. In mid-2022, between eight and 30 Swedish children are reported to be still imprisoned in the detention camps in northeast Syria.[30] As early as March 2019, the Swedish Government – through the Minister for Justice and Migration and the Minister for Home Affairs – expressed concerns for these children:[31]

> In the middle of this, there are also children who were born on the site or who were forced to follow when their parents left Sweden to join the IS. The child perspective is central to the government. However, the opportunities to act on site are limited due to the security situation. The Foreign Service's staff cannot operate in the conflict area. If a Swedish citizen were to go to a Swedish foreign service mission, Swedish foreign service missions may have the opportunity to assist with consular support. The situation for the children is complicated, both legally and in terms of security, and is further analysed. In cases where the children have already returned to Sweden, the social services must be involved, and the children's situation investigated so that appropriate efforts can be decided.

As the statement indicates, the Swedish children in the detention camps found themselves not only in detention but also in the intersection of several subareas of statutory rights. These include family law (regarding paternity, maternity, and parental responsibilities); public law (regarding citizenship, population registration, and issuing of passports); municipality law and social law (to identify a Swedish municipality responsible for a child protection order under the Care of Young Persons Act); and international private law and criminal law (in terms of the CRC, Articles 1–12, 14, 18–22, 24–27 and 37 are at stake here).

As stated by the Ministers, as Swedish subjects these children are in principle protected by statutory rights. All the same, the Swedish state, like several other European states, has repeatedly referred to its inability 'under the law' to repatriate Swedish subjects from the camps.

---

30 Ferhatovic, M. 'Så många svenska kvinnor och barn har återvänt från IS i Syrien', *Dagens Nyheter* (Stockholm, Sweden), 5 March 2022.

31 Johansson, M. and Damberg, M., 'Komplicerad situation för IS-återvändares barn', DN-Debatt, *Dagens Nyheter* (Stockholm, Sweden) 11 March 2019.

7 UN vs. Sweden

Several calls have been made by the UN and NGOs to urge European states to repatriate their child subjects from the detention camps. These calls of the UN Special Representative for Children and Armed Conflict for immediate repatriation of all minor children to the states from which they or their parents originated proved to be a test of how far national and international child protection legislation goes to protect the rights of children of citizens who are suspected of crimes against humanity. The requests did not result in the Swedish state repatriating its subjects.

In January 2021, through the High Commissioner of Human Rights, the United Nations expressed its concern in a 26-page Joint Communication from Special Procedures.[32] The communication was prompted by a 'registration and verification exercise' in the Al-Hol detention camp in June 2020. The UN, represented by 12 Special Rapporteurs and one working group, presented the concerns to the Swedish government and urged it once more to repatriate the country's underage citizens.

The Swedish response to the UN's plea amounted to this: Sweden has neither an obligation nor the capacity to repatriate its subjects because Sweden lacks jurisdiction in Syrian territory.[33] The Swedish government stated:

> 44. At the same time, the Government recognises the complexity of the situation and wishes to reiterate that women in the camps may have committed serious crimes, including associating with Daesh. The importance of accountability for the serious crimes committed in Syria and Iraq must be acknowledged.

The Swedish Government also suggested an alternative interpretation of the concept of jurisdiction and Sweden's legal obligations to fulfil children's rights.

---

32 United Nations Human Rights Council. Swedish Government Observations 210326 SP Joint Communication (AL SWE 1/2021). https://spcommreports.ohchr.org/TmSearch/Results. Accessed 9 August 2022. See also Holm, F. and Wistrand Johansson, E., 'Hanteringen av svenska IS-resenärer i Syrien ur folkrättsligt perspektiv', *Svensk Juristtidning* (2022): 250–277.

33 UD2021/01294, 26 March 2021. The Swedish government does not have an ambition to establish a legal mechanism to prosecute people who fought for the terrorist group Daesh on the ground in Syria and Iraq.

> 45. While appreciating the references to key principles of human rights law, the Government respectfully disagrees with the legal reasoning and conclusions in the Communication, in particular concerning the fundamental concept of jurisdiction and Sweden's legal obligations.

Sweden has not (yet) ratified the 3rd Optional Protocol to the Convention on the Rights of the Child on a communications procedure. Therefore, complaints regarding Sweden cannot be heard by the Committee on the Rights of the Child. However, complaints under the CRC regarding children in the camps for former IS members have been directed towards Finland and France who are signatory states to this optional protocol.[34] In 2019, in response to a communication to the UN Committee on the Rights of the Child, the French Government took a similar view as its Swedish counterpart regarding the scope of jurisdiction. In its decision, the Committee on the Rights of the Child states:[35]

> 9.6 The Committee is being called upon to determine if the State party has competence *ratione personae* over the children detained in the camps in north-eastern Syrian Arab Republic. The Committee recalls that, under the Convention, States have the obligation to respect and ensure the rights of the children within their jurisdiction, but the Convention does not limit a State's jurisdiction to 'territory'. (…) A State may also have jurisdiction in respect of acts that are performed, or that produce effects, outside its national borders. In the migration context, the Committee has held that under the Convention, States should take extraterritorial responsibility for the protection of children who are their nationals outside their territory through child-sensitive, rights-based consular protection. In its decision on *C.E. v. Belgium*, the Committee considered that Belgium had jurisdiction to ensure the rights of a child located in Morocco who had been separated from a Belgian-Moroccan couple that had taken her in under the *kafalah* system.

34 No. 100/2019 Finland, No.79/2019 and No. 109/2019 France.

35 *L.H. et al v. France*, communications No.79/2019 and No. 109/2019, CRC/C/85/D/79/2019. CRC/C/85/D/109/2019 2 November 2020. https://www.ejiltalk.org/wp-content/uploads/2020/12/CRC_C_85_D_79_2019_E-1.pdf. Accessed 9 August 2022. See also https://tbinternet.ohchr.org/Treaties/CRC/Shared%20Documents/FRA/CRC_C_89_D_77-79-109-2019_33552_F.pdf. Accessed 9 August 2022.

Based on a joint submission from a group of 31 academics, the Committee on the Rights of the Child favoured a 'flexible and child-rights focused approach to the extraterritorial application of the Convention'.[36] Consequently, the Committee found that a State party, in this case France, does exercise jurisdiction over minor nationals outside their territory. The Committee on the Rights of the Child thus stresses the responsibilities of a state to bring home its minor citizens. The Committee's approach has been criticized for stretching state jurisdiction and prioritizing nationality while other children are left in dire need.[37]

In its answer to the UN, the Swedish Government has stated that as an alternative to repatriation of Swedish children detained in the camps, it will continue work to improve the humanitarian situation in northeast Syria, including the al-Hol and Roj camps. The Government stresses that consular work by Swedish authorities is ongoing in the camps and that staff of the Swedish Ministry of Foreign Affairs have made so-called 'Reports of concern' (*orosanmälan*) to the social services authorities in the relevant Swedish municipalities. It is unclear how the reports will help the detained children, as the territorial jurisdiction of Swedish municipalities is by no means more far-reaching than that of the state of Sweden; on the contrary, municipal jurisdiction is normally limited to the municipality's territory (Chapter 2 of the Social Service Act). In cross-border cases, child protection is a matter of cross-border cooperation or negotiation. In relation to the state parties to the Convention of 19 October 1996 on Jurisdiction, Applicable Law, Recognition, Enforcement and Co-operation in respect of Parental Responsibility and Measures for the Protection of Children (HCCH 1996 Child Protection Convention), the procedure is somewhat more predictable than for non-member states of this convention, such as Syria.

All the same, children who have been wrongfully taken to or detained in states that are not members of the 1996 Child Protection Convention are occasionally brought home to Sweden after negotiations with local authorities (examples include the Kurdistan Region) or expulsion. In these cases, the abducting parent may stand trial for child abduction and the child is returned

36 L.H. et al v France CRC/C/85/D/79/2019, CRC/C/85/109/2019. Decision on 2 November 2020. # 8.8, see also # 8.1–8.7.

37 Marko Milanovic, M., 'Repatriating the Children of Foreign Terrorist Fighters and the Extraterritorial Application of Human Rights' https://www.ejiltalk.org/repatriating-the-children-of-foreign-terrorist-fighters-and-the-extraterritorial-application-of-human-rights/ November 10, 2020. Accessed 9 August 2022.

to the parent from whom the child was taken.[38] In other cases, children returning with their mothers are taken into compulsory care according to the Care of Young Persons Act. These care proceedings initiated by reports of concern issued by the Swedish Security Service.[39]

8 In Conclusion: 'A Right in Its Fundamental Sense Is Power Held by the Powerless'[40]

The frequently debated situation for children in the detention camp for former IS members has been analysed in order to examine the statement that, regardless of the plurality of human rights, states are largely at liberty to decide whose presence in their territories and whose agency they will recognize.[41] Article 4 CRC appears to be drafted as to encourage states to be generous in the entitlement of rights for children. It provides that the states shall, within the maximum extent of their resources and within the framework of international cooperation, ensure that the rights of the child according to the CRC are implemented.

In regard to the legal argumentation described in this chapter, the right of children in the detention camps in northeast Syria to have rights – based on their Swedish nationality, Swedish citizenship, and Swedish statutory rights – has been key for bringing the children over the border and into Sweden. However, this right to have rights does not appear to have been decisive in bringing the children out of the camps: what made a difference were the steps taken by the Autonomous Administration of North and East Syria to release the Swedish children and their mothers from the camp and to expel them from Syria to Sweden, thereby forcing Swedish authorities to act once the children arrived in Sweden.

Thus, the rejection of the right of the children to remain in Syria was a key factor for the children's possibility to be present in Swedish territory. It is

38 The Court of Appeal over Skåne and Blekinge, 24 June 2021 Case B 747-21; Lund District Court, Case B 5335-14, 8 Mars 2021. In September 2021, a returned woman was detained, suspected of a serious violation of international law and a serious war crime.

39 The Administrative Court in Malmö, Case 15266-20 19 January 2021; the Administrative Court in Gothenburg, Cases 16160-20 and 16166-20 26 January 2021; the Administrative Court in Stockholm, Cases 27048-20 and 27178-20 1 February 2021; and the Administrative Court in Jönköping, Cases 1502-21 and 1503-21 3 May 2021.

40 Federle, K., 'Rights flow downhill', *The International Journal of Children's Rights* 2, no. 4 (1994): 343–368, 345.

41 Field, S.M. (2019).

questionable to what extent these children were entitled to agency in Sweden. Another question is how, in the long run, statutory rights originating from human rights could be expected help to protect children's relationships that are significant for their identity and sense of personhood.[42]

References

Abramson, Bruce. 2008. *Article 2: The Right of Non-discrimination*. Brill.

Arendt, Hannah. 1973. *The Origins of Totalitarianism*. New York: Harcourt Inc.

Bhabha, Jacqueline. 2009. "Arendt's Children: Do Today's Migrant Children Have a Right to Have Rights?", *Human Rights Quarterly* 31(2): 410–51.

Brittle, Ruth, and Ellen Desmet. 2020. "Thirty Years of Research on Children's Rights in the Context of Migration", *The International Journal of Children's Rights* 28(1): 36–65.

Condry, Rachel, and Shona Minson. 2020. "Conceptualizing the effects of imprisonment on families: Collateral consequences, secondary punishment, or symbiotic harms?", *Theoretical Criminology* 25(3): 540–558.

Dane, Louise. 2015. "Europadomstolen och barnets bästa", *Förvaltningsrättslig tidskrift*, 2: 193–224.

Elsrud, Torun, Sabine Gruber, and Anna Lundberg. 2021. *Rättssäkerheten och solidariteten – vad hände? En antologi om mottagande av människor på flykt*. Linköping University Electronic Press.

Faghfouri Azar, Leila. 2019. "Hannah Arendt: The Right to Have Rights", *Critical Legal Thinking, Key Concepts,* https://criticallegalthinking.com/keyconcepts/ accessed 1 Mars 2022.

Federle, Katherine Hunt. 1994. "Rights flow downhill", *The International Journal of Children's Rights* 2(4): 343–368.

Ferhatovic, Marina. (2022). "Så många svenska kvinnor och barn har återvänt från IS i Syrien", *Dagens Nyheter,* 5 Mars 2022.

Field, Sarah M. 2019. "Law of Peace and Children's Right to have Rights", *The International Journal of Children's Rights* 27(3): 425–454.

Government's Official Investigations 2016: 19 *Barnkonventionen blir svensk lag* (SOU 2016: 19).

Grahn-Farley, Maria. 2017. "Högsta domstolens rättighetspraxis från 2003 till 2015: utmaningar och möjligheter med en inkorporering av Barnkonventionen", *Europarättslig tidskrift* (3): 651–669.

42 Condry, R. and Minson, S., 'Conceptualizing the effects of imprisonment on families: Collateral consequences, secondary punishment, or symbiotic harms?', *Theoretical Criminology* 25, no. 3 (2020): 540–558, 549.

Hanson, Karl, and Laura Lundy. 2017. "Does Exactly what it says on the Tin? A Critical Analysis and Alternative Conceptualisation of the so-called 'General Principles' of the Convention on the Rights of the Child", *International Journal of Children's Rights* 25(2): 285–306.

Harris, Georgina. (2022). "Rädda barnen larmar: Barnens situation i al-Hol ohållbar", *Dagens Nyheter* (Stockholm, Sweden), 25 Mai 2022, accessed 28 June 2022.

Hermansson, Linus, Anna Lundberg, Sabine Gruber, Andrew Jolly, Jacob Lind, Erica Righard, and Hanna Scott. 2020. "Firewalls: A necessary tool to enable social rights for undocumented migrants in social work", *International Social Work* 00(0): 1–15.

Hoffman, Simon, and Rebecca Thorburn Stern. 2020. "Incorporation of the UN Convention on the Rights of the Child in National Law", *The International Journal of Children's Right* 28(1): 133–156.

Holm, Fanny, and Emil Wistrand Johansson. 2022. "Hanteringen av svenska IS-resenärer i Syrien ur folkrättsligt perspektiv", *Svensk Juristtidning* 2022: 250–277.

Johansson, Morgan, and Mikael Damberg. 2019. "Komplicerad situation för IS-återvändares barn", *Dagens Nyheter*, 11 Mars 2019.

Legislative Bill 1975:26 Regeringens politik om riktlinjer för invandrar- och minoritetspolitiken m.m. (Prop. 1975:26).

Legislative Bill 2009/10:80 En reformerad grundlag (Prop. 2009/10:80).

Legislative Bill 2017/18:186 Inkorporering av fn:s konvention om barnets rättigheter (Prop. 2017/18:186).

Milanovic, Marko. "Repatriating the Children of Foreign Terrorist Fighters and the Extraterritorial Application of Human Rights", www.ejiltalk.org/repatriating-the-children-of-foreign-terrorist-fighters-and-the-extraterritorial-application-of-human-rights/ November 10, 2020, accessed 7 September 2021.

Moyn, Samuel. 2014. *Human Rights and the uses of history*. London and New York: Verso.

Office of the United Nations High Commissioner for Human Rights, *Legislative History of the Convention on the Rights of the Child: Vol. 1* (New York, UN, 2007).

Schiratzki, Johanna. 2013. *Föräldraansvar i välfärdsrätten*. Stockholm: Norstedts Juridik.

Schiratzki, Johanna. 2020. "Children's Right to Family Life and the Swedish Constitution", in Trude Haugli, Anna Nylund, Randi Sigurdsen, and Lena R.L. Bendiksen (Eds.), *Children's Constitutional rights in the Nordic Countries,* 357–373. Leiden: Koninklijke Brill.

Schiratzki, Johanna. 2020. "Clarification of Concepts – The Four General Principles of the CRC", in Trine Schultz, Anne Mørk and Hanne Hartoft (Eds.), *Children's Rights – an anthology about the impact of the Convention on the Rights of the Child in Danish law,* 59–71. Copenhagen: DJOF Forlag.

Schiratzki, Johanna. 2020. "The Elusive Best Interests of the Child and the Swedish Constitution", in Trude Haugli, Anna Nylund, Randi Sigurdsen, and Lena R.L.

Bendiksen (Eds.), *Children's Constitutional rights in the Nordic Countries*, 185–198. Leiden: Koninklijke Brill.

Sundén, Jesper. "Därför kommer inte IS-barnen hem", *Svenska Dagbladet* (Stockholm, Sweden), 13 April 2021, www.svd.se/darfor-kommer-inte-is-barnen-hem, accessed 28 June 2022.

United Nations Committee on the Rights of the Child. *Decision adopted by the Committee under the Optional Protocol to the Convention on the Rights of the Child on a communications procedure, concerning communications*, No. 79/2019 and No. 109/2019 CRC/C/85/D/79/2019, CRC/C/85/D/109/2019, 2 November 2020.

United Nations Human Rights Council. Swedish Government Observations 210326 SP Joint Communication (AL SWE 1/2021).

Zillén, Kavot. 2019. *Barn i välfärdsstatens utkant, Om rätten till sjukvård för barn som är unionsmedborgare och som lever i ekonomisk utsatthet i Sverige*. Uppsala: Iustus.

A Response to Johanna Schiratzki

Sandra Karlsson

In her chapter, Johanna Schiratzki presents a discussion on the statutory rights of children with a weak status in respect to Swedish law, and the recurrent dilemma of protecting the rights of non-citizen children. Schiratzki draws on Hannah Arendt's famous discussion on 'the right to have rights'[1] to demonstrate how the paradox of human rights protection in a world of nation states is still a very urgent matter. In her chapter, Schiratzki suggests that children's statutory rights are highly important, especially for children with Swedish citizenship and who are detained in camps in Syria. The chapter focuses on the political and legal framework for protection of Swedish children in these camps, and in particular how a human rights framework could be used to bring these children home from the detention camps for former IS-members in northeast Syria.

Schiratzki's study relates to the work of human rights scholar Jaqueline Bhabha[2] who has inquired if 'Arendt's children'– today's migrant children – have 'the right to have rights'. Bhabha concludes that children who are functional or *de facto* stateless have a weak status as rights holders. Schiratzki presents a similar and interesting legal discussion on these issues in the Swedish context and a current child rights issue that highlights how some children's status as a rights holder is weaker than others. The chapter illustrates how, for immigrants, entitlements to rights entails different levels of inclusion. Schiratzki shows how the first level of inclusion involves being recognized as an asylum-seeker, that is, having a right to reside in a state while seeking asylum, but it is the next level of inclusion, that is the residence permits, that provides a legal connection to Sweden. This connects to Yuval-Davis (2006) discussion on asylum-seekers right to enter a state territory of a political community and, once inside, the right to remain there.[3]

The legal framework problematized by Schiratzki, constitutes an important background for understanding also the conditions of children's rights in Swedish asylum contexts. In addition to these legal issues, the fieldwork

---

1 Arendt, H., *The origins of totalitarianism* (Schocken Books, 1951).

2 Bhabha, J., 'Arendt's children: Do today's migrant children have a right to have rights?', *Human Rights Quarterly* 31, no. 2 (2009): 410–451.

3 Yuval-Davis, N. 'Belonging and the politics of belonging', *Patterns of Prejudice* 40, no. 3 (2006): 197–214.

I discuss in Chapter 10, this volume, was conducted in the midst of a political context that has been framed as 'the refugee crisis', in which Sweden abandoned a human rights perspective and instead enforced immigration control. In this context, the social rights to which asylum-seeking children in Sweden are entitled were infringed upon in both policy and practice. The new status of the United Nations Convention on the Rights of the Child (CRC) in Sweden may lead to a strengthening of the protection of children, but, children in asylum reception systems still tend to have weak connections to rights.

Schiratzki's chapter also clarifies that it is not only the CRC that is important for the rights of children, but also the Charter of the European Union (CFR), and the European Convention on the Fundamental Human Rights and Freedoms (ECHR), from which she gives examples of the right to equal treatment and the right to life. This reminds the reader of the importance of first and foremost viewing children as human beings and that it is not always in the best interest of the child to separate children from adults when striving for special protection for young people.

References

Arendt, Hanna. 1951. *The origins of totalitarianism* (Schocken Books).

Bhabha, Jaqueline. 2009. "Arendt's children: Do today's migrant children have a right to have rights?", *Human Rights Quarterly* 31(2): 410–451.

Yuval-Davis, Nira. 2006. "Belonging and the politics of belonging", *Patterns of Prejudice* 40(3): 197–214.

CHAPTER 2

Child Rights without Substance? – Swedish Public Welfare and the Invisibility of Children in Economic Support Cases

Pernilla Leviner and Tim Holappa

1 Introduction[1]

Children have the right to social security and an adequate standard of living. This follows from Articles 26 and 27 of the United Nations (UN) Convention on the Rights of the Child (CRC), but also from a series of other international conventions regulating social rights for all, including children.[2] For many countries, combating poverty and economic vulnerability – often with a focus on supporting parents as being responsible for their children – has been and remains a clear objective, articulated for example in the UN sustainability goals.[3] Eliminating poverty has been a central aspect in the construction of Sweden's modern welfare state, and a cornerstone of the Swedish 'folk home' that emerged in the 20th century, with its strong emphasis on self-sufficiency through labour. In addition, various types of support were introduced for families with the purpose of achieving equality and good health in the population. A particular objective in this case was that children should grow up under favourable circumstances and be given equal opportunities.[4]

The ambition of the Swedish welfare state to create fair living standards for the nation's residents is ultimately manifested in Chapter 1 Section 2 of Sweden's constitution – the Instrument of Government (*Regeringsformen*).

1 We want to thank colleagues Laura Carlson, Aoife Daly and Johanna Schiratzki for valuable comments on earlier drafts on this chapter. An article dealing with the same theme and questions as this chapter has been published by the authors in Swedish. See Holappa, T. & Leviner, P., 'Barns villkorade rätt till skälig levnadsstandard – om rättsligt osynliggörande av barn i ärenden om ekonomiskt bistånd', *Förvaltningsrättslig tidskrift*, no. 2 (2022): 239–263.

2 See Article 25 of the UN Declaration of Human Rights and Article 11 of the International Covenant on Economic, Social and Cultural Rights.

3 United Nations, 'Sustainable Development Goal No. 1: No poverty'. Accessed 7 March 2022, http://www.un.org/sustainabledevelopment/poverty/.

4 For a general description of the politics of the Swedish welfare state see Hirdman, Y., *Att lägga livet till rätta – studier i svensk folkhemspolitik* (4th ed.). (Stockholm: Carlssons, 2018).

According to this section, the state is to particularly ensure the right to employment, housing, and education, as well as endeavour to provide social security and the prerequisites for good health. The same section also states that the rights of children are to be respected. This is now further emphasized by the 2020 incorporation of the CRC into Swedish law. According to the Swedish government, the incorporation stresses the importance of ensuring that the rights of children are realized in Sweden.[5] Overall, Sweden often strives to be considered as one of the most child-friendly countries in the world.[6]

Consistent with the ambitions of the Swedish welfare state, a series of various general (or in other words universal) support initiatives and subsidies are offered to all families with children, including child subsidies, childcare cost ceilings, and free school meals. More selectively focused, means-tested benefits also exist. These welfare support benefits function as a social safety net, and individuals who cannot support themselves in any other manner may apply for economic support from municipal social services.

This comprehensive social safety net might appear to be in accordance with the CRC's requirement on ratifying states to ensure that children have an adequate standard of living as well as the aim stated in Sweden's Instrument of Government to prevent poverty and economic vulnerability for children in Sweden today.[7] Nevertheless, while Sweden is one of the world's wealthiest countries on a per-capita basis, child poverty is still a problem. Against this background, this chapter poses these questions: What do the regulations in the international conventions and in Swedish law concerning the right to an adequate standard of living for *all* children actually mean in Sweden today? How, more concretely, is this right for children constructed in Swedish law, and how does the law relate to the general regulations in the Swedish constitution and the CRC? Are there legal challenges that can explain the economic vulnerability

5 See Legislative Bill 2017/18:186 *Inkorporering av FN:s konvention om barnets rättigheter*.

6 The goal of being the absolutely best country in which to grow up has been mentioned, for example, by Prime Minister Stefan Löfvén in the Government Declaration given during the fall of 2014. This was one of the reasons for the CRC incorporation, The Government of Sweden, 'Regeringsförklaringen'. Accessed 7 March 2021, www.regeringen.se/49b6d2/contentassets/436960c05f524109b8a020b879efd76b/regeringsforklaringen-3-oktober-2014. However, it can be noted that according to UNICEF's child wellbeing measurement, Sweden ranks only tenth after countries such as the Netherlands, Norway, Denmark, Switzerland, and Finland – see UNICEF Innocenti, 'Worlds of Influence: Understanding what shapes child well-being in rich countries', *Innocenti Report Card 16* (UNICEF Office of Research, Innocenti, Florence, 2020).

7 The terms 'poverty' and 'economic vulnerability' are discussed further below.

of some children in Sweden, and the inequalities that have emerged between different groups of children?

The chapter focuses on the outermost social safety net and the responsibility of the municipal social services – in other words, the means- and needs-based focused support that can be provided to families when general welfare contributions are not sufficient, and therefore offer support to the most economically vulnerable children in Sweden. Children's right to an adequate standard of living and the legal regulation of a social safety net for the individual child are analysed from a critical legal perspective that draws on childhood sociology to problematise the realization of children's rights in the Swedish context. We frame this theoretical exploration within literature on welfare conditionality and welfare-state typologies. The objective is to reveal underlying assumptions in the law that create a risk of undermining the realization of children's rights, and which can even create a type of silent acceptance of how certain children are poor in one of the world's richest countries. Sweden is used here as an example of how the welfare state, with its ideological premises and 'child-friendly self-image', is challenged by the requirement of realizing children's rights, not least in terms of the CRC's principle of non-discrimination. Although the focus is on Sweden, the discussion and findings are of broader interest as the realization of children's right to an adequate standard of living entails inherent challenges in any legal system of a welfare state.

The chapter starts with a description of theoretical starting points that guide our analysis and conclusions. This is followed by a short summary of previous research and reports regarding child poverty in Sweden and the social services' administration of municipal economic support to families with children. The legal regulations are then analysed against this background. The focus is on the CRC and its significance in Swedish law, the rights and responsibilities of parents as guardians, and municipal economic support according to the Social Services Act. The chapter concludes with a discussion of legal challenges with respect to achieving an adequate standard of living for children through rights.

2 Theoretical Premises

The legal analysis in this chapter is carried out through a social justice lens that focuses on risks connected to viewing children and childhood in unjust ways.[8] Such a perspective underscores the 'age order' in society, in which

8 For further explorations on the conditions of childhood from a child rights perspective, see Mayall, B., *Towards a sociology for childhood: thinking from children's lives* (Buckingham: Open University Press, 2002). Conditions of childhood and unjust treatment

childhood risk being regarded primarily as a preparatory phase to adulthood, and that children, rather than being seen as independent actors, are viewed largely as belonging to a family and parents in a process that has been referred to as 'familization'.[9] As will be discussed further in this chapter, through such familization processes in the decision-making by public authorities and courts, children risk being rendered invisible, which can lead to discriminatory practices. Such discrimination of children because they are children is sometimes referred to as 'childism'.[10]

Against the back-drop of these view-points and perspectives we examine how the legal regulation "handles" children's right to an adequate standard of living and how the law can ascertain that children in practice are seen as independent rights holders. In line with this view, we also invoke the perspective encouraged in critical children's rights studies: acting as 'critical proponents' when it comes to children's rights.[11] Simply emphasizing children's rights, for example by reference to the CRC, is not sufficient to create adequate living standards for children and therefore, the role of research must be to analyse more closely the impediments to the realization of an adequate living standards for children. Here, legal research in child law has an important

---

of children in relation to adults has been discussed by many other scholars, see for example Närvänen, A. and Näsman, E., 'Age Order and Children's Agency'. In Wintersberger, H. et al., (Eds.), *Childhood, Generational Order and the Welfare State: Exploring Children's Social and Economic Welfare*. Children's Welfare (Odense: University Press of Southern Denmark, 2007): 225–229.

9 Alanen, L., *Modern childhood?: exploring the 'Child question' in sociology* (Jyväskylä: Institute for Educational Research, University Press, 1992).

10 Childism can be described as having two sides: 1) childism to describe discrimination; compare with sexism; and 2) childism to describe the struggle for equality and empowerment; compare with feminism. See further Adami's contribution in this book, but also Young-Bruehl, E., *Childism: confronting prejudice against children*. (New Haven: Yale University Press, 2012), as in contrast to Wall, J., 'From Childhood Studies to Childism: Reconstructing the Scholarly and Social Imagination', *Children's Geographies* 20, no. 83 (2022): 257–270. See also Daly, A., Thorburn Stern, R. & Leviner, P., *UN Convention on the Rights of the Child, Article 2 and Discrimination on the basis of Childhood: The CRC Paradox?*, Nordic Journal of International Law, Volume 91, 2022, s. 419–452.

11 See for example Reynaert, D., Bouverne-De Bie, M., and Vandevelde, S., 'Between "believers" and "opponents" – Critical discussions on children's rights', *International Journal of Children's Rights* 20, no. 1 (2012): 155–168; and Vandenhole, W. (Ed.), *The Routledge International Handbook of Children's Rights Studies* (Abingdon: Routledge International, 2015).

task in detecting legal impediments – both in the formulation of rights and in the regulations that impose responsibility for the realization of these rights.[12]

The understanding that different welfare systems have diverse focus and structures that influence how the actualization of different rights can occur – in this case in the Swedish context – forms a basis for the analysis in this chapter. According to Esping-Andersen's oft-cited work, *The Three Worlds of Welfare Capitalism*,[13] and in later literature seeking to define different typologies of welfare states, the Swedish welfare system differs from liberal systems' (in countries such as the US and Great Britain) and 'conservative systems' (as in Germany and France). The Swedish welfare system is defined with Esping-Andersen's terms as 'social democratic', characterized by the focus on generous, broad, and non-needs-tested social initiatives for the citizens of the country. Equality among people is the central theme in this type of system (although generally not achieved by claiming rights) and efforts are put into giving citizens a relatively high degree of independence by limiting their dependence on the family and the market.[14] In this type of welfare state, there is a particular risk of poverty being associated with shame as there is an expectation that everyone is to contribute jointly to the system by working and paying taxes, and that individuals who do not pull their weight are a burden. It is thus generally held that today's Swedish welfare state is based on the work/support policy (*arbetslinjen*).[15] Being self-sufficient is the goal, and consequently, imposing requirements on those applying for support is viewed as correct and reasonable. The idea that welfare support systems are conditional in different ways is not unique to the Swedish system, and in international research this has been referred to as welfare conditionality.[16]

In this chapter, we investigate potential effects on children resulting from the conditions placed on receiving welfare support in the Swedish system,

12 See, for a discussion on the role and objectives of child law research in the Swedish context, Leviner, P., 'Barnrätt: ett rättsvetenskapligt ämne, tema eller perspektiv?'. In Arvidsson, R. et al., (Eds.), *Festskrift till Wiweka Warnling Conradson* (Stockholm: Jure, 2019).

13 Esping-Andersen, G., *The Three Worlds of Welfare Capitalism* (Princeton, Princeton University Press, 1990).

14 However, as we show in this chapter, children are dependent to a significant degree on their parents for actualizing the right to an adequate standard of living, which in itself can lead to discrimination.

15 Fernqvist, S., et al., *Barnfattigdom: barnfamiljers och professionellas perspektiv* (2nd ed.). (Lund: Gleerups, 2020).

16 See Watts, B., and Fitzpatrick, S. *Welfare conditionality* (Abingdon: Routledge, 2018) and the website for the large British research project on the theme: Department of Social Policy & Social Work, University of York 'Welfare Conditionality', accessed 7 March 2022, www.welfareconditionality.ac.uk.

for example the requirement on parents to submit a certain number of job or residence applications. We argue that these requirements risk leading to situations where children whose parents do not live up to the conditions and requirements will not get or lose their municipal economic support. Children in this situation become subjected to a sort of legally accepted discrimination that may violate the principles of non-discrimination and equal treatment, and which risk rendering invisible the specific needs of these children.

3 Briefly on Child Poverty in Sweden and the Administration of Municipal Economic Support to Families

What poverty and economic vulnerability constitutes and how the terms should be defined is not self-evident. The terms *absolute* and *relative* poverty are sometimes used to distinguish different types of economic vulnerability. Absolute poverty refers to a situation where the household income is not sufficient to pay for housing and necessary living expenses, while relative poverty concerns living in considerably worse economic circumstances (a lower income) in comparison to the median income of the population.[17] Both terms – poverty and economic vulnerability – are used in this chapter.

According to a recent report from the Swedish Social Insurance Agency, 8 percent of households with children live in absolute poverty. Among households with a single parent the number is 17 percent. Apart from households living in absolute poverty, 17,8 percent of households with children live in relative poverty.[18] The statistics reveal that children who live with a single parent (the mother) and children with a foreign background are the most vulnerable.[19]

As research on this in Sweden is limited, it is difficult to measure what it means for a child to grow up in poverty and what the resulting immediate and long-term consequences for children are. One difficulty in measuring child poverty is that poverty is often measured based on the parents' resources, thus

17 The threshold is usually at 60 % of the median income in Sweden. For a further discussion on the term 'poverty', see Fernqvist, S., et al. (2020), 14 ff.

18 Försäkringskassan [Swedish Social Insurance Agency], *Barnhushållens ekonomi – Resultatindikatorer för den ekonomiska familjepolitiken 2021*, (2021).

19 Fernqvist, et al. (2020); Köhler-Olsen, J., 'Growing up in families with low income – the state's legal obligation to recognize the child's right to adequate standard of living'. In Pellissery, S., Mathew, B., Govindjee A., and Narrain, A. (Eds.), *Transformative Law and Public Policy* (London: Routledge, 2019): 151–170, 161 concerning similar overrepresentation in Norway.

obscuring the actual situation of children.[20] What we do know from research is that poverty is a risk factor in that long-term poverty increases risks for both social and health-related problems.[21] Economically vulnerable children also live to a higher degree in unsafe environments, and in uncertain and short-term housing, with less access to food, clothing, play, and leisure time than other children.[22] It has also been observed that children to parents receiving economic support have a considerably greater risk of being placed in out-of-home care than other children.[23]

Different types of support exist, as noted, to assist parents economically, and the economic support administered by Swedish municipal social services is envisioned as an outermost social safety net. Several studies have examined whether a child perspective has been taken into account in economic support cases. For example, one study of administrative court judgments regarding municipal economic support to families with children shows that even where it was demonstrated that a child had needs that the support could fulfil, the child was seldom considered an independent actor. The child's own views and capabilities were not discussed to any great extent, in what could be viewed as a process of 'familization' where the child was simply considered as part of a family.[24] Similar conclusions are found in studies of the municipal social services' administration of economic support cases.[25] Studies focusing on children's participation in such cases show that children are very seldom given the opportunity to be heard, and the conclusion is that children are made invisible in such cases.[26]

By way of conclusion, studies on economic vulnerability in Sweden show that certain groups of children are affected more than others and we also know that to a significant degree, children are rendered invisible in municipal economic support cases. In the next section, we discuss how children's right to an

20 C.f. Fernqvist, et al. (2020), 16.

21 Wiklund, S., and Pålsson, D., "Barn i ekonomisk utsatthet – om barnperspektiv och ekonomiskt bistånd". In Bruno, L., and Becevic, Z. (Eds.), *Barn & unga i utsatta livssituationer: perspektiv från forskning och praktik* (Stockholm: Liber, 2020): 59–69.

22 C.f. Fernqvist, et al. (2020), 27; and Barnombudsmannen [The Ombudsman for Children in Sweden], *Inget rum för trygghet* (2016).

23 Schiratzki, J. *Barnrättens grunder* (7th ed.). (Lund: Studentlitteratur, 2019), 137; and Government Official Report Series 2009:68 *Care of Young Persons Act*, 340.

24 Fernqvist, et al. (2020), 211.

25 Näsman, E. 'Barnperspektiv på ekonomiskt bistånd'. In Hjort, T. (Ed.), *Det yttersta skyddsnätet: om arbete med socialbidrag* (Lund: Studentlitteratur, 2019): 247–268.

26 Heimer, M., and Palme, J., 'Rethinking Child Policy Post-UN Convention on the Rights of the Child: Vulnerable Children's Welfare in Sweden', *Journal of Social Policy* 45, no. 7 (2016): 435–452; Wiklund, S., and Pålsson, D. (2020).

adequate standard of living is legally constructed and how the right is legally conditioned, and by way of extension, we examine the legal aspects that can explain the process of familization.

4 The Right to an Adequate Standard of Living According to the CRC

Under Article 27 of the CRC, ratifying states are to recognize each child's right to a standard of living as required for the child's physical, psychological, spiritual, moral and social development. Parents, in their role as guardians, have the primary responsibility for realizing the child's right, but states are obligated to take suitable measures to assist parents and other guardians in a manner that is consistent with national circumstances and within the framework of states' resources.[27] The states shall also provide material support and support programmes when needed, particularly when it comes to food, clothing, and housing, but also to ensure the child's right to a standard of living as required for the child's physical, psychological, spiritual, moral, and social development.[28]

It should be noted that the obligations according to Article 27 are arguably also central to fulfilling the requirements of Article 6 CRC – one of the general principles of the Convention – which states the right to life, survival, and development. Adequate living conditions are evidently also a premise for other rights, such as the right to an education and to good health.[29] The UN Committee on the Rights of the Child has not published any general comments giving specific guidance as to the various obligations on ratifying states based on Article 27 (nor Article 6) CRC, but the Committee has referred to this article in several general comments on other topics. For example, the Committee has stated that Article 27 is applicable to all children, regardless of migration

27 UN Committee on the Rights of the Child, however, has interpreted Article 27 in such a manner that it does not prohibit an obligation for the states to give support, when necessary, directly to children, for example for children living on the streets, without guardians, or in violent family circumstances. UN Committee on the Rights of the Child. *General comment No. 21 (2017) on children in street situations*, CRC/C/GC/21, para. 49.

28 Alen, A., Vande Lanotte, J., Verhellen, E., Ang, F., Berghmans, E. and Verheyde, M., 'Interpretation and Application of Article 27'. In Eide, A. (Ed.), *Article 27: the rights to an adequate standard of living* (Martinus Nijhoff, Leiden, 2006): 15–44, 17; Nolan, A. 'Art.27 The Right to a Standard of Living Adequate for the Child's Development'. In Tobin, J. (Ed.), *The UN convention on the rights of the child: a commentary* (1st ed.). (Oxford: Oxford University Press, 2019): 1022–1055.

29 For a discussion on this see Dahlqvist, J., and Leviner, P. 'Barns rätt till liv, överlevnad och utveckling'. In Åhman, K., Leviner, P., and Zillén, K. (Eds.), *Barnkonventionen i praktiken: rättsliga utmaningar och* möjligheter (Stockholm: Norstedts juridik, 2020): 90–101.

status.[30] Important to note in this context is also that states are obligated in accordance with Article 4 to use their resources to the fullest extent to take the necessary measures to realize CRC rights.

By emphasizing in Article 27, that states must recognize *all* children's right to a necessary standard of living, this article is consistent with Article 2 on equal treatment and non-discrimination. According to this general principle of the Convention states are to respect and ensure that *each* child within their jurisdiction can exercise the rights in the Convention without discrimination of any kind, irrespective of the child's or his or her parent's or legal guardian's race, colour, sex, language, religion, political or other opinion, national, ethnic, or social origin, property, disability, birth, or other status. The Committee has emphasized that Article 2 means that no discrimination of any kind may occur, by for example pointing specifically to the rights of children residing in a country without legal permission.[31] The Committee has also noted the importance of positive treatment of particularly vulnerable groups, as well as the need to combat prejudices and stigmatization.[32]

These statements by the Committee with respect to Article 2 – which could have great significance for the application of Article 27 – can seem clear. However, while the principle of non-discrimination is one of the four general principles of the Convention, its actual content has not received much

---

30 The UN Committee on the Rights of the Child. Twenty-fourth session, *Consideration of Reports Submitted by States Parties under Article 44 of the Convention, Concluding observations of the Committee on the Rights of the Child Norway 2000*, (CRC/C/15/Add.126) regarding Norway's second periodic report; and UN Committee on the Rights of the Child. *General Comment No. 6 (2005) Treatment of Unaccompanied and Separated Children Outside their Country of Origin*, CRC/C/GC/2005/6, para. 12. See also the *Joint General Comment No. 4 (2017) of the UN Committee on the Protection of the Rights of All Migrant Workers and Members of their Families* and the UN Committee on the Rights of the Child. *No. 23 (2017) on the states' obligations regarding the human rights of children within the framework for international migration in the countries of origin, transit, destination and return*, CMW/C/GC/4-CRC/C/GC/23, section G.

31 For example, the Committee issued a principally important statement in the concluding observation with respect to Norway in 2000 that a State's responsibility includes all children within the jurisdiction, see CRC/C/15/Add.126. Thereafter, in its *General Comment No. 6* (2005), the Committee emphasized that no discriminatory treatment of children on the basis of nationality, citizenship, migrations status, or statelessness may occur, see UN Committee on the Rights of the Child. *General Comment No. 6 (2005)*, para. 12.

32 UN Committee on the Rights of the Child. *General Comment No. 11 (2009) Indigenous children and their rights under the Convention [on the Rights of the Child]*. CRC/C/GC/11, para. 24; UN Committee on the Rights of the Child. *General comment No. 6 (2005)*, para. 18, and UN Committee on the Rights of the Child. *General comment No. 5 (2003) General measures of implementation of the Convention on the Rights of the Child.* CRC/GC/2003/5, para.12.

attention in the Committee's statements, periodic state reports, or in legal literature.[33] Article 2 has also been described as problematic because it was both poorly drafted ('not well written') and difficult to understand owing to some confusion concerning the principle of non-discrimination ('people make too much of the right, while at the same time making too little of it').[34]

A reasonable interpretation of Article 27 in light of Article 2 would be that states need to direct particular support to children who are most vulnerable and in the greatest need.[35] In line with this, the principle of non-discrimination means that in addition to prohibiting discrimination, states also need to ensure that all children can enjoy their rights under the Convention.[36] In other words, 'those groups of children that are most disadvantaged in enjoying their rights', for example living in poverty, 'require the highest standard of protection'.[37]

From a more general non-discrimination perspective, it is also important to question whether states accept a system in which children are discriminated against in a non-legitimate manner, because they are children and compared to how adults are treated.[38] As has been pointed out earlier, studies show that too often, children in economic support cases are considered only in the

---

33 For a discussion on this see Lundy, L., and Byrne, B., 'The four general principles of the United Nations Convention on the Rights of the Child: the potential value of the approach in other areas of human rights law'. In Brems, E., Desmet, E., and. Vandenhole, W. (Eds.), *Children's Rights Law in the Global Human Rights Landscape: Isolation, Inspiration, Integration* (Abingdon: Routledge, 2017): 52–70; Schiratzki, J. 'Clarifications of Concepts – On the Four General Principles of the CRC'. In Schultz, T., Mork, A., and Hartoft, H. (Eds.), *Children's Rights – the Convention on the Rights of the Child in Danish Law* (Copenhagen: Djof Publishing 2020): 59–71.

34 Abramson, B., *A Commentary on the United Nations Convention on the Rights of the Child, Article 2: The Right of Non-Discrimination* (Leiden: Martinus Nijhoff, 2008), 147. See also Lainpelto, K., Chapter 4 in this volume.

35 C.f. Nolan, A. (2019).

36 Thorburn Stern, R. 'Skydd mot diskriminering'. In Åhman, K., Leviner, P., and Zillén K. (Eds.), *Barnkonventionen i praktiken: rättsliga utmaningar och möjligheter* (Stockholm: Norstedts juridik, 2020): 51–71.

37 This is emphasized by Croke, R., and Crowley, A., "Human Rights and Child Poverty in the UK – Time for Change". In Invernizzi, A., and Williams, A. (Eds.), *The Human Rights of Children – From Visions to Implementation* (Abingdon: Routlege, 2016): 250–270. See also the analysis presented in Leviner, P., 'Våra barn och andras ungar – om solidaritet och (o)likabehandling av barn i det svenska välfärdssystemet'. In Erhag, T., Leviner, P., and Lind, A. (Eds.), *Socialrätt under omvandling – om solidaritetens och välfardsstatens gränser* (Stockholm: Liber förlag 2018): 94–131.

38 C.f. Adami, R., Chapter 6 this volume. This is an issue that is focused on in the on-going research project, 'Treated like a child', conducted by Daly, A., Thorburn Stern, R., and Leviner, R. financed by Ragnar Söderbergs stiftelse.

context of the family rather than as individuals with rights of their own. This can be seen as discrimination against children.[39]

5 Parental Primary Responsibility and Gatekeeping Function in Swedish Law

Just as in the CRC – and most likely the majority of legal systems in the world – Swedish law is based on parents, in their role as guardians, serving as the first-hand fulfillers of children's rights and needs. Chapter 6 Section 1 and 2 of the Swedish Parental Code (*föräldrabalken*) state that children's guardians have the responsibility for the child's personal circumstances and needs, ensuring that the child receives the necessary supervision, and ensuring that the child has sufficient support and education.[40]

In line with parent's responsibility as guardian according to Chapter 6 Section 11 of the Parental Code, the rights and responsibilities on deciding issues concerning a child's personal matters are also included, but guardians are to make greater consideration for the child's views and wishes in keeping with the child's increasing age and development. As shown in the next section, this also means that the guardian is the one who must apply for family support benefits, and it is up to the guardian to determine how any financial resources are to be distributed within the family.

Thus, guardians have the primary responsibility for ensuring that their children's basic needs are met and that they receive the appropriate support, while the ultimate responsibility for the situation and living circumstances of children lies with the municipal social services. This can be seen in Chapter 2 Section 1 and Chapter 4 Section 1 of the Social Services Act (*socialtjänstlagen*), which state that the municipal social services are responsible for ensuring that all persons – including children – who reside in the municipality and who cannot provide for themselves in any other manner are given various types of support to achieve a reasonable standard of living as set out by law. The

---

39 See further Adami, R., Chapter 6 this volume.

40 Non-guardian parents also have a responsibility for support, and to the degree a parent fails to pay maintenance for their children, maintenance support can be paid to the other parent by the Swedish Insurance Agency. The support responsibility is regulated in Chapter 7 of the Parental Code, and the regulation of maintenance by the Swedish Insurance Agency is found in the Social Insurance Code (2010:110) (*Socialförsäkringsbalken*). The support responsibility of parents remains in place until the child has completed a high school education, but can be extended to when the child reaches 21 years of age, see Chapter 7, Section 1(2) of the Parental Code.

specific responsibility of the social services for children and youth is set out in Chapter 5 Section 1 of the Social Services Act, which states (among other things) that this responsibility – in addition to preventive and supportive measures at home – also includes placing children outside the home if doing so is necessary to protect children from harm and will serve the best interests of the child.

A basic premise for all social services is that they are to be voluntarily available – in other words, consensual.[41] It is only when children are at risk of serious harm in certain specific circumstances that the social services can act without consent and thus against the will of the guardian.[42] As long as the requirements in the Care of Young Persons Act (*lag med särskilda bestämmelser om vård av unga,* LVU) are not fulfilled, it is the guardian who decides whether to apply for and accept support, both economic and other types of measures. This follows from Chapter 6 Section 11 of the Parental Code as mentioned above. According to Chapter 11 Section 10 of the Social Services Act, children have legal standing when they reach the age of 15 years, which gives children and youths certain possibilities to apply on their own for and consent to certain types of support from social services.[43]

Nevertheless, even if older children have legal standing in these issues, the fact remains that a child's independent right is limited to a large extent by parents' authority in their role as guardians to decide over their children. This authority means that in their roles as guardians, parents act as gatekeepers, choosing whether to apply for municipal economic support and even reject any offered support. It also lies within the authority of parents in their role as guardians to use the received economic support as they wish; in other words, there is no guarantee that the municipal economic support will benefit the children. The question is then whether this outermost social safety net – in the form of the social services' responsibility – is truly designed to guarantee children a reasonable standard of living. This question is examined in the next section.

41 See Chapter 3 Section 5 of the Social Services Act.

42 See the Care of Young Persons Act.

43 Under Swedish law, children's legal standing depends on the legal issue at hand. See further Schiratzki, J. (2019).

6 The Social Services (Act) Guaranteeing but Conditioning the Outermost Social Safety Net

As described above in the introduction, the Swedish welfare system offers various types of support to families with children. The right to an adequate standard of living according to Article 27 CRC does not provide a basis for a claim; that is, children (or parents) cannot use this Article to make a claim for support from the social services. This is not changed by the fact that the CRC was incorporated into Swedish law in 2020. Instead, the right is to be realized through more concrete, legally regulated support. For those who are most vulnerable, the thought is that adequate standard of living is to be achieved through the municipal economic support regulated by the Social Services Act.

As already mentioned, municipal economic support is conceptualized to serve as an outermost social safety net when all other possibilities for support are exhausted. Individuals who cannot support themselves or cannot meet their own needs in any other way have the right to receive such support to achieve and maintain a reasonable standard of living.[44] Self-sufficiency is nevertheless the goal and, as noted, this support can be conditioned in different ways and the objective is to provide the support only during a short period.

With respect to families with children, the municipal economic support is adjusted in order to meet the basic needs of the children, but the starting point remains: parents are to support their children, and in their role as guardians, parents are responsible for applying for support for their children.[45] When seeking support, parents are also expected to demonstrate the child's need of support in the application and during the investigation by social services.[46] An important aspect to emphasize here is that the regulations on economic support in the Social Services Act are based on principles of consent and self-determination. No one can be forced to accept support. Children (and their families) can therefore have a need and may formally fulfil the requirements for support according to the Social Services Act, but if the parents do not apply for support nor demonstrate the child's needs, support to which the child (and the family) would have been eligible for will not be given.

In addition to this extension of parents' responsibility to apply for support, the right to support must be viewed primarily in relation to the entire household.[47] This means that when a parent applies for economic support for

---

44 Chapter 4 Section 1 of the Social Services Act.

45 C.f. Näsman, E. (2019), 257.

46 Ibid., 259.

47 This has been emphazised by the Supreme Administrative Court in case, HFD 1995 ref 79.

themselves and their children, the household is assessed as a unit and not on the basis of its individual members. A child's individual needs are certainly a basis for the form of the support – primarily in terms of the amount of municipal economic support the household is to receive – but in general, qualification for municipal economic support is assessed in relation to the household as a whole. Consequently, the legal construction of how the right to support is to be assessed is characterized by an adult perspective, in which the child can clearly be said to be rendered invisible through what has been called a 'familization process'.[48]

When it comes to requirements for being eligible for economic support from the social services, applicants only have the right to municipal economic support if they *cannot* support themselves economically in another way, for example through employment, unemployment benefits or sickness benefit. Furthermore, in cases where support is granted, the support is not given without fulfilling certain conditions.[49] These conditions are justified by the goal that individuals who receive municipal economic support in the long term are to become self-sufficient.[50] The conditions are set out in the Social Services Act and stipulate (among other things) that as a main rule, the individual receiving municipal economic support must be at the disposal of the labour market. This basically entails doing whatever is necessary to get a job. The social services can also require the applicant's participation in adult education such as Swedish-language courses for immigrants.[51] The intent in the Social Services Act is thus that conditions should be placed on the benefits recipient, and there are no exceptions from this conditionality when the person applying for support has children.

In addition to these conditions, the social services can place requirements on the support recipient which are not directly regulated in the Social Services Act.[52] One example of added requirements involves persons who receive

48 C.f. Näsman, E. (2019), 247.

49 This follows, as we will show below, from how the text of the legislation is formulated. See further Socialstyrelsen, *Ekonomiskt bistånd Handbok för socialtjänsten* [National Board of Health and Welfare: The handbook for the Social Services on economic support] (2021). A part of the support that children who live with separated parents receive is the maintenance subsidy or maintenance support the guardian under certain conditions has the right to.

50 Socialstyrelsen (2021), 81.

51 Such requirements are however not imposed if the person for some reason, for example for health reasons, cannot be at the disposal of the labour market.

52 This can be considered as a part of self-responsibility, c.f. Kjellbom, P., and Alexius, K., 'Socialrättsliga principer vid risk för vräkning: finns det i Sverige en rätt till boende, bostad eller ett hem?', *Juridisk tidskrift* no. 2 (2011): 273–289.

help with housing through the social services. Sweden does not have a social housing sector, and individuals who cannot arrange housing on their own are instead directed to apply to the social services for support. However, no explicit right to housing exists in the Social Services Act. Nevertheless, case law from the Administrative Supreme Court shows that individuals who are entirely without housing and who have specific difficulties in arranging housing on the housing market have the right to housing under the Social Services Act.[53] In practice, such arrangements are conditioned upon different requirements, for example the acceptance of supervision by the social services[54] or specific obligations to attempt to arrange housing on one's own in the housing market by viewing available dwellings.[55]

An example of such specific obligations (or in other words conditionality), is found in a case dealt with by the Administrative Court of Stockholm concerning a single mother with three children.[56] In the case, the social services had required the mother to demonstrate that she had applied for twenty apartments in one week in order to continue living in the apartment that the social services had provided for her and her children. The mother had applied for significantly fewer apartments during a two-week period and the social services almost immediately terminated the family's housing. The mother appealed the decision, which was upheld by the court because the mother did not fulfil the requirement for receiving support in the form of housing, 'even taking into consideration the perspective of the best interests of the child'.

This case illustrates how the conditions and requirements imposed on parents in the Social Services Act trump children's best interests and their right to an adequate standard of living – even when it comes to such a fundamental need as suitable housing. Other examples of requirements and conditions placed on single parents include the obligation to apply for housing throughout the entire country, which by way of extension means that the child's right to housing is pitted against the right to contact and visitation with a

53 HFD 1990 ref. 119 and HFD 2004 ref. 130.

54 The Parliamentary Ombudsmen's decisions 25 September 2014, dnr 4930-2012, 28 June 2018 dnr 7179-2016 and 28 June 2018 dnr 7595-2016.

55 For an in-depth study on how alike conditions effect single mothers, see Samzelius, T., *A vicious circle of silent exclusion Family homelessness and poverty in Sweden from a single-mother perspective* (Malmö University, 2020).

56 The Administrative Court of Stockholm's judgment case number 1894–18, 14 March 2018. There is no information available about what happened to this family. To our knowledge there are no studies having looked at what happens to families who are denied support. See further Schiratzki, J., Chapter 1 in this volume about the Swedish court system.

non-custodial parent, or for that matter other important care-givers.[57] This is also illustrative of how the proportionality and suitability of conditional welfare can be questioned from a child's perspective.

In this context, it is important to note that when it comes to children in Sweden who lack a residence permit, which is a very vulnerable group, there are no clear regulations on the right to municipal economic support according to the Social Services Act. This has been confirmed by a 2017 judgment from the Supreme Administrative Court.[58] The judgment, which has been debated,[59] concerned a single mother with three children who had applied for and had been denied permanent residency in Sweden. After being denied residency, the family remained in the country without permission and hid in order to avoid deportation. The mother applied for support for herself and her children, but this was ultimately denied by the Supreme Administrative Court. For children in Sweden, the right to an adequate standard of living is consequently conditioned on legal status and their parents' decision to remain in the country without permission. This is in contrast to the statement of the UN Committee on the Rights of the Child, that children should enjoy the rights in the Convention regardless of migration status.[60]

It is interesting and important to note that the conditional character of the right to a reasonable standard of living is not concretely affected by the principle of the best interests of the child and the child's right to participation according to Articles 3 and 12 CRC, also found in the Social Services Act (Chapter 11 Section 10 and Chapter 1 Section 2). These principles mean that a child's needs and interests are to be taken into consideration when authorities make decisions in cases concerning children. However, the conditions discussed above

---

57 The Parliamentary Ombudsmen's decision 29 June 2018 dnr 1126–2017.

58 Supreme Administrative Court, HFD 2017 ref. 33. See further Schiratzki, J., Chapter 1 in this volume.

59 See Holappa, T. 'Barns rätt till social trygghet och skälig levnadsstandard'. In Åhman, K., Leviner, P., and Zillén, K. (Eds.), *Barnkonventionen i praktiken: rättsliga utmaningar och möjligheter* (Stockholm: Norstedts juridik, 2020): 200–221; Kjellbom, P., and Lundberg, A. 'Olika rättsliga rum för en skälig levnadsnivå?: En rättskartografisk analys av SoL och LMA i domstolspraktiken', *Nordisk Socialrättslig tidskrift*, no. 17–18 (2018): 39–71; Glotz Stade, N., 'Rättsfallskommentar: HFD 2017 ref. 33. Socialnämndens yttersta ansvar i akuta nödsituationer – ett negligerat ansvar?', *Förvaltningsrättslig tidskrift*, no. 1 (2018): 123–135.

60 CRC/C/15/Add.126 and UN Committee on the Rights of the Child. *General comment No. 6 (2005)*, para. 12. See also the *Joint General comment No. 4 (2017) of the UN Committee on the Protection of the Rights of All Migrant Workers and Members of their Families*, and the UN Committee on the Rights of the Child. *No. 23 (2017) on the states' obligations regarding the human rights of children within the framework for international migration in the countries of origin, transit, destination and return*, CMW/C/GC/4-CRC/C/GC/23, section G.

are more concretely regulated, which means that as long as no clear statement is set out in the law, stipulating that a different assessment is to be made when it comes to families with children, the conditions on parents trump children's needs, best interests and rights to municipal economic support. This can be seen as a clear example of 'welfare conditionality' described above. As noted, conditioning welfare seems justified either through the idea that everyone should – or at least try to – contribute to society and not be a 'burden' on it, or the idea that it is in the recipients' best interest to support themselves, as this encourages individuals to become self-sufficient.[61] One central question in this context, is whether the conditions imposed on parents are reasonable and proportionate from a child's perspective. We return to this discussion in the last section of this chapter.

Our analysis shows that the conclusions drawn in the research described above on how the social services' handles applications of economic support can be seen as being confirmed or even sanctioned by the legal system. The notion that children are rendered invisible in the practices of the social services is thus consistent with how legislation is formulated and applied. It is clear that the outermost social safety net for children – and by extension children's right to an adequate standard of living – is conditional. This situation has been referred to as '[un]deserving parents make children undeserving of society's support'.[62] Even if ensuring that children are heard in the procedures for economic support (for example by social workers speaking with children) would provide a clearer child perspective in the legislation and subsequent practices, the result would probably be the same unless the conditions for support were changed. Whatever children say, the requirements and conditions have so far been given stronger weight and, in other words, trump children's right to an adequate standard of living and the strive for economic equality.

In cases where a guardian does not take parental responsibility and fails to apply for support when children require it, or does not fulfil the conditions imposed on them by social services, there is currently no possibility for the social services to give support directly to children.[63] The authority to intervene with support and protection for children who are at risk of serious harm is regulated as described above in the Care of Young Persons Act and is tied to types of deficiencies in the home other than poverty. In general terms, the Care of

61 Watts, B., and Fitzpatrick, S., (2018), 113.

62 Näsman, E. (2019), 258.

63 Only in exceptional cases can support be paid out directly to youths over 18 but under 21 years of age who are still covered by the guardian's duty to support; C.f. Socialstyrelsen (2021), 154–155. C.f. Näsman, E. (2019).

Young Persons Act concerns parental abuse and neglect and not economic vulnerability. Only if there is a tangible risk that a child can be seriously harmed can the social services intervene without the guardian's consent (according to the Care of Young Persons Act), and such interventions mean that the child will be placed in a family home or an institution. There is no known case law concerning out-of-home placement solely on the basis of the consequences of poverty, at least from an appellate court, but it is not impossible that such cases will arise in the future. It should be noted, however, that as mentioned above, children in families who receive support are overrepresented among those children who are placed in social care outside the home.

In summary, regulations concerning the care of children are constructed on the premise that the 'system' is to ensure that families have sufficient economic means to meet basic needs such as housing and food. However, when we know that children's right to an adequate standard of living is conditioned by how 'deserving' their parents are, and when poverty is an increasing problem in Sweden, the question is this: what does this situation mean for the child protection system? Should child protection regulations be adjusted so that children to a higher degree can be placed in out-of-home-care due to economic vulnerability, to guarantee the right to an adequate standard of living? Many would oppose to such regulations and there are probably better ways of ensuring an adequate and equal standard of living for children. The next section offers reflections on how the present system could be challenged and what changes are needed.

7 Conclusions – Layers of Conditions and Legal Invisibility

As can be seen from the examination and analysis in this chapter, there is a discrepancy between the legal ambition of ensuring on the one hand, that everyone in Sweden – and not least children – can enjoy an adequate standard of living, and on the other hand, the hard reality that there are children in Sweden who live in economic vulnerability. Beyond the studies mentioned earlier demonstrating that it is not unusual for children in Sweden to live in poverty, we do not know much about either the consequences of poverty or how authorities and courts handles and reasons when assessing needs and when deciding on the eligibility of municipal economic support for families with children who are living in economic vulnerability. As described, there are some studies showing that children are largely invisible in the management of and decisions in such cases. Legal academic research in Sweden in this area is generally lacking, as is more systemic legal academic review of the case law. We have only scratched the surface here by including a few illustrative cases.

Our overall conclusion is that the invisibility of children described in previous research on the case-management and decisions by the social services and courts is not surprising. Instead, this invisibility can be seen as accepted by the legal system. As we have shown, the current Swedish regulations impose a series of requirements and conditions which, from a child's perspective, entail clear limitations as to the possibility to realize children's right to an adequate standard of living. This state of affairs can be described as layers of problematic assumptions and conditions that risk rendering children's specific needs and rights invisible.

Children's rights in this respect are actualized primarily through their parents, with support and contributions based on the parents' application for support and acceptance of offered contributions. Above all, support to families with children is made conditional through specific requirements imposed on parents, and from a child's perspective these requirements can be both unreasonable and disproportional. In this manner the above-mentioned depiction by Näsman that '[un]deserving parents can make children undeserving of support' can be said to be sanctioned and reproduced by the legal system.[64]

The objective of this chapter has been to discuss how the Swedish legal structure handles the most economically vulnerable children's right to an adequate standard of living. The basic assumptions, requirements and conditions that we have revealed and examined here pierce a hole in the Swedish outermost social safety net. As we have shown, this give rise to a (silent) acceptance of a situation in which not all children are ensured an adequate standard of living and that children are discriminated against (compared to adults) based on the ability and capacity of their parents to ensure that standard of living.

The principle of the best interests of the child and children's right to participation are intended in part to address the fact that children in Sweden currently lack an independent, claimable right to an adequate standard of living. However, as long as the legal regulations entail that the described requirements and the conditionality involved, continually trumps children's rights, the principle of the best interests of the child and children's right to participation as such do not have sufficient 'legal effectiveness' to challenge the limitations of the right to an adequate standard of living. This has not changed by the fact that the CRC is incorporated in Swedish law. However, the legal regulations can be challenged from a child's perspective. It would be desirable to receive

64 Näsman, E. (2019).

clarification from the Swedish legislator regarding what a child's right to an adequate standard of living means in practice in Sweden today, and how that right should be fulfilled. In the absence of such political initiatives, the hope is that cases will be brought to the courts.

Our child protection system – in other words, the authority and obligation to intervene to protect children who are at risk for serious harm – does not adequately address children who are living in poverty, and it is generally accepted that children should *not* be placed in out-of-home care based on poverty. At the same time, society cannot silently watch and accept that children are affected by the short- and long-term consequences to which poverty can lead. There is no self-evident solution for the problems that have been described here, and the way forward is not clear. One immediate shift could be for the social services to properly assess the proportionality when setting conditions on parents applying for municipal economic support.[65] In such assessments of children's rights, the best interest of the child and the child's needs must be taken into consideration. One thing, however, is certain: there are good arguments supporting the view that the current system does not create reasonable and equal living conditions for all children in Sweden today, despite the country's status as one of the world's wealthiest nations and its child-friendly self-image. Therefore, the definition of the right to an adequate standard of living for children in Sweden today must be clarified, and the corresponding responsibility of society must be more accurately defined.

References

Abramson, Bruce. 2008. *Commentary on the United Nations Convention on the Rights of the Child, Article 2: The Right of Non-Discrimination*. Leiden: Martinus Nijhoff.

Administrative Court of Stockholm's judgment case number 1894–18, 14 March 2018.

Alanen, Leena. 1992. *Modern childhood?: Exploring the 'Child question' in sociology*. Jyväskylä: University Institute for Educational Research: University Press.

Alen, André, Johan Vande Lanotte, Eugeen Verhellen, Fiona Ang, Eva Berghmans, and Mieke Verheyde. 2006. "Interpretation and Application of Article 27", in Asbjørn Eide (Ed.), *Article 27: the rights to an adequate standard of living*, 15–44. Leiden: Martinus Nijhoff.

65 Helmius, I., 'Proportionalitetsprincipen'. In Marcusson, L. (Ed.) *Offentligrättsliga principer* (4th ed). (Uppsala: Iustus, 2020).

Croke, Rhian, and Anne Crowley. 2016. "Human Rights and Child Poverty in the UK – Time for Change", in Antonella Invernizzi, and Jane Williams (Eds.), *The Human Rights of Children – From Visions to Implementation*, 250–270. London: Routledge.

Dahlqvist, Julia, and Pernilla Leviner. 2020. "Barns rätt till liv, överlevnad och utveckling", in Karin Åhman, Pernilla Leviner, and Kavot Zillén (Eds.), *Barnkonventionen i praktiken: rättsliga utmaningar och möjligheter*, 90–101. Stockholm: Norstedts juridik.

Daly, Aoife, Rebecca Stern & Pernilla Leviner. 2022. "UN Convention on the Rights of the Child, Article 2 and Discrimination on the basis of Childhood: The CRC Paradox?", *Nordic Journal of International Law* 91: 419–452.

Esping-Andersen, Gøsta. 1990. *The Three Worlds of Welfare Capitalism*. Cambridge: Princeton University Press.

Fernqvist, Stina, Marie Flinkfeldt, Elisabet Näsman, and Christina Ponton von Gerber. 2020. *Barnfattigdom: barnfamiljers och professionellas perspektiv*. Malmö: Gleerups.

Försäkringskassan [Swedish Social Insurance Agency]. 2021. *Barnhushållens ekonomi – Resultatindikatorer för den ekonomiska familjepolitiken 2021*.

Glotz Stade, Natalie. 2018. "Rättsfallskommentar: HFD 2017 ref. 33. Socialnämndens yttersta ansvar i akuta nödsituationer – ett negligerat ansvar?" *Förvaltningsrättslig tidskrift*, 1: 123–135.

Government of Sweden, Government Declaration, Stefan Löfvén, October 2014, www.regeringen.se/49b6d2/contentassets/43696oco5f524109b8a020b879efd76b/regeringsforklaringen-3-oktober-2014 accessed 9 September 2021.

Government's Official Investigations. 2009. *Lag om stöd och skydd för barn och unga* (SOU 2009:68).

Heimer, Maria, and Joakim Palme. 2016. "Rethinking Child Policy Post-UN Convention on the Rights of the Child: Vulnerable Children's Welfare in Sweden", *Journal of Social Policy* 45(3): 435–452.

Helmius, Ingrid. 2020. "Proportionalitetsprincipen", in Lena Marcusson (Ed.), *Offentligrättsliga principer* (4th ed). Uppsala: Iustus.

Hirdman, Yvonne. 2018. *Att lägga livet till rätta – studier i svensk folkhemspolitik*. Stockholm: Carlssons.

Holappa, Tim. 2020. "Barns rätt till social trygghet och skälig levnadsstandard", in Karin Åhman, Pernilla Leviner, and Kavot Zillén (Eds.), *Barnkonventionen i praktiken: rättsliga utmaningar och möjligheter*, 200–221. Stockholm: Norstedts juridik.

Kjellbom, Pia, and Katarina Alexius. 2011. "Socialrättsliga principer vid risk för vräkning: finns det i Sverige en rätt till boende, bostad eller ett hem?", *Juridisk tidskrift*, 2: 273–289.

Kjellbom, Pia, and Anna Lundberg. 2018. "Olika rättsliga rum för en skälig levnadsnivå?: En rättskartografisk analys av SoL och LMA i domstolspraktiken", *Nordisk Socialrättslig tidskrift*, 17–18: 39–71.

Köhler-Olsen, Julia. 2019. "Growing up in families with low income – the state's legal obligation to recognize the child's right to adequate standard of living", in Sony Pellissery, Babu Mathew, Avinash Govindjee, and Arvind Narrain (Eds.), *Transformative Law and Public Policy*, 151–170. London: Routledge India.

Legislative Bill 2017/18:186 *Inkorporering av fn:s konvention om barnets rättigheter* (Prop. 2017/18:186).

Leviner, Pernilla. 2018. "Våra barn och andras ungar – om solidaritet och (o)likabehandling av barn i det svenska välfärdssystemet", in Thomas Erhag, Pernilla Leviner, and Anna-Sara Lind (Eds.), *Socialrätt under omvandling – om solidaritetens och välfärdsstatens gränser*, 94–131. Stockholm: Liber förlag.

Leviner, Pernilla. 2019. "Barnrätt: ett rättsvetenskapligt ämne, tema eller perspektiv?", in Richard Arvidsson, Pernilla Leviner, Jane Reichel, Mauro Zamboni, and Karin Åhman (Eds.), *Festskrift till Wiweka Warnling Conradson*, 193–206. Stockholm: Jure.

Lundy, Laura, and Bronagh Byrne. 2017. "The four general principles of the United Nations Convention on the Rights of the Child: the potential value of the approach in other areas of human rights law", in Eva Brems, Ellen Desmet, and Wouter Vandenhole (Eds.), *Children's Rights Law in the Global Human Rights Landscape: Isolation, Inspiration, Integration*, 52–70. Abingdon, Oxon: Routledge.

Mayall, Berry. 2002. *Towards a sociology for childhood: thinking from children's lives*. Buckingham: Open University Press.

Nolan, Aoife. 2019. "Art.27 The Right to a Standard of Living Adequate for the Child's Development", in John Tobin (Ed.), *The UN convention on the rights of the child: a commentary*, 1022–1055. Oxford: Oxford University Press.

Närvänen, Anna-Liisa, and Elisabet Näsman. 2007. "Age Order and Children's Agency", in Helmut Wintersberger, Leena Alanen, Thomas Olk, and Jens Qvortrup (Eds.), *Childhood, Generational Order and the Welfare State: Exploring Children's Social and Economic Welfare*, 225–229. Odense: University Press of Southern Denmark.

Näsman, Elisabet. 2019. "Barnperspektiv på ekonomiskt bistånd", in Torbjörn Hjort (Ed.), *Det yttersta skyddsnätet: om arbete med socialbidrag*, 247–268. Lund: Studentlitteratur.

Ombudsman for Children in Sweden (2016) *Inget rum för trygghet*. https://www.barnombudsmannen.se/stallningstaganden/publikationer/inget-rum-for-trygghet--barn-och-unga-om-vrakningar-och-hemloshet/ accessed 30 July 2022.

Parliamentary Ombudsmen's decision 25 September 2014 dnr. 4930-2012.

Parliamentary Ombudsmen's decision 28 June 2018 dnr. 7179-2016.

Parliamentary Ombudsmen's decision 28 June 2018 dnr. 7595-2016.

Parliamentary Ombudsmen's decision 29 June 2018 dnr. 1126-2017.

Reynaert, Didier, Maria Bouverne-De Bie, and Stijn Vandevelde. 2015. "Between 'believers' and 'opponents' – Critical discussions on children's rights", *International Journal of Children's Rights* 20(1):155–168.

Samzelius, Tove. 2020. *A vicious circle of silent exclusion Family homelessness and poverty in Sweden from a single-mother perspective.* Malmö: Malmö University Press.

Schiratzki, Johanna. 2019. *Barnrättens grunder.* Lund: Studentlitteratur.

Schiratzki, Johanna. 2020. "Clarifications of Concepts – On the Four General Principles of the CRC", in Tine Schultz, Anne Mørk, and Hanne Hartoft (Eds.), *Children's Rights – the Convention on the Rights of the Child in Danish Law,* 59–71. Copenhagen: Djof Publishing.

Socialstyrelsen [National Board of Health and Welfare], *Ekonomiskt bistånd Handbok för socialtjänsten* [The handbook for the Social Services on economic support], 2021.

Supreme Administrative Court of Sweden, HFD 1990 ref. 119.

Supreme Administrative Court of Sweden, HFD 1995 ref. 79.

Supreme Administrative Court of Sweden, HFD 2004 ref. 130.

Supreme Administrative Court of Sweden, HFD 2017 ref. 33.

Thorburn Stern, Rebecca. 2020. "Skydd mot diskriminering", in Karin Åhman, Pernilla Leviner, and Kavot Zillén (Eds.), *Barnkonventionen i praktiken: rättsliga utmaningar och möjligheter*, 51–71. Stockholm: Norstedts juridik.

UNICEF Innocenti. 2020. 'Worlds of Influence: Understanding what shapes child well-being in rich countries', *Innocenti Report Card 16*, UNICEF Office of Research. Innocenti, Florence.

United Nations Committee on the Protection of the Rights of All Migrant Workers and Members of their Families and UN Committee on the Rights of the Child. *Joint general comment No. 4 (2017) of the Committee on the Protection of the Rights of All Migrant Workers and Members of Their Families and No. 23 (2017) of the Committee on the Rights of the Child on State obligations regarding the human rights of children in the context of international migration in countries of origin, transit, destination and return.* CMW/C/GC/4-CRC/C/GC/23 (16 November 2017).

United Nations Committee on the Rights of the Child. *General comment No. 5 (2003). General measures of implementation of the Convention on the Rights of the Child.* CRC/GC/2003/5 (27 November 2003).

United Nations Committee on the Rights of the Child. *General comment No. 6 (2005). Treatment of Unaccompanied and Separated Children Outside their Country of Origin*, CRC/C/GC/2005/6 (1 September 2005).

United Nations Committee on the Rights of the Child. *General comment No. 11 (2009) Indigenous children and their rights under the Convention [on the Rights of the Child]* CRC/C/GC/11. (12 February 2009).

United Nations Committee on the Rights of the Child. *General comment No. 21 (2017) on Children in Street Situations.* CRC/C/GC/21 (20 June 2017).

United Nations Committee on the Rights of the Child, Twenty-fourth session. *Consideration of Reports Submitted by States Parties under Article 44 of the Convention*

Concluding observations of the Committee on the Rights of the Child Norway 2000, CRC/C/15/Add.126.

Vandenhole, Wouter (Ed.). 2015. *The Routledge International Handbook of Children's Rights Studies* Abingdon: Routledge International.

Wall, John, 2022. "From Childhood Studies to Childism: Reconstructing the Scholarly and Social Imaginations", *Children's Geographies* 20(83): 257–270.

Watts, Beth, and Suzanne Fitzpatrick. 2018. *Welfare conditionality*. Abingdon: Routledge.

Wiklund, Stefan, and David Pålsson. 2020. "Barn i ekonomisk utsatthet – om barnperspektiv och ekonomiskt bistånd", in Linnéa Bruno, and Zulmir Becevic (Eds.), *Barn & unga i utsatta livssituationer: perspektiv från forskning och praktik*, 56–69. Stockholm: Liber.

Young-Bruehl, Elisabeth. 2012. *Childism: confronting prejudice against children*. New Haven: Yale University Press.

A Response to Pernilla Leviner and Tim Holappa

Lars Lindblom

In their aptly titled chapter *Child Rights without Substance*, Leviner and Holappa identify an important aspect of welfare conditionality and its detrimental effect on children. Economic support for children in or near poverty is delivered to through municipal social services, but whether children in need actually receive such support is dependent on two conditions. First, the child's parent must choose to apply for such support and, second, the parent must act in a manner that satisfies the conditions for being granted support.

As a consequence of organizing economic support in this fashion, a limitation has been placed on the economic rights of children in poverty: these children may have a right to 'have their economic interests looked after', but given *how* this kind of aid is structured, it may be far from certain that children receive the support to which they are entitled. In general, to have a right is to have a guarantee, but in the case of children – due to conditionality – no such guarantee exists. In other words, this is a case of children's rights without substance.

The first condition mentioned above (parents' ability and choice to seek support) raises issues about an arguably confused way that we tend to think about responsibility and childhood, and the second condition (parents' qualifying behaviour for receiving support) illustrates how the notion of conditionality may conflict with standard accounts of moral justifications of the family. In addition to writing on an issue of utmost practical importance, Leviner and Holappa have delivered a chapter with much to offer for those of us with an interest in the core issues of the philosophy of childhood.

A common way of thinking about responsibility and children is that for at least two reasons, children should not be held responsible in the same way that may be suitable for holding adults to account: children are not sufficiently developed and they are vulnerable. It is generally held that on the one hand, children may have yet to develop the capacities for autonomous choice that are preconditions for responsibility, and on the other hand, since children are in a vulnerable developmental state, it may be inappropriate to hold them responsible. Now, let us consider the following picture of how conditionality may influence individual responsibility in relation to welfare rights. A person can choose to abide by the conditions of welfare conditionality or choose to refrain from doing so. If the person chooses not to abide by the conditions, then any negative consequences thereof are regarded the responsibility of the individual. This in turn assumes that the person satisfies three criteria of responsible choice: 1) that s/he can act voluntarily (and is not subject to coercion), 2) s/he is informed (and knows the alternatives and outcomes), and 3) s/he has the capacity to make choices (and has achieved a sufficient level of autonomy). This ensures that the agent's choice is her or his own.

The connection between conditionality and responsibility breaks down in several ways in the cases that Leviner and Holappa investigate. First, conditionality directly for children is inappropriate, given that we have reasons – either vulnerability or autonomy – not to hold children responsible in the manner prescribed by this conditionality. Secondly, the notion of responsibility here is one of one's own choice, but what welfare conditionality of economic support for children in fact does is to hold some people (children) responsible for the choices of other people (the parents). This seems an inconsistent use of ideas of responsibility, and one that drains children's rights of substance.

However, the parent and the child are family. Could this play a role in justifying conditionality? Perhaps, but it seems implausible for other reasons that the chapter also brings to the fore. This has to do with the near-draconian conditions that parents sometimes face, as well as the moral justification of the family. There is a bit of a mystery in how some people get to decide over others without the consent of those others; why do parents have authority over their children? A standard answer is that the justification of this comes from the welfare interests of the children.[1] It is good for children to have at least one person in their lives with such authority over them.

Moreover, it could also be good for parents to have such responsibilities, because the parent-child relationship can be deeply valuable. If this is true, then it could make some sense to channel the implementation of children's rights via parents, as parents have such responsibilities and can be assumed to be motivated. However, this story is reliant on it being possible for the parent to carry out his or her parenting in a way that furthers the interests of the child.

The demand, for instance, of sending out twenty applications a week for housing seems to be a condition that most people, if put under pressing circumstances, would at some point fail to satisfy. If this is so, then this kind of welfare conditionality would also threaten to undermine the institution of the family, in the rather strong sense of being inconsistent with letting the family do its intended work for children. Practically speaking, such conditions would make it impossible for parents to safeguard the rights of children. Leviner and

1 Brighouse H. and Swift, A., *Family Values: The Ethics of Parent-Child Relationships* (Princeton: Princeton University Press, 2014).

Holappa's chapter shows the importance of placing more substance into children's rights.

Reference

Brighouse, Harry, and Adam Swift. 2014. *Family Values: The Ethics of Parent-Child Relationships*. Princeton: Princeton University Press.

CHAPTER 3

Children's Participation in Legal Proceedings – Conditioned by Adult Views of Children's Capacity and Credibility?

Anna Kaldal

1 Introduction and Purpose

Article 12 in the UN Convention on the Rights of the Child (CRC) is often said to emphasize children's participation rights, yet the article does not explicitly mention participation or specify how 'children's influence' might be defined.[1] The aim of this chapter is to discuss challenges in realizing children's right to participate in the legal proceedings of family-law disputes (concerning custody, residence, and contact – hereinafter referred to as *custody disputes*) and in criminal cases, where a child is either a witness to or a victim of violence.[2] The discussion concerns children in vulnerable life situations related to their family and/or caregiver: children in custody disputes between their parents and children exposed to domestic violence and sexual abuse in criminal cases. Focus is on the child's narrative and the influence this might have on the outcome of the case. In a custody case, this is described as the child's *view* and is treated in relation to the assessment of the child's *capacity*.[3] In a criminal case, the child's *narrative* is the child's description of a crime; it is the child's *statement*, which is not related to the child's formal position in a criminal proceeding as a victim or a witness, but to the child's assessed *credibility*.[4]

---

1 As Lindkvist discusses in his chapter in this volume, special participation rights for children can be seen as weaker participation rights than the typical categories in human rights law: civil and political on the one hand, and economic and social and cultural rights on the other. He also questions whether participation rights can be meaningful if they do not lead to improved conditions for children. See also Lundy and Peleg in this volume.

2 The reason that both child witnesses and child victims are included in this discussion on participation in criminal cases is that the definition of when a child exposed to domestic violence is perceived as a victim of or a witness to a crime depends on formalities of criminal law and in criminal law proceedings. This is discussed further later in this chapter.

3 E.g. the UN Committee on the Rights of the Child. *General comment No. 12 (2009). The right of the child to be heard,* CRC/C/GC/12, para. 44.

4 E.g. the UN Economic and Social Council 2005/20. *Guidelines on Justice in Matters Involving Child Victims and Witnesses of Crime*, 22 July 2005, para. 18.

DOI:10.1163/9789004511163_008

The weight that the child's views should be given in custody cases, the child's capacity, and children's credibility as victims or witnesses in criminal cases have long engaged legislation, case law, and legal science in Sweden.[5] In this chapter, I will discuss how empirical studies and Swedish case law show that children's participation in legal proceedings is still a challenge, and that the emphasis in law on child participation has not necessarily led to children being given more influence or believed in legal proceedings.

The discussion in this chapter on children's participation rights applies a procedural-law perspective. For any individual, the prospect of participation in legal proceedings cannot be viewed solely as the consequence of a particular right to participate. Rather, participation is linked to the (procedural) capacities of predefined roles in the (often extensive) procedural framework. Thus, the perceived capacities of the parties concerned (e.g. the victim,[6] plaintiff, or defendant), their agents or representatives, and witnesses[7] will affect the

---

5 Case law in this chapter refers to court decisions from the Swedish Supreme Court (*Högsta domstolen*). These decisions are considered binding or at least to have a strong guidance. In this Chapter 1 discuss several court decisions from the Swedish Supreme Court. These decisions are public judgments that are made available on the courts' websites as well as through court databases. However, the judgments often contain sensitive personal data. In accordance with the Act (2003: 460) on research relating to humans (the Ethical Review Act), as interpreted by the Central Ethics Review Board, research that includes such material must be ethically reviewed and special requirements placed on the handling of sensitive material. In this chapter the Supreme Court rulings are not analyzed per se but referred to when discussing the principle that can and have been drawn from the rulings. In accordance with good research practice as described in e.g. the Swedish Research Council, Good research practice, Report 2017, I have applied for and received permission for nearby research projects in which the cases in this chapter have been referenced and discussed, see decision from the Regional Ethics Review Board in Stockholm Dnr. 2015/1551-31/5 and Dnr. 2018/2041-31/5. The rulings referred to in this chapter have furthermore been discussed in 1procedural law-, evidential law- and child law literature (e.g. Sutorius, H., *Bevisprövning vid sexualbrott* (Stockholm: Norstedts juridik, 2013); Kaldal, A., *Parallella Processer. En rättsvetenskaplig studie av riskbedömningar i vårdnads- och LVU-mål* (Stockholm: Jure förlag, 2010); Lainpelto, K., *Stödbevisning* (Stockholm: Jure förlag, 2013); Schiratzki, J., *Barnrättens grunder* (Lund: Studentlitteratur, 2019)). The cases in this chapter have not been compiled in any register or the like but have been read directly on the legal data's website. In sum, several measures have been taken that comply with required ethical considerations.

6 Participating in a legal proceeding as a victim comes with formal procedural rights. These procedural rights differ in different legal system, see e.g. Braun, K., *Victim Participation Rights. Variation Across Criminal Justice Systems* (Cham: Palgrave Maximilian, 2019). The Swedish system provides the victim with strong procedural rights such as a right to prosecute and become a party in the criminal case alongside with the prosecutor, which gives the victim the right to evoke evidence, argue the case and appeal.

7 Witnesses normally also have rights linked to the position as a witness, e.g. the right not to testify against a family member, witness protection and witness support.

extent to which participation rights can be exercised. As such, participation for all concerned parties is also heavily dependent on relevant substantive-law provisions, which in this chapter are defined as family law (custody disputes) and criminal law. For example, even if the child is a witness to a crime committed by a parent, the child can also be a victim of that crime depending on whether exposing a child to domestic violence is criminalized or not.[8] In light of international-law developments – e.g. the influence of Article 6 in the European Convention on Human Rights (ECHR), on the right to a fair trial – procedural participation rights have become part of the human-rights discourse. This discourse includes procedural participation rights and access to justice for victims; these are discussed in several international documents as well as in decisions from the European Court of Human Rights (ECHR).[9] Alongside this development, and as a consequence of a strengthening of children's rights in general, children's right to participate in legal proceedings has become part of the human-rights discourse. However, the discussion of children's right to participate in legal procedures has taken place mainly in child-rights literature and not in procedural-law literature, which is why the concepts and distinctions established in procedural law are not always mirrored in child-rights literature.

In the following two sections, I provide an overview of the Swedish legal discussion concerning the child's right to participation in custody cases and as victims or witnesses in criminal proceedings. Finally, in the concluding section, I discuss children's right to participation in legal proceedings and the tension between the law and realities of childhood.

8 See further below in this chapter.

9 E.g. the UN Declaration of Basic Principles of Justice for Victims of Crime and Abuse of Power, 29 November 1985 and Directive 2012/29/EU the Victim Rights Directive of Establishing Minimum Standards on the Rights, Support and Protection of Victims of Crime (the Victim Rights Directive). Se further in European Parliamentary Research Service, The Victims' Rights Directive. European Implementation Assessment (Brussels, 2017). Also European Court of Human Rights case law provides several examples where the rights of victims and witnesses have been tried under Article 6. E.g. Case of Y. v. Slovenia, 28 May 2015 (Application no. 41107/10). See also, Wergens, A., "Human rights for victims of non-state crime. Taking victims seriously?" (Oisterwijk: Wolf Legal Publishers, 2014).

2 Children's Right to Participation in Custody Cases

2.1 *Challenges to Procedural Rights for Children in Custody Cases*

Literature on child participation in custody cases has focused to a large extent on the child's right to be heard and to have their views given due weight in decisions made by courts.[10] This clearly relates to the aim of CRC Article 12. The challenges of realizing the child's right to participation in custody disputes, as described in the literature, are several. One aspect is the division in Article 12 between the right to be heard on the one hand, and on the other the due weight to be given to a child's view.[11] In practice, children's right to participation can be seen as conditioned in the article itself.[12] As noted by the UN Committee on the Rights of the Child, assessing the child's *capacity* is necessary when applying the article. The Committee also emphasise that the provision applies to parental separation and custody disputes.[13] Children's right to participate and the scope of interpretation given in Article 12 has, however, been problematized in relation to the matter of children in custody disputes. Another, closely related aspect in custody disputes is the ambivalence towards involving children, due to the risk of drawing them into their parents' conflict, and how to handle situations when there is a suspicion that a child is being influenced by one or the other parent.[14]

In Swedish custody cases, children are not a party to the case; they have neither an appointed legal representative nor a lawyer. Nevertheless, children's

---

10 Tisdall, E, Kay M., 'Challenging competency and capacity? Due weight to children's views in family law proceedings', *The International Journal of Children's Rights,* 26 (2018): 159–182; Henderson-Dekort, E., Smits, V. and van Bakel, H., 'The Meaningful Participation and Complex Capacities of Children in Family Law: Based on transdisciplinary perspectives and articles of the United Nations convention on the rights of the child', *The International Journal of Children's Rights* 29 (2021): 78–98.

11 Tisdall, E. Kay M., 'Children and Young People's Participation: A critical consideration of Article 12'. In Reynaert, D., Desmet, E., Lembrechts, S. and Vandenhole, W. (Eds.), *Routledge International Handbook of Children's Rights Studies* (London: Routledge, 2015): 185–200; Tisdall, K. (2018); Singer, A., 'Alla talar om barns rätt'. In Ryberg-Welander, L. (Ed.), *Rätt, social utsatthet och samhälleligt ansvar: festskrift till Anna Hollander* (Stockholm: Norstedts juridik, 2012); Schiratzki, J., *Barnrättens grunder* (Lund: Studentlitteratur, 2019).

12 See e.g. Leviner, P., 'Voice but No Choice – Children's Right to Participation in Sweden'. In Haugli, T, Nylund, A., Sigurdsen, A. and Bendiksen, L. R. (Eds), *Children's Constitutional Rights in the Nordic Countries* (Leiden: Brill Nijhoff, 2019): 269–294; Grahn-Farley, M. *Barnkonventionen: en kommentar* (Lund: Studentlitteratur, 2019).

13 UN Committee on the Rights of the Child. *General comment No.* 12, para. 32 and 44 (2009).

14 Tisdall, K. (2018); Tisdall, K. (2015); Barnes, A., 'A Genealogy of the CRC'. *Minnesota Journal of International Law* 2, no. 3 (2014): 1–46; Daly, A., 'Assessing Children's Capacities', *International Journal of Children's Rights* 28 (2020): 471–499.

right to participation and to express their view as well as the court's responsibility to take the child's view into account have been strengthened in the Swedish Parental Code (*föräldrabalken*) several times in recent decades. The right to participation in custody disputes has been constructed in the Parental Code as a responsibility or duty directed to the court to let the child present his or her view and a responsibility of the court to consider this view in accordance with the child's age and maturity (Chapter 6 Section 2b). The child's right to be heard (e.g. interviewing the child) is formulated as an instruction to the investigator (normally the family-law unit of the social services) to try and clarify the child's view, unless doing so is deemed inappropriate (Chapter 6 Section 19).

Since the judge's responsibility to consider the child's view was implemented in the Parental Code in 1998,[15] the child's right to express his or her view and have his or her view taken into account has been emphasized through a number of amendments. In 2006, for example, the right to be heard was moved to the portal section of the chapter in the Parental Code that regulates custody, residence, and contact.[16] By including the right to participation in the portal section, making this right applicable to all decisions concerning custody, residence, and contact. The latest amendments concerning the child's right to participation include both a clarification of the responsibility to provide the child with information (Chapter 6 Section 2b), and gives the social services' family-law unit the authority to interview the child without the consent of the custodians (Chapter 6 Section 20b).[17]

2.2 *Participation in Accordance with the Child's Age and Maturity – in the Best Interest of the Child?*

The strengthening of children's right to participate in custody cases in Sweden has mainly concerned the child's right to be heard, whereas the question of the impact of the child's view on the decision has not been explicitly strengthened.[18] The right to participate in custody disputes is explicitly set out in legislation (the Parental Code Chapter 6 Section 2b) with the same wording as in CRC Article 12, and relativized in the same way by the child's age and maturity (capacity). Thus, the assessment of the child's capacity and the weight that the child's view should be given ultimately lie in the hands of the adult decisionmaker. Consequently, children's possibility to influence a decision can be

15 Legislative Bill 1997/98:7 *Vårdnad, boende och umgänge.*
16 Legislative Bill 2005/06:99 *Nya vårdnadsregler.*
17 Legislative Bill 2020/21:150 *Ett stärkt barnrättsperspektiv i vårdnadstvister.*
18 Legislative Bill 2020/21:150 *Ett stärkt barnrättsperspektiv i vårdnadstvister.*

limited with reference to the child's lack of capacity and by asserting that limiting the child's influence is in the child's best interest.[19] As definitions do not exist for the concept of either a child's 'sufficient capacity' or the 'best interest of the child', any assessment of the weight that the child's view should be given runs the risk of being subjective and influenced by the decisionmaker's own views on capacity and best interest.[20]

2.3 *Swedish Law on Children's Right to Participation in Custody Cases*

As mentioned above, according to the Swedish Parental Code, the child must be heard in custody cases and the child's view considered, with respect to the child's age and maturity (Parental Code Chapter 6 Section 2b). Normally the courts hand over the responsibility for hearing the child to the social services' family-law unit. The child interview then becomes a part of the so-called custody inquiry that the family-law unit submits to the court. According to the Parental Code, the social services' family-law unit is responsible for hearing the child, unless doing so is inappropriate (Chapter 6 Section 19). The phrase 'unless it is inappropriate' gives the family-law investigator a scope of interpretation as to *when, how,* and *if* it would be in the best interest of the child to be heard. The phrasing to 'consider the child's view in accordance with the child's age and maturity' gives the judge a similarly broad scope of interpretation regarding the extent to which the child's view should influence the court decision.

In Swedish case law, the Supreme Court (*Högsta domstolen*) has tried only a few cases where the question centred on the extent to which the child's view should influence a decision on custody or contact. In one case, where the court found that the child was under strong influence from one parent, the court decided that the view of the 9-year-old child should not be given weight in the decision, as this was not in the best interest of the child.[21] In two cases, where the child was 13 years old, the court stated that a parent cannot be expected to force a child to act against the child's will, and that the child's view can be decisive as long as it does not put the child at risk. This indicates that an older child's view should be given great importance in a decision.[22] Worth noting is that two of the cases are from 1992 and 1995. However, one of the cases concerning a 13year-old is from 2017, and it confirms the court decision from 1995.[23]

19 E.g. Tisdall, K. (2015).

20 E.g. Henderson-Dekort, E., Smits, V. and van Bakel, H. (2021).

21 NJA 1992 p. 666.

22 NJA 1995 p. 398; NJA 2017 p. 557.

23 In NJA 2017 p. 557, the 13-year-old daughter had refused go back to her father, who had sole custody, after visiting her mother. The mother was prosecuted for the crime of arbitrary

How children's participation rights according to the CRC should be understood in custody disputes is discussed in Swedish literature.[24] A cautious assumption is that the right to participate according to Article 12 – e.g. being one of the four ground principles of the Convention – is stronger than this right as implemented in the Swedish Parental Code. The incorporation of the Convention can therefore be seen as a strengthening in Swedish law of the child's right to participation.[25]

2.4 *Empirical Studies on Children's Participation in Custody Cases*

Several empirical studies have been carried out on children's participation in custody cases in Sweden.[26] Social-science research stresses that children's participation in custody disputes is a complex matter, and the influence of a child's narrative on a court decision is often conditional. An empirical study of court decisions from 2007 found that after the implementation of the child's right to be heard in the Parental Code in 2006, courts showed a greater tendency to give more weight to the child's opinion.[27] In the examined cases, however, the child's participation was conditioned by the age of the child, and the expressed views of the child could be waived with reference to the influence of a parent (usually the mother). The court argued in these cases that children's narratives could be interpreted as an expression of the parents' conflict rather than the child's experience of a parent.[28]

In a study of custody decisions from 2010–2011, the importance of close and positive contact with both of the child's parents was given greater weight

---

conduct concerning a child (*egenmäktighet med barn*). The Supreme Court found the mother not guilty and stated that a parent could not be expected to force a 13-year-old child to act against the child's own will.

24 Leviner, P., 'Barns rätt till delaktighet'. In Åhman, K., Leviner, P. and Zillén, K. (Eds.), *Barnkonventionen i praktiken: rättsliga utmaningar och möjligheter* (Stockholm: Norstedts Juridik, 2020): 102–124, Schiratzki, J. (2019).

25 Kaldal, A., 'Barnet i vårdnadstvister – särskilt principen om barnets bästa och rätten att komma till tals'. In Åhman, K., Leviner, P. and Zillén, K. (Eds.), *Barnkonventionen i praktiken: rättsliga utmaningar och möjligheter* (Stockholm: Norstedts Juridik, 2020): 145–175.

26 E.g. Eriksson, M., *I skuggan av Pappa. Familjerätten och hanteringen av fäders våld* (Stehag: Gondolin, 2003); Dahlstrand, L., *Barns deltagande i familjerättsliga processer* (Uppsala: Uppsala University, 2004); Ingrids, H., *Dilemmas in child custody disputes: the child's best interest in courtroom discourse* (PhD diss., Stockholm University, 2014); Röbäck, K., *Barns röster i vårdnadstvister: om verkställighet och professionellas riskbedömningar* (PhD diss., Gothenburg University, 2012); Bruno, L., 'Contact and Evaluations of Violence: An Intersectional Analysis of Swedish Court Orders', *International Journal of Law Policy and the Family* 29, (2015): 167–182.

27 Röbäck, K. (2012).

28 Röbäck, K. (2012).

than the child's expressed wish to have limited or no contact with one of the parents.[29] Yet another study that examined children's participation in custody cases in six municipalities during 2011–2013 came to similar conclusions. This study showed that the views of children who expressed the desire for extended contact with a parent were taken seriously, while the views of children who wanted reduced or no contact was not given due weight.[30]

Another empirical study from 2014 analysed audio recordings from the main hearing in custody disputes. A recurring theme in the recordings was an apparent lack of child participation and voice. The parties (the child's parents) discussed – in the child's absence – whether the child's expressed views were genuine or related to their idea of the best interests of the child. In addition, the child's voice or experiences could be used by both parents to support the blame directed towards the other parent (e.g. accusations of violence, maltreatment, mental problems, substance abuse etc.). Another theme in the recordings was that a parent's reference to the child's view could be perceived by the other party and the involved professionals as dragging the child into the conflict between the parents.[31] In a study from 2017 regarding custody disputes including 215 children, most children met with the family-law unit, and nearly all children from six years of age met with the social worker without the presence of the parents. For 54 percent of the children, the child's view was presented to the court, and for 41 percent of the children, the view of the child appeared in the judgment.[32] The child's view was taken into consideration and discussed in the judgments concerning 38 percent of the 215 children. For 73 percent of these children, the court decision was in accordance with the child's view. The older the child, the more common it was that the child's view appeared in the decision, was taken into consideration, and was given weight in the decision of the court. The study stated that even if more children are heard than previously, children's rights to participate in custody disputes still needs to be strengthened.[33]

---

29 Bruno, L. (2015).

30 Stiftelsen allmänna barnhuset, *Slutrapport – Barnets rättigheter i vårdnadstvister* (2015), 32. Similar results have been shown in international research, e.g. Crosby-Currie, C. A. 'Children's involvement in contested custody cases: Practices and experiences of legal and mental health professionals', *Law and Human Behavior* 20, no. 3 (1996): 289–311; Smart, C., Neale, B. and Wade, A., *The Changing Experience of Childhood, Families and Divorce* (Oxford: Polity Press, 2001).

31 Ingrids, H. (2014).

32 Government's Official Investigations 2017:6 *Se barnet!*

33 In the Government's Official Investigations 2017:6 *Se barnet!*, the investigation suggested several amendments to the law; indeed several amendments followed; see above in this chapter (2.3).

A more recent study shows similar results. The Swedish Gender Equality Agency conducted a study to determine the extent to which, and in what way, information about violence or other abuse by one parent against another other parent or a child has been presented in cases involving custody, residence, and contact or visitation.[34] The study examined the extent to which the child was heard and the extent to which the child's view was given weight in the decision. In 57 percent of the cases, the child's views were not included in the judgement. In interviews conducted with children who had experienced a custody proceeding that included information about violence or other abuse, several children emphasized the importance of participation. The children who discussed the violence to which they had been exposed and their desire not to be with an abusive father found it difficult to understand why they had not been protected from contact with that parent.

All in all, developments have moved towards a formal strengthening of children's right to participation in custody disputes. According to the empirical studies presented here, the strengthening of children's right to participate in custody disputes has resulted in more children being heard; children's views are given greater influence. However, the studies show that children's participation in proceedings and influence on the court's decision is still conditioned. In conclusion, the referred studies show that the assessment of the capacity of the child to have a view of its own and an impact on the court decision risks being relativized by whether the decisionmaker considers the child's view to be accurate (and not influenced by a parent), and whether the child's view corresponds to the predominant norm of good and close contact with both parents. In essence, this way of limiting the child's influence on the decision affirms the notion that it would be in the child's best interest not to allow the child to influence the decision.

3 Children's Participation in Criminal Proceedings

3.1 *Participation through the Child's Statement – a Prerequisite for Access to Justice*

Children's participation in criminal proceedings has been discussed in terms of children in conflict with the law. The CRC explicitly addresses this group

34 The Swedish Gender Equality Agency, *Uppgifter om våld är inget undantag i vårdnadstvister*, Rapport 2022:1. 198 cases were investigated. The population included 285 children (0–17 years).

of children.[35] Children's participation in criminal proceedings when they are victims of and/or witnesses to a crime is also discussed in child-rights literature,[36] but is not addressed specifically in the CRC.[37] The UN Committee on the Rights of the Child nonetheless describes the right to participate in a judicial proceeding, as a victim of or a witness to a crime, as an outflow of Article 12, and both national and international policy developments to achieve a more child-friendly justice have sprung from this article.[38] The General Comments of the UN Committee on the Rights of the Child and other international policy documents have focused on protecting the child from re-traumatization as a result of being subjected to adult legal proceedings; such protection includes avoiding exposure to repeated interrogation and cross-examination in court, access to crisis support, and a child-friendly environment.[39] Because there are rarely any witnesses to sexual abuse and domestic violence, the child's statement is crucial in order to prosecute these crimes. Therefore, the child's participation as a victim or witness is a prerequisite for the child's access to justice. The importance of treating the child as a credible witness, without presumption that the child's testimony is unreliable solely because of the child's age, is pointed out in several international documents.[40]

Historically, children were not seen as credible witnesses and therefore were not allowed to give testimony in the Scandinavian criminal law system.[41]

---

35 CRC Article 37 and 40. The participation rights and access to justice of this vulnerable group of children has – in a global perspective – met great challenges from e.g. the perspective of the right to a fair trial as well as the age of criminal reasonability and right to rehabilitation. See Lainpelto, K., Chapter 4 in this volume.

36 According to Swedish criminal proceedings, the position as witnesses and/or plaintiffs is more or less the same when it comes to how the child's testimony is handled. The expression 'witness' will be used throughout the chapter when discussing children in criminal proceedings.

37 De Bondt, W. and Lauwereys, H., 'Children's rights and child participation in criminal proceedings'. In Pereira, R., Engel, A., and Miettinen, S. (Eds.), *The Governance of Criminal Justice in the European Union, Transnationalism, Localism and Public Participation in an Evolving Constitutional Order* (Cheltenhamn: Edward Elgar Publishing, 2020): 232–268.

38 UN Committee on the Rights of the Child. *General comment No. 12 (2009)*, e.g. para. 32, 62–64; The UN Economic and Social Council 2005/20; The Council of Europe Convention on Protection of Children against Sexual Exploitation and Sexual Abuse (The Lanzarote Convention); Council of Europe, *Guidelines of the Committee of Ministers of the Council of Europe on child-friendly justice*, 2010.

39 Ibid.

40 The UN Economic and Social Council 2005/20, para, 18, 41; Council of Europe, *Guidelines of the Committee of Ministers of the Council of Europe on child-friendly justice*, 2010, e.g. para. 70, 73.

41 Myklebust, T. 'The Nordic Model of Handling Children's Testimonies?'. In Johansson, S. et al. (Eds), *Collaborating Against Child Abuse: Exploring the Nordic Barnahus Model*

Today, in a criminal proceeding, child victims and witnesses have the same formal position as adults.[42] How and when to interview a child witness, however, has invigorated discussions in Swedish criminal case law for some fifty years, and the child's credibility as a witness has been the core question in several Supreme Court decisions.[43]

Challenges related to the credibility of the child's statement in a criminal proceeding is probably the reason that the most extensive research on child victims and witnesses in criminal proceedings is found in the fields of psychology and psychiatry. Such research has a long history of dealing with children's credibility as witnesses and has provided the basis for developing appropriate techniques for interviewing children.[44]

3.2 *The Duty to Testify Regardless of Age*

In criminal cases, the child statement is evidence invoked by either the prosecutor or the defendant. Therefore, from a strict criminal-law perspective, this statement is not a matter of fulfilling the child's right to participation or considering the child's view, but of *investigating the crime.* In contrast to the right to participation stated in Article 12 CRC, according to which the right to be heard is not a duty, but a fundamental right of every child to express their views without pressure, participating in a criminal proceeding as a witness is

---

(Cham: Palgrave Macmillian, 2017): 97–119. Several crimes such as corporal punishment and incest where also originally not seen as crimes against children. See e.g. Sutorius, H., *Bevisning vid sexualbrott* (Stockholm: Norstedts juridik, 2013), Mykelbust, T. (2017); Johansson, S., Stefansen, K., Bakketeig, E. and Kaldal, A. 'Implementing the Nordic Barnahus Model: Characteristics and Local Adaptations'. In Johansson, S. et al. (Eds), *Collaborating Against Child Abuse: Exploring the Nordic Barnahus Model* (Cham: Palgrave Macmillan): 1–31.

42 Sutorius, H. (2013).

43 NJA 1963 p. 555, NJA 1993 p. 68, NJA 1993 p. 616, NJA 2010 p. 671 and NJA 2017 p. 316.

44 Lamb, M.E., La Rooy, D.J., Malloy, L.C., and Katz, C., *Children's testimony: A handbook of psychological research and forensic practice* (Oxford: John Wiley & Sons, 2011); Powell, M. B., and Snow, P. C., 'A guide to questioning children during the free-narrative phase of an interview about abuse', *Australian Psychologist* 41, no. 1 (2007): 57–65; Goodman, G.S. and Melinder, A., 'Child witness research and forensic interviews of young children: A review', *Legal & Criminological Psychology* 12, no. 1 (2007): 1–19; Bruck, M., Ceci, S.J., and Hembrooke, H., 'The nature of children's true and false narratives', *Developmental Review* 22 (2002): 520–554; Vrij, A., Granhag, P.A., and Porter, S., 'Pitfalls and opportunities in nonverbal and verbal lie detection', *Psychological Science in the Public Interest* 11, no. 3 (2010): 89–121; Magnusson, M., *Interviewing preschoolers: Facilitators and barriers to young children's legal testimony* (University of Gothenburg, 2020).

a *duty* (duty to testify) for the child. According to Swedish law, this duty also applies to a victim of crime.[45]

The duty to testify according to Swedish law applies to all individuals, whether a child or an adult. The relationship between the right to participation according to Article 12 in the CRC and the duty to testify according to the Swedish Code of Judicial Procedure (*rättegångsbalken*) is not clear, but is often described as a right to a *child-friendly justice*.[46] In other words, this comprises a legal proceeding adapted to the child's needs, in the sense that the investigation and proceedings (such as interviewing the child in a child-friendly environment) are adapted to the child's sensibility.[47]

The duty to testify as a witness is limited by the right not to testify against a family member. When the witness is a child, the question arises of whether a child has the legal capacity to invoke this right, or if this right must be invoked by the child's legal guardian. This is not explicitly addressed in Swedish law; therefore, a child's legal guardian can decide against the wishes of the child to provide witness testimony.

Thus, in domestic violence cases where a child has witnessed violence between parents (and legal guardians), the question of the child's legal capacity presents a significant problem: the same person accused of violence, as the legal guardian of the child, can invoke the child's right not to testify – despite the child's expressed desire to testify.[48] Because the right not to testify against a family member applies only to witnesses and not victims of crimes, a new crime was introduced in the Swedish Penal Code (*brottsbalken*): the crime of *violation of a child's integrity* (*barnfridsbrottet*). This criminalizes violence against a family member in the presence of a child and gives the child the position as a victim of crime.[49] The child thus participates as a victim of crime

---

45 The duty to give a statement has some exceptions that apply to witnesses but not to victims, such as the right not to testify against a family member, Chapter 36 section 6 the Swedish Code of Judicial Procedure. A witness or victim can of course choose not to speak during an interview or at the main hearing in court.

46 Council of Europe, *Guidelines of the Committee of Ministers of the Council of Europe on child-friendly justice*, 2010; European Union Agency for Fundamental Rights (FRA) *Child-friendly justice – Perspectives and experiences of professionals on children's participation in civil and criminal judicial proceedings in 10 EU Member States*, 2015.

47 The development of a child-friendly justice must proceed in accordance with the principle of due process, especially the defendant's right to a fair trial; see below.

48 The right not to testify against a family member applies only to witnesses and not victims of crimes.

49 Legislative Bill 2020/21:170 *Barn som bevittnar brott*.

and not a witness, and is not dependent on the parent's consent to the child being heard.

3.3 *The Evidential Value of the Child's Statement*

There are likely several reasons underlying the well-established practice of hearing children in criminal cases. One particularly important reason is that in most cases, as mentioned above, the child's statement is necessary to prosecute crimes against children. Therefore, the discussion in recent decades has not dealt with whether the child should be heard, but *how* the child should be interviewed as well as the *evidential value* of the child's statement. Almost 60 years have passed since these aspects were first highlighted by the Swedish Supreme Court in 1963.[50] Since then, several cases concerning children's statements have been brought to the Swedish Supreme Court. The core questions have involved the evidential value of the statement and interview methods, as well as the defendant's right to a fair trial, when the child's testimony is not given at the main hearing. The Supreme Court has stated that the burden of proof beyond reasonable doubt applies in all criminal cases, and no relief of evidence is allowed for more difficult-to-prove cases or categories of crimes which, for one reason or another, are considered particularly important to prosecute.[51] The conclusion is that even if crimes against children are often difficult to prove, the standard of proof cannot be lowered. The Supreme Court has also stated that a testimony that is fully reliable can be sufficient to meet the high standard of proof, which is an important precedent for domestic-violence and sexual-abuse cases – cases in which the only evidence is often the victim's testimony.[52] However, subsequent statements from the Supreme Court show a clear shift towards a demand on evidence to corroborate the statement of the victim, especially if the victim is a child (this is discussed further in Section 3.4 below).[53]

Given the characteristic circumstances of domestic-violence and sexual-abuse cases, prosecuting and convicting a perpetrator is often difficult. There are seldom any witnesses other than the victim, and physical evidence is rarely available or has low evidential value. In addition, a child may lack sufficient

50 In NJA 1963 p. 555, the Swedish Supreme Court stated that the child is not required to appear in court to give testimony; instead, the child interview can be recorded in the police investigation and presented to the court at the main hearing.

51 See NJA 1990 p. 555; Ekelöf, P.-O., Edelstam, H., Heuman, L., *Rättegång IV* (Stockholm: Norstedts Juridik, 2009).

52 See NJA 1992 p. 446 and NJA 1993 p. 68.

53 See NJA 2009 p. 447 and NJA 2010 p. 671; Lainpelto, K. (2013).

references to realize that a crime has been committed, possess limited language for expression, and feel loyal to or afraid of the suspected perpetrator. The consequence is that in practice, children often do not tell anyone about the abuse, and if they do so, their statement often lacks concrete details – e.g. information about where and when the crime (crimes) were committed or detailed descriptions of the act itself. This means that it can be difficult to obtain a statement from the child of sufficiently high evidential value and because strong corroborating evidence is seldom available, most police investigations do not lead to prosecution. In addition, the conviction rate for these cases is low compared to other crimes.[54]

In evidential-law literature, the discussion about the evidential value of an oral statement is that a statement shall be evaluated for its reliability – an aspect which in turn must be held separate from the credibility of the witness. Reliability of a statement is about the content of the statement itself, such as the amount of detail, consistency, and clarity, whereas credibility is about the individual giving the statement, such as whether the person is known to be trustworthy, the appearance of the witness etc.[55] The reason behind this division is the importance of non-discrimination, rationality, and objectivity, because assessing the evidential value of a statement based on the credibility of the witness has weak scientific support. Aspects such as a person's lack of maturity, memory disorder, mental illness, or neuropsychiatric diagnoses are aspects that relate to the person and can therefore influence perceived witness credibility. Statistically, these are aspects that can affect one's capacity to give a reliable statement, but the value of a certain statement must be assessed on the basis of the statement itself. As mentioned above, children's rights of access to justice includes their statements not being given lower evidential value solely because the witness or victim is a child.[56] This can require the court to have knowledge concerning trauma reactions and psychological development of children. Judging the reliability of a statement through the lens of credibility opens the door for a bias assessment. This has e.g. been shown in research where the evidential value of statements given by children was determined to

54 Kaldal, A., Diesen, C., Beije, J. and Diesen, E. F., *Barnahusutredningen 2010* (Stockholm: Jure, 2010); Sutorius, H. (2013); Swedish National Council for Crime Prevention (*Brottsförebyggande rådet*) statistics 2021, Barnmisshandel, https://www.bra.se/statistik/statistik-utifran-brottstyper/barnmisshandel.html/ accessed 10 August 2022.

55 Schelin, L., *Bevisvärdering av utsagor i brottmål* (Stockholm University; 2006); Bruck, M., Ceci, S.J., and Hembrooke, H. (2002); Vrij, A., Granhag, P.A., and Porter, S. (2010).

56 The UN Economic and Social Council 2005/20, para, 18, 41; Council of Europe, *Guidelines of the Committee of Ministers of the Council of Europe on child-friendly justice*, 2010, e.g. para. 70, 73.

be lower when the judge was informed that the child witness had received a neuropsychiatric diagnosis.[57]

Because the child's statement often comprises the main evidence in cases of sexual abuse, much attention has focused on *how* to assess the evidential value of such statements, especially when the statement is given by a child. The reasons that are most frequently given in Swedish case law are that a child is more sensitive to influence, is more suggestible than an adult, has limited references, and is hampered by less developed language.[58] Therefore, considerable interest has involved interview methods that exclude suggestive elements.[59] In other words, because the child is perceived as a sensitive witness – but can still be the only, or at least an important, source of information – interview methods must take the child's sensibility into consideration.

3.4 *The Defendant's Right to a Fair Trial and the Principle of Precaution*

The Swedish Supreme Court has also stated that because children are not heard in court (their statement is recorded during the criminal investigation and then presented to the court at the main hearing), such statements must be evaluated with caution (the precautionary principle).[60] This makes it more difficult to meet the standard of proof in criminal cases where the main evidence is a statement of a child. In a number of decisions, the Swedish Supreme Court has discussed the probative value of the child's statement presented to the court through a video recording, and the consequence of a witness not being cross-examined at the main hearing. In summary, the Swedish Supreme Court states that evidence based mainly on an oral statement alone can fulfil the evidentiary requirement beyond a reasonable doubt, provided that the statement is sufficiently reliable and that the defendant's right to a fair trial is satisfied,

---

57 Lindblad, F., and Lainpelto, K., 'Sexual Abuse Allegations by Children with Neuropsychiatric Disorders', *Journal of Child Sexual Abuse*, no. 20 (2011): 182–95. See Lainpelto, K., Chapter 4 in this volume.

58 The above-mentioned case law; Sutorius, H. (2013).

59 This is a challenge because children can have difficulties in giving statements without support from the person conducting the interview. Balancing the child's need of support during an interview as well as the importance of not instructing the child is discussed in the literature: E.g. Baugerud, G. A. and Sinkerud Johnson, M., 'The NICHD Protocol: Guide to Follow Recommended Investigative Interview Practices at the Barnahus?'. In Johansson, S. et al. (Ed.), *Collaborating Against Child Abuse: Exploring the Nordic Barnahus Model*, (Chm: Palgrave Macmillian): 121–143; Langballe, Å., and Davik, T., 'Sequential Interviews with Preschool Children in Norwegian Barnahus'. In Johansson, S. et al., (Eds.), *Collaborating Against Child Abuse: Exploring the Nordic Barnahus Model* (Cham: Palgrave MacMillan, 2017): 165–183.

60 See NJA 1992 p. 532, NJA 1993 p. 68 and NJA 1993 p. 616; Kaldal, A. (2010).

e.g. by the defence being given the opportunity to pose supplementary questions to the child during the police investigation. The Court also states that a consequence of the oral statement being presented through video at the main hearing is that the statement must be interpreted with caution. The European Court of Human Rights came to a similar conclusion when hearing a Swedish case, in which a child was interviewed during the criminal investigation and the interview was admitted as evidence.[61]

In the past decade, the Swedish Supreme Court has handed down rulings that demonstrate greater caution in assigning high evidential value to a child's statement. In these cases, the Court emphasizes absence of details, less developed language, and the principle of caution.[62] The Supreme Court's step towards greater caution when assessing the evidential value of a child's statement – despite improved child interview protocols, more research on children as witnesses, and increased efforts to strengthen children's access to justice – is probably one of the reasons that prosecution and conviction rates are still low.

4 Conclusion: Child Participation in Legal Proceedings – a Zero-Sum Game?

As presented above, law amendments and developments in practice over recent decades have aimed to strengthen child participation in both custody cases and criminal proceedings. In custody cases, the emphasis on children's right to participation has been continuedly strengthened – not by giving the child the position of a party or securing legal representation, but through the adoption of legislation that gives the courts and social services' family-law units a responsibility to investigate the child's view, and which emphasizes the responsibility to give that view due weight in the decision. In criminal proceedings, the child's right to participate has been met by striving for a more child-friendly justice, by e.g. implementing more child-friendly proceedings, such as interviewing the child in a child-friendly environment, developing interview methods, giving the child the right to independent legal representation when the child is a victim of crime, and introducing a new crime in the Penal Code, giving child witnesses to domestic violence status as a victim and not merely as a witness.

61 European Court of Human Rights Case of *S.N. v. Sweden*, 2 July 2002 (Application no. 34209/96).

62 NJA 2010 p. 671 and NJA 2017 p. 316.

Despite these developments, research on children's participation in custody cases and Swedish case law in criminal proceedings show that greater legislative emphasis on children's participation in legal proceedings does not necessarily lead to children being given more influence on the decision; nor are children more often believed or taken seriously. This paradox is not obvious or clear, mainly because legal decisions (judgments, decisions, or assessments of the child's capacity in custody investigations and credibility in criminal investigations) seemingly present a rational reason to explain why the child was not heard, why the child's view was not considered, or why the child's statement was not found sufficiently credible.

Even though child participation serves different purposes in custody and criminal cases, the dilemmas of the impact or weight that the child's narrative should be given in the legal outcome demonstrate certain similarities. As the chapter shows, the focus in family law is on the child's *capacity,* and in criminal cases on as the child's *credibility*. Even if these concepts are different (capacity to have a view versus credibility as a witness), the discussions are similar. Firstly, the assessment of capacity and credibility gives the decisionmaker a discretionary space, and secondly, on closer inspection, the assessments of capacity and credibility are similar. The lack of consideration of the child's view in custody cases is often motivated by claims that the child is too young to be heard, the child's view is not in the child's best interest, and/or the child's expressed view is not the child's own because of influence from an adult (normally one of the child's parents). Frequently given reasons in criminal cases for lack of credibility in children's statements cite that the standard of proof is high and that the principle of precaution (e.g. the defendant's right to cross-examination) must be considered, and that the child's statement, which more often than adult statements lacks details, must be supported with corroborating evidence. The seemingly rational basis here is the content of the statement and the defendant's right to a fair trial – not the notion that children in general are less credible.

A summative reflection is that in both custody proceedings and criminal cases, we see similar reasoning concerning the outcome of the cases: the simple assumption is that a child is a child, and a child's narrative lacks impact. The child is said to be too young, too immature, and/or influenced by others. Of course, judgments, decisions, and assessments exist where this is indeed the case. However, when children's right to participate is strengthened in laws, but without due weight being given to their view or adequate belief in their statements in practice, the question is whether this is an expression of a discriminatory bias towards children in terms of their capacity to form views and ability to give credible statements. In other words, this is a view of children as not being capable and competent. If this is the case, children's right to participate is conditioned –but not as a result of legal barriers.

We need to ask ourselves whether this is a question of attitude and power. Do decision-makers' prejudiced attitudes prevail over legislation? If so, a follow-up question is this: Why is this so? Has the development towards stronger child-participation rights in legal proceedings led to – or even been counteracted by – a greater questioning of children's capacity and credibility? If stronger emphasis on the right to participate does not seem to foster a stronger view of children's capacity and credibility, we may even risk silencing children instead of the other way around. Is this a question of discrimination of children?[63]

References

Andersson, Malou, and Anna Kaldal. 2021. "Barnkonventionens genomslag i rättstillämpningen. Barn som utsatts för våld inom familjen – Kartläggning av brottsmålsavgöranden från tingsrätt", in Malou Andersson, and Anna Kaldal (Eds.), *Barn i brottmål: En antologi*, 17–123. Stockholm: Jure förlag AB.

Barnes, Ashleigh. 2014. "A Genealogy of the CRC", *Minnesota Journal of International Law* 23(3):1–46.

Baugerud, Gunn Astrid, and Miriam Sinkerud Johnson. 2017. "The NICHD Protocol: Guide to Follow Recommended Investigative Interview Practices at the Barnahus?", in Susanna Johansson, Kari Stefansen, Elisiv Bakketeig, and Anna Kaldal (Eds.), *Collaborating Against Child Abuse: Exploring the Nordic Barnahus Model*, 121–143. Cham: Palgrave Macmillian.

Braun, Kerstin. 2019. "Victim Participation Rights. Variation Across Criminal Justice Systems". Cham: Palgrave Macmillian.

Bruck, Maggie, Stephen Ceci, and Helene Hembrooke. 2002. "The nature of children's true and false narratives", *Developmental Review* 22: 520–554.

Bruno, Linnea. 2015. "Contact and Evaluations of Violence: An Intersectional Analysis of Swedish Court Orders", *International Journal of Law Policy and the Family* 29: 167–182.

Council of Europe. 2010. *Guidelines of the Committee of Ministers of the Council of Europe on child-friendly justice.* Council of Europe.

Crosby-Currie, Catherine A. 1996. "Children's involvement in contested custody cases: Practices and experiences of legal and mental health professionals", *Law and Human Behavior* 20(3): 289–311.

63 See Adami, R., Chapter 6 in this volume.

Dahlstrand, Lotta. 2004. *Barns deltagande i familjerättsliga processer*. Faculty of Law, Uppsala University.

Daly, Aoife. 2020. "Assessing Children's Capacities", *International Journal of Children's Rights* 28: 471–499.

De Bondt, Wendy, and Heleene Lauwereys. 2020. "Children's rights and child participation in criminal proceedings", in Ricardo Pereira, Annegret Engel, and Samuli Miettinen (Eds.), *The Governance of Criminal Justice in the European Union, Transnationalism, Localism and Public Participation in an Evolving Constitutional Order*, 232–268. Cheltenhamn: Edward Elgar Publishing.

Ekelöf, Per Olof, Henrik Edelstam, and Lars Heuman. 2009. *Rättegång IV*. Stockholm: Norstedts Juridik AB.

Eriksson, Maria. 2003. *I skuggan av Pappa. Familjerätten och hanteringen av fäders våld.* Stehag: Gondolin.

European Court of Human Rights Case of S.N. v. Sweden, 2 July 2002 (Application no. 34209/96).

European Court of Human Rights Case of Y. v. Slovenia, 28 May 2015 (Application no. 41107/10).

European Parliamentary Research Service. 2017. *The victims' rights directive. European Implementation Assessment.* Brussels: European Union.

Goodman, Gail. S., and Annika Melinder. (2007). "Child witness research and forensic interviews of young children: A review", *Legal & Criminological Psychology* 12(1): 1–19.

Government's Official Investigations 2017: 6 *Se barnet!* (SOU 2017:6).

Henderson-Dekort, Emmie, Veronica Smits, and Hedwig van Bakel. 2021. "The Meaningful Participation and Complex Capacities of Children in Family Law: Based on transdisciplinary perspectives and articles of the United Nations Convention on the Rights of the Child", *The International Journal of Children's Rights* 29(1): 78–98.

Ingrids, Henrik. 2014. *Dilemmas in child custody disputes: the child's best interest in courtroom discourse*. PhD dissertation. Stockholm University.

Johansson, Susanna, Kari Stefansen, Elisiv Bakketeig and Anna Kaldal. 2017. "Implementing the Nordic Barnahus Model: Characteristics and Local Adaptions", in Susanna Johansson, Kari Stefansen, Elisiv Bakketeig, and Anna Kaldal (Eds.), *Collaborating Against Child Abuse: Exploring the Nordic Barnahus Model*, 1–31. Cham: Palgrave Macmillian.

Kaldal, Anna. 2010. *Parallella processer – En rättsvetenskaplig studie av riskbedömningar i vårdnads- och LVU-mål.* Stockholm: Jure förlag AB.

Kaldal, Anna. 2020. "Barnet i vårdnadstvister – särskilt principen om barnets bästa och rätten att komma till tals", in Karin Åhman, Pernilla Leviner, and Kavot Zillén (Eds.), *Barnkonventionen i praktiken: rättsliga utmaningar och möjligheter*, 145–175. Stockholm: Norstedts Juridik AB.

Kaldal, Anna, Christian Diesen, Johan Beije, and Eva F. Diesen. 2010. *Barnahusutredningen 2010.* Stockholm: Jure förlag AB.

Lainpelto, Katrin, 2013. *Stödbevisning i brottmål,* Stockholm: Jure förlag AB.

Lamb, Michael, David J. La Rooy, Lindsay C. Malloy, and Carmit Katz. 2011. *Children's testimony: A handbook of psychological research and forensic practice.* Oxford: John Wiley & Sons.

Langballe, Åse, and Tone Davik. 2017. "Sequential Interviews with Preschool Children in Norwegian Barnahus", in Susanna Johansson, Kari Stefansen, Elisiv Bakketeig, and Anna Kaldal (Eds.), *Collaborating Against Child Abuse: Exploring the Nordic Barnahus Mode,* 165–183. Cham: Palgrave Macmillian.

Legislative Bill 2020/21:150 *Ett stärkt barnrättsperspektiv i vårdnadstvister* (Prop. 2020/21:150).

Legislative Bill 1997/98:7 *Vårdnad, boende och umgänge* (Prop. 1997/98:7).

Legislative Bill 2005/06:99 *Nya vårdnadsregler* (Prop. 2005/06:99).

Legislative Bill 2020/21:170 *Barn som bevittnar brott* (Prop. 2020/21:170).

Leviner, Pernilla. 2020. "Barns rätt till delaktighet", in Karin Åhman, Pernilla Leviner, and Kavot Zillén (Eds.), *Barnkonventionen i praktiken: rättsliga utmaningar och möjligheter,* 102–124. Stockholm: Norstedts Juridik AB.

Leviner, Pernilla. 2019. "Voice but No Choice – Children's Right to Participation in Sweden", in Trude Haugli, Anna Nylund, Randi Sigurdsen, and Lena R.L. Bendiksen (Eds.), *Children's Constitutional Rights in the Nordic Countries,* vol. 5: 269–294. Leiden: Brill Nijhoff.

Lindblad, Frank, and Katrin Lainpelto. 2011. "Sexual Abuse Allegations by Children with Neuropsychiatric Disorders", *Journal of Child Sexual Abuse* 20: 182–95.

Magnusson, Mikaela. 2020. *Interviewing preschoolers: Facilitators and barriers to young children's legal testimony.* PhD dissertation. University of Gothenburg.

Myklebust, Trond. "The Nordic Model of Handling Children's Testimonies?", in Susanna Johansson, Kari Stefansen, Elisiv Bakketeig, and Anna Kaldal (Eds.), *Collaborating Against Child Abuse: Exploring the Nordic Barnahus Model,* 97–119. Cham: Palgrave Macmillan.

Powell, Martine B., and Pamela C. Snow. 2007. "A guide to questioning children during the free-narrative phase of an interview about abuse", *Australian Psychologist* 41(1): 57–65.

Röbäck, Karin. 2012. *Barns röster i vårdnadstvister: om verkställighet och professionellas riskbedömningar.* PhD dissertation. Gothenburg: Gothenburg University.

Schelin, Lena. 2006. *Bevisvärdering av utsagor i brottmål,* PhD dissertation. Stockholm: Stockholm University.

Schiratzki, Johanna. 2019. *Barnrättens grunder.* Lund: Studentlitteratur.

Singer, Anna. 2012. "Alla talar om barns rätt", in Lottie Ryberg-Welander (Ed.), *Rätt, social utsatthet och samhälleligt ansvar: festskrift till Anna Hollander,* 73–86. Stockholm: Norstedts juridik.

Smart, Carol, Bren Neale, and Amanda Wade. 2001. *The Changing Experience of Childhood, Families and Divorce*. Oxford: Polity Press.

Stiftelsen Allmänna Barnhuset. 2015. *Slutrapport – Barnets rättigheter i vårdnadstvister*. Stockholm: Stiftelsen Allmänna Barnhuset.

Supreme Court, NJA 1963 p. 555.

Supreme Court, NJA 1992 p. 532.

Supreme Court, NJA 1992 p. 446.

Supreme Court, NJA 1992 p. 666.

Supreme Court, NJA 1993 p. 68.

Supreme Court, NJA 1993 p. 616.

Supreme Court, NJA 1995 p. 398.

Supreme Court, NJA 1990 p. 555.

Supreme Court, NJA 2009 p. 447

Supreme Court, NJA 2010 p. 671.

Supreme Court, NJA 2017 p. 316.

Supreme Court, NJA 2017 p. 557.

Sutorius, Helena. 2013. *Bevisning vid sexualbrott.* Stockholm: Norstedts juridik.

Swedish Gender Equality Agency. 2022. *Uppgifter om våld är inget undantag i vårdnadstvister*. Rapport 2022:1.

Swedish National Police Board. 2009. *Guidelines for children's participation in Barnahus.*

Swedish National Council for Crime Prevention (*Brottsförebyggande rådet*) statistics 2021, Barnmisshandel, https://www.bra.se/statistik/statistik-utifran-brottstyper/barnmisshandel.html accessed 10 August 2022.

Tisdall, E. Kay M. 2015. "Children and Young People's Participation: A critical consideration of Article 12", in Didier Reynaert, Ellen Desmet, Sara Lembrechts, and Wouter Vandenhole (Eds.), *Routledge International Handbook of Children's Rights Studies,* 185–200. London: Routledge.

Tisdall, E. Kay M. 2018. "Challenging competency and capacity? Due weight to children's views in family law proceedings", *The International Journal of Children's Rights* 26: 159–182.

United Nations Committee on the Rights of the Child (CRC). *General comment No. 12* (2009): The right of the child to be heard. CRC/C/GC/12 (20 July 2009).

United Nations Economic and Social Council (ECOSOC), UN Economic and Social Council 2005/20. Guidelines on Justice in Matters Involving Child Victims and Witnesses of Crime. E/RES/2005/20 (22 July 2005).

Vrij, Aldert, Pär Anders Granhag, and Stephen Porter. 2010. "Pitfalls and opportunities in nonverbal and verbal lie detection", *Psychological Science in the Public Interest* 11(3): 89–121.

Wergens, Anna. 2014. *Human rights for victims of non-state crime. Taking victims seriously?* Oisterwijk: Wolf Legal Publishers.

A Response to Anna Kaldal

Linde Lindkvist

In the chapter, 'Children's Participation in Legal Proceedings', Anna Kaldal provides an insightful view of how children's participation rights are approached in Swedish criminal law and custody cases. In these areas, Kaldal argues, there are no apparent legal barriers to the realization of the child's right to be heard and to have an impact on the outcome of individual cases. However, the credibility of the child's testimony and the assessment of the child 'capacity' is always at stake. Children's participation as witnesses is firmly established in criminal law. Here, the main questions have been *how* children's testimonies should be gathered and what evidential value they should be given, especially considering the law's high standard of proof. In custody cases, the main rule says that the child should be heard and that the child's views should influence the court's decision. Nevertheless, the law provides investigators with an escape route if hearing the child is considered 'inappropriate'. Similarly, the law gives judges a margin of interpretation by prescribing that the child's views should be considered 'in accordance with the child's age and maturity'.

Citing empirical studies on the application of children's participation rights, Kaldal reveals how in practice such legal windows serve to condition the child's influence in several ways. The child is frequently considered too young, too immature, too incoherent, too dependent on others, and too ignorant to be heard, believed, or have an impact. Therefore, the real obstacle to children's participation rights is not the law as such, but a more profound scepticism toward 'children's ability to give credible statements and have independent views'. What needs to change is essentially the attitude among investigators and judges, who need to regard children as competent human beings.

The Swedish case thus points to the limits of law as a means of realizing children's rights. We can allocate ever more rights to children, but without effective institutional procedures for enforcement, such rights will remain empty and without effect. Institutions put in place to safeguard rights must have adequate resources, time, management, and competence. They must also be staffed by people who know how to fulfil their responsibilities, including attending to the needs and capabilities of those whose rights they are meant to protect. This points to the political dimension of human rights – the importance of providing sufficient economic, administrative, and educational resources to duty-bearing institutions. It also opens the gate for ethics in the sense of greater attention to the responsibilities of civil servants to treat persons of all ages with dignity and respect.

There are parts of Kaldal's chapter that point in a somewhat different direction. In the conclusion, she notes how legal decisions frequently offer seemingly rational reasons why a child was not heard or why a child's statements or views were not considered. She asks whether this betrays a deeper paradox, and whether strengthened legal protection of children's participation rights may sometimes have the opposite effect. Instead of a greater appreciation of children's views, child rights legislation perhaps leads to greater questioning of children's ability and credibility.

Kaldal might disagree, but I think her question here points to one of the central tensions of contemporary child rights discourse: namely, that of the right to participation versus ideas of children's immaturity. Children's rights are frequently seen as revolving around the child of the CRC's Article 12 – the child who is sufficiently competent to have a say on all issues of concern to his or her person. At the same time, child rights discourse has not been able to free itself from the best-interest principle. Much of the activism in this field is premised on a strong belief in the utilitarian value of rights – the idea that children's rights are justified in so far as they promote children's wellbeing. As Kaldal shows, the degree to which the courts consider the child's views frequently depends on how well those views align with social norms on what is typically in the child's best interest (e.g. contact with both parents in custody cases).

Put boldly, Kaldal's chapter thus actualizes the radical question of whether children's participation rights can ever be realized as long as the best-interest principle remains an integral part of children's rights.

Another aspect that explains some of the disappointing results from efforts to realize participation rights is the concept of 'evolving capacities'. Swedish law, following the CRC, has made this a ground for assessing the weight of the child's views in certain cases. What is often overlooked is how the CRC – by tying rights of participation and due process to capacity – depart from general human rights law, where age and maturity are not treated as legitimate grounds for discrimination.

Therefore, we should consider whether children's rights, especially in the context of participation, are better protected under general human rights law than under the CRC. In legal reasoning, children are perhaps better off not as children, but as human beings.

CHAPTER 4

Societal Unease and the Right to Non-discrimination for Youths with Foreign Background Who Are in Conflict with the Law

Katrin Lainpelto

1 Introduction

The political and societal discourses in Europe have been dominated in recent years by questions related to migration. Through cultural affiliation, young refugees and asylum seekers have not been left out of the discussion on crime; instead, this group has been pointed out as a specific risk to social order. The purpose of this chapter is therefore to examine whether heightened societal unease regarding a particular group in society affects the group members' right to fair treatment and a fair trial in practice and in the application of the law, compared to the majority population.

The propensity to associate a certain group of the population with social problems is deeply rooted; historically, this association has often been ascribed to those considered the 'newly arrived'.[1] This form of so-called 'vilification' defines certain groups as a threat to society and social order, and such classifications can form the perceptions and treatment of these groups.[2] Perceiving certain groups as a threat to society and social order is often based on prejudices[3] and these prejudices are in turn often linked to the group members' cultural affiliation and cultural beliefs.[4]

1 See Shamir, R., 'Without Borders? Notes on Globalization as a Mobility Regime', *Sociological Theory* 23, no. 2 (2005): 197–217.

2 Klapp, O. E., 'Notes Toward the Study of Vilification as a Social Process', *The Pacific Sociological Review* 2, no. 2 (1959): 71–76, 71.

3 See Adami, R., Chapter 6 in this volume. C.f. Stephan, W. G. and Stephan, C. W., 'An Integrated Threat Theory of Prejudice'. In Oskamp, S. (Ed.), *Reducing, Prejudice and Discrimination* (Lawrence Erlbaum Associates Publishers 2000): 23–45.

4 Stephan, W. G., Diaz-Loving, R. and Duran, A., 'Integrated Threat Theory and Intercultural Attitudes – Mexico and the United States', *J of Cross-Cultural Psychology* 31 (2000): 240–249, 240, 241.

 | DOI:10.1163/9789004511163_010

Several researchers seem to agree that the events in Cologne during New Year's Eve 2015 marked a turning point in the European debate on migration.[5] On the night in question, more than a thousand women reported that they had been sexually assaulted and that they had had their belongings stolen. The perpetrators were described as young migrants from the Middle East and North Africa.[6] Within a few days, reports of similar incidents in other European cities spread in the media.[7] In the debate that followed, the assaults were described as planned, organized, and part of a new 'terror strategy'.[8] Therefore, the debate was framed by a securitization of migration, in which migrants – especially those with a Muslim background and in a clearer way than ever before – were painted as a substantive security threat.[9] Young asylum seekers and young refugees were also associated with a number of social problems, especially criminality.[10]

The chapter begins with a discussion concerning the principle of non-discrimination in the UN Convention on the Rights of the Child (CRC) to create an interpretive framework regarding the rights and procedural safeguards that are assured for children in conflict with the law. Two legal studies will be presented in the chapter,[11] which examine how the Swedish judiciary system

5 Hestermann, T., 'Refugee and Migrants in the Media – The Black Hole'. In Kury, H., and Redo, S. (Eds.), *Refugee and Migrants in Law and Policy – Challenges and Opportunities for Global Civic Education* (Cham: Springer, 2018): 125–136, 128.

6 C.f. Witold K., Lévay, M., Rzeplińska, I. and Scheinost, M., 'Refugees and Asylum Seeks in Central European Countries – Reality, Politics and the Creation of Fear in Societies'. In Kury, H., and Redo, S. (Eds.), *Refugees and Migrants in Law and Policy – Challenges and Opportunities for Global Civic Education* (Cham: Springer 2018): 457–494.

7 Melnyk, I., '"Something is Immensely Rotten in the Media Republic" – The Information Dimension of the Refugee Crisis in Europe', *Social Communication* 3, no. 1 (2017): 40–53.

8 C.f. Adam, E. K., Heissel, J. A., Zeiders, K. H., Richeson J. A., Ross, E. C., Ehrlich, K. B., Levy, D. J., Kemeny, M., Brodish A. B., Malanchuk O., Peck S., C., Fuller-Rowell, T. E., and Eccles, J. S., 'Developmental Histories of Perceived Racial Discrimination and Diurnal Cortisol Profiles in Adulthood – A 20-Year Prospective Study' *Psychoneuroendocrinology* 62 (2015): 279–291.

9 C.f. De Genova, N., 'The "Migrant Crisis" as Racial Crisis – Do Black Lives Matter in Europe?', *Ethnic and Racial Studies* 41, no. 10 (2018): 1765–1782.

10 See for example Sinram, J., '"I am not a Racist, but ..." – The Phenomenon of Hate Comments on Refugees in Germany and How to Deal with Them'. In Jünemann, A., Scherer, N., and Fromm, N. (Eds.), *Fortress Europe? – Challenges and Failures of Migration and Asylum Policies* (Wiesbaden: Springer 2017) 159–165, 160.

11 These legal studies have been presented in an earlier publication, see Lainpelto, K. 'Ett dömande eller ett fördömande rättsväsendet? – En fråga om integration' ['A judicial or condemning judiciary? – A question regarding integration?']. In Helander, K., and Leviner, P. (Eds.), *Barn, migration och integration i en utmanande tid* [*Children, migration and integration in a challenging time*] (Ragulka Press, 2019): 127–158.

handles youth suspected of and charged with sexual harassment – a crime that has been linked in some aspects of the public debate to increased migration from certain regions. The main question investigated through these two studies is whether members of the court are influenced by the ethnic or cultural background of the youth involved and, if so, the ways in which this influence manifests itself during the evaluation of evidence. Finally, the results of the studies are discussed in the light of children's rights when children come in conflict with the law.

2 Children's Right to Non-discrimination

The principle of non-discrimination is built on the recognition of the inherent dignity and the equal and inalienable rights of all members of the human family.[12] According to Article 2(1) of the CRC, the States Parties shall respect the rights set forth in the Convention and ensure these rights are fulfilled for each child[13] within their jurisdiction[14] without discrimination of any kind.[15] The expressions 'discrimination of any kind' and 'or other status' suggest that the list of grounds for discrimination is not exhaustive. Therefore, other grounds for discrimination could be included.[16]

12 See the Preamble to the CRC.

13 A child means every human being below the age of 18 years; see Article 1 of the CRC.

14 Sutherland writes: '(…) the child's presence is the controlling factor and how the child came to be there – whether by legal or illegal means – is irrelevant', Sutherland, E. 'Article 2 of the United Nations Convention on the Rights of the Child – Non-Discrimination and Children's Rights'. In Skivenes, M., and Søvig, K. (Eds.), *Child Rights and International Discrimination Law – Implementing Article 2 of the UN Convention on the Rights of the child* (New York: Routledge 2019): 23–41.

15 Article 2(1) of the CRC uses the term 'discrimination', as does Article 14 of the European Convention on Human Rights (ECHR), in contrast to Article 2(1) of the International Covenant on Civil and Political Rights (ICCPR) and Article 2 of the Universal Declaration of Human Rights (UDHR), which refer to 'without distinction'. Today, it is accepted that both terms refer to the same kind of differentiation without reason, see Besson, S. 'The Principle of Non-Discrimination in the Convention on the Rights of the Child', *International Journal of Children's Rights* 13 (2005): 433–461, 447.

16 See UN Committee on the Rights of the Child. *General Comment No 15*. CRC/C/GC/15, para. 8, which mentions 'sexual orientation, gender identity and health status'. See also the UN Office of the High Commissioner for Human Rights, *Manual on Human Rights Reporting Under Six Major International Human Rights Instruments* (HR/PUB/91/1 1997), 418.

Article 2(1) of the CRC uses the same structure and wording that can be found in other international human-rights instruments.[17] This reflects the CRC's intention to relate to and comply with international anti-discrimination law.[18] On the other hand, Article 2 of the CRC can be described as a unique provision because Article 2(2) offers protection not only against discrimination that is directed specifically to the child, but also against discrimination related to status of the child's parents or guardians. This child-specific dimension acknowledges children's special status and needs.

The principle of non-discrimination is one of the general principles of the CRC; all these principles are included as important elements in the realization of the child-rights perspective.[19] Therefore, Article 2 must be read in the light of the other general principles of the Convention, while at the same time, the article provides an interpretative framework for application of the other provisions of the Convention. Article 2(1) can thus be described as non-autonomous: the provision covers only discrimination in relation to the other rights enshrined in the Convention.[20]

The same does not apply, however, to Article 2(2), which by its application to all forms of discrimination and punishment on the basis of the position, activities, expressed views, or beliefs of parents, guardians, or family members, can instead be described as autonomous. In other words, the scope of Article 2(2) is greater because the provision can be applied independently in all areas where discrimination can take place (including those that fall outside the

---

17 A similar wording is used in the International Bill of Human Rights; see Article 2 of the UDHR, Article 2(1) of the ICCPR (see also Article 24(1), which concerns children specifically), and Article 2(2) of the International Covenant on Economic, Social and Cultural Rights (ICESCR). See also the Convention on the Rights of Persons with Disabilities (CRPD), the International Convention on the Elimination of All Forms of Racial Discrimination (CERD), and the Convention on the Elimination of All Forms of Discrimination against Women (CEDAW). CRC adds the discrimination ground disability. Regarding disability, see Article 23 of the CRC and CRC/C/GC/9. Note: General comments of the CRC are not binding on States Parties, but the views expressed in these comments are widely regarded as non-binding norms that add detail to the rights and obligations contained in the treaty.

18 Besson, S., (2005), 445. From a pronounced child perspective, Article 2(1) of the CRC is also in line with what is stated in rule 2(1) of the United Nations Standard Minimum Rules for the Administration of Juvenile Justice (the Beijing Rules).

19 UN Committee on the Rights of the Child. *General Comment No 5. General measures of implementation of the Convention on the Rights of the Child.* CRC/GC/2003/5, para. 12. The other general principles are the child's best interest (Article 3), the right to life, survival, and development (Article 6), the right to be heard (Article 12).

20 Article 2(1) of the CRC is similar to Article 2(1) of the ICCPR, Article 2(2) of the ICESCR, and Article 14 of the ECHR. Cf. Article 26 of the ICCPR. See also Leviner, P., and Holappa, T. Chapter 2 this volume.

scope of the CRC), while Article 2(1) must be applied in relation to other convention rights.[21] At the same time, Article 2(1) can also be described as being of a binding nature owing to its lack of subjective qualification requirements, thus leaving little scope for a more discretionary assessment of whether the discrimination is justified, proportionate, or acceptable. In this way, Article 2(1) resembles more of a rule than a principle.

The requirement on States Parties, in accordance with Article 2(1), to 'respect and ensure' the right set forth in the Convention creates both positive and negative (mandatory) obligations. The requirement for 'respect' implies that the States Parties shall 'abstain from adopting measures that may preclude the exercise of such rights or may violate them', while the obligation to 'ensure' implies an 'an affirmative and immediate obligation to take all necessary measures to enable individuals to enjoy and exercise the relevant rights, including the removal of possible obstacles to the enjoyment of those rights'.[22] Article 2(2) states that the States Parties 'shall take all appropriate measures'.

Thus, the first paragraph generates negative obligations of respect and positive obligations of results, while the second paragraph deals exclusively with positive obligations of results. Article 2 does not specify the manner in which the States Parties shall ensure these relevant rights; therefore, it must be deduced from the provision dealing with the right in question, together with Article 4, which stipulates that the States Parties shall undertake all appropriate legislative, administrative, and other measures for the implementation of the rights recognized in the Convention.

The CRC does not clarify what is meant by 'discrimination'; nor has the UN Committee on the Rights of the Child made a specific comment on Article 2. However, there is a consensus that discrimination in the context of children's rights implies a difference of treatment in similar situations or similar treatment in different situations, irrespective of whether the discrimination is intentional.[23]

Further, not all forms of differential treatment are discriminatory. The UN Committee on Human Rights has stated that there may be good reasons for

---

21 Besson, S. (2005), 447.

22 UN Office of the High Commissioner for Human Rights, *Manual on Human Rights Reporting Under Six Major International Human Rights Instruments* (HR/PUB/91/1 1997), 417.

23 Besson, S. (2005), 451. See also UN Committee on the Rights of the Child. *General comment No. 1 Article 29 (1) The aims of education*, 17 April 2001, CRC/GC/2001/1,10.

differential treatment[24] and the UN Committee on the Rights of the Child has accepted differential treatment, provided that the distinction is lawful, proportionate, legitimate, and in line with the best interests of the child and international human-rights standards. In Swedish law, for example, a number of provisions imply that children should be treated differently compared to adults.[25] This differential treatment is legitimized by the acceptance of children's immaturity and need for special protection and care.

3 Children in Conflict with the Law

As mentioned in the previous section, the general principle of non-discrimination shall guide the interpretation and application of the other provisions of the CRC. This also applies to the special rights of children in conflict with the law, which are set out mainly in Articles 37 and 40. This chapter will discuss certain paragraphs of CRC Article 40 in more detail.

Article 40 concerns the right to a dignified and child-friendly criminal procedure and penal system. The provision implies a necessary balance between protection and participation of children who are in conflict with the law and is permeated by a respect for the rights of the child and a recognition of the child's developmental abilities.

Article 40 (1) clarifies three principles of importance for promoting the child's sense of wellbeing. Every child alleged as, accused of, or recognized as having infringed the penal law shall be treated in a manner which (i) is consistent with the promotion of the child's sense of dignity and worth, (ii) reinforces the child's respect for human rights and fundamental freedoms of others, and (iii) takes into account the child's age and the desirability of promoting the child's reintegration and the child's acceptance of a constructive role in society. These three principles are related and interdependent with respect to the realization of the child's human dignity and rights.[26] Although an important purpose of the criminal process is to demand accountability and thus achieve

---

24 United Nations Committee on Human Rights, *General comment no. 13 (2011), The right of the child to freedom from all forms of violence*, CCPR, 18 Apr. 2011; United Nations Committee on Human Rights, *General Comment No. 18, Non-discrimination*, CCPR, 10 November 1989.

25 For example, the protection for children under the age of 15 against sexual offences differs from the protection for children over the age of 15, and children under the age of 15 cannot be sentenced, even when found guilty of a crime. See also Leviner, P., and Holappa, T., Chapter 2; and Kaldal, A., Chapter 3 this volume.

26 Manco, E., 'Protecting the Child's Right to Participate in Criminal Justice Proceedings' *Amsterdam Law Forum* 8, no. 48 (2016): 48–77, 52.

general and individual prevention, the Committee on the Rights of the Child suggests that this purpose should be achieved by applying the principles of justice for children set forth in the Convention because crimes committed by children and youths tend to decrease when these principles are considered.[27]

The principle that the child should be treated in a way that is (i) consistent with the promotion of the child's sense of dignity and worth during all stages of the criminal process[28] is a direct reference to the most basic requirements of the CRC: every child should be recognized and respected as a human being with rights. The Committee on the Rights of the Child states that such treatment reflects the fundamental rights enshrined in Article 1 of the Universal Declaration of Human Rights (UDHR), which provides that people are born free and equal in dignity and rights.[29]

The principle that the child should be treated in a way that (ii) reinforces the child's respect for human rights and fundamental freedoms of others is in line with what is expressed in the Preamble to the CRC, i.e. children should be brought up in the spirit of the ideals proclaimed in the Charter of the United Nations.[30] The treatment and education of children shall be directed to the development of respect for human rights and freedoms.[31] At the same time, full respect for and implementation of the guarantees of a fair trial listed in Article 40(2) are required. The Committee on the Rights of the Child emphasizes that if key actors do not fully respect and protect these guarantees during all stages of the criminal process, the child cannot be expected to respect the human rights and fundamental freedoms of others.[32]

Finally, there is the principle that children should be treated in a way that (iii) takes into account the child's age and the desirability of promoting the child's reintegration and the child's acceptance of a constructive role in society. Consideration of the child's age is an important element in the promotion of the child's wellbeing. The child's wellbeing serves both individual and societal interests. From a societal perspective, the child's wellbeing enables the child to participate actively and fully assume responsibilities, and in addition take on a constructive role within the community. Even if the term

27 UN Committee on the Rights of the Child. *General Comment No. 24 (2019). Children's Rights in the Child Justice System.* CRC/C/GC/24, para. 3.

28 UN Committee on the Rights of the Child. *General Comment No. 10 (2007). Children's Rights in Juvenile Justice.* CRC/C/GC/10, para. 13.

29 UN Committee on the Rights of the Child. *General Comment No. 10 (2007)*, para. 13.

30 See also Article 29(1)(b).

31 UN Committee on the Rights of the Child. *General Comment No. 10 (2007)*, para. 13.

32 UN Committee on the Rights of the Child. *General Comment No. 10 (2007)*, para. 13.

'rehabilitation' is found in several human-rights instruments, the CRC uses the word 'reintegration'.

The Committee on the Rights of the Child does not develop further the concept of 'social integration'. Van Bueren is of the opinion that the focus on social integration, rather than rehabilitation, reflects an approach that recognizes that children's difficulties are not necessarily individually conditioned, but instead require that children's social environments and social relationships must be taken into account.[33]

The Riyadh Guidelines are also permeated by the approach that children should be helped to develop a sense of responsibility, and that this can be achieved only when the child develops a sense of belonging. The Committee has stated that the principle must 'be applied, observed and respected'. The wording is sharper here than that found in the Committee's statements regarding the child's value and dignity ('respected and protected').[34] Manco argues that the sharper statement may be due to the principle's acknowledgement of the developmental abilities of the child.[35] On the other hand, the principle should not be interpreted in a way that relieves children of criminal liability; instead, the process of accountability must take place in the light of children's developmental abilities. It is thus a matter of creating a balance between general and individual prevention, societal protection, the interests of the crime victim, and the child's capacity for reintegration. Therefore, it is important to take measures to prevent circumstances that could hinder children's opportunities for participation, such as stigmatization, social isolation, and negative publicity.[36]

Article 40(2) lists the rights and guarantees aimed at ensuring every child fair treatment and a fair trial. These rights and guarantees consist of the following: no retroactive application of child justice (2)(a); presumption of innocence (b)(i); prompt and direct information regarding the charge (b)(ii); legal or other appropriate assistance (b)(ii); decisions without delay and with the

---

33 Van Bueren, G. 'Article 40: Child Criminal Justice'. In Alen, A., Vande Lanotte, J., Verhellen, E., Ang, F., Berghmans, E, Verheyde, M. (Eds.), *A Commentary on the United Nations Convention of the Rights of the Child, Article 40; Child Criminal Justice* (Leiden: Martinus Nijhoff Publishers, 2006).

34 UN Committee on the Rights of the Child. *General Comment No. 10* (2007), para. 13.

35 Manco, E., *The United Nations Convention on the Rights of the Child – Are Children 'In Conflict with the Law' Really Protected? – A Case Study of Republic of Albania's Juvenile Justice System* (University of Sheffield, 2013), 186.

36 UN Committee on the Rights of the Child. *General Comment No. 10* (2007), para. 29. See also UN Committee on the Rights of the Child. *General Comment No. 24* (2019), para.70 and 76.

involvement of parents or guardians (b)(iii); freedom from compulsory self-incrimination (b)(iv); presence and examination of witnesses (b)(iv); right of review or appeal (b)(v); assistance of an interpreter without cost (b)(vi); and respect of privacy (b)(vii).[37] In addition, it is a fundamental right of the child to be heard at all stages of the criminal process (Article 12 of the CRC). The child also has the right to remain silent.[38]

The enumeration is based inter alia on Article 14(2) of the International Covenant on Civil and Political Rights (ICCPR) and Article 6 of the European Court of Human Rights (ECHR). Therefore, these human-rights instruments can be used as sources for the interpretation of Article 40(2). Furthermore, the Beijing Rules can be used as an interpretative aid with regard to a child perspective on the right to a fair trial.[39] According to the Committee on the Rights of the Child, an important part of fulfilling these guarantees is that the professionals involved in the criminal process for children should be able to work in interdisciplinary teams and should be well informed about the physical, psychological, mental, and social development of children and adolescents, as well as the special needs of the most marginalized children.[40]

Although not explicitly stated in Article 40(2), both children and adults have the right to equality before the courts. This right includes equal access, equality of arms, and ensuring that the parties are treated without any form of discrimination.[41] In other words, the child must not be placed at a procedural disadvantage compared to the counterparty. This condition emphasizes that procedural equality in question has greater priority than equality before the law.

Article 40(2)(b)(iii) sets out the right to have the matter determined by a competent, independent, and impartial authority or judicial body in a fair hearing without delay. With regard to the requirement of 'without delay', the time that elapses between the alleged crime and the conclusion of the proceedings should be as brief as possible.[42] The greater the time interval, the more likely it is that the judicial reaction will lose its positive effects, and at the same time the child runs the risk of stigmatization. The Committee on the Rights of the Child has therefore recommended that the States Parties set

37 See UN Committee on the Rights of the Child. *General Comment No. 24* (2019), para. 42–71.
38 UN Committee on the Rights of the Child. *General Comment No. 24* (2019), para. 44 and 45.
39 Manco, E. (2013), 180.
40 UN Committee on the Rights of the Child. *General Comment No. 24* (2019), para. 39.
41 See Article 14(1) of the ICCPR and CCPR/C/GC/32, para. 8.
42 UN Committee on the Rights of the Child. *General Comment No. 24* (2019), para. 54. Cf. Article 14(3) ICCPR.

and apply time limits, and that these limits should be shorter than those for adults – while fully guaranteeing the legal safeguards.[43]

Like Article 6 of the ECHR, Article 40(2)(b)(iii) is based on Article 14(1) of the ICCPR and ultimately seeks to ensure the right to a fair trial. The requirement of impartiality is addressed by the Human Rights Committee, and the Committee emphasizes both a subjective and objective appearance of impartiality. According to the Committee, a subjective appearance of impartiality means that judges must not allow judgements to be influenced by personal biases or prejudice. Judges shall not harbour preconceived notions about the particular case before them, or act in ways that improperly promote the interests of one of the parties to the detriment of the other. An objective appearance of impartiality means that to a reasonable observer, the authority or judicial body must appear to be impartial.[44]

4 The Swedish Justice System's Treatment of Youths with Foreign Background

4.1 *The Aim of the Studies*

This section of the chapter presents the main results of two studies, which have examined how the Swedish justice system treats youths with foreign background, between the ages of 15 and 17, who have been suspected of and charged with sexual harassment. The purpose of these studies has been to investigate whether an increased societal unease regarding a certain group of youths affects the group members' right to fair treatment and a fair trial.

4.2 *An Experimental Study*

The first study examined whether legally qualified Swedish judges and lay judges are influenced by perpetrators' ethnic and cultural backgrounds in their evaluation of evidence and, if so, how this influence might manifest itself.[45] The respondents were informed that a 13-year-old girl had been the victim of an alleged sexual harassment at a public swimming pool. The suspect was a 16-year-old boy, previously unknown to the victim. Apart from the victim's

43 UN Committee on the Rights of the Child. *General Comment No. 24* (2019), para. 55.

44 UN Committee on the Rights of the Child. *General Comment No. 32* (2007), CCPR/C/GC/32, para. 21.

45 The study was carried out within the framework of a research project in the form of a degree project at the Department of Law, Stockholm University, see Bisso, R., *Fördomar mot utlandsfödda i brottmålsprocessen* (Stockholm: Stockholm University Press, 2017).

statement, there was no other evidence to support the allegations. Thereafter the recorded police interrogation with the young suspect was presented to the respondents. The experimental design of the study included a police interrogation that was recorded in two versions: one where the young suspect was played by a person with a Swedish background, and one where the young suspect was played by a person with non-Swedish background.

In terms of content, the questions asked during the interrogation were identical, but the young suspect with foreign background expressed his statement with an accent. After hearing the police interrogation with the young suspect, the respondents were asked to answer questions concerning the suspect's credibility, the reliability of suspect's statement, how much discomfort the respondents experienced based on the alleged crime, and the perceived degree of guilt. Because so few legally qualified judges participated in the study (n=34), the presentation below focuses mainly on the results from the lay judges (n= 320).

The respondents judged the young suspect with a Swedish background to be significantly more credible than the young suspect with a foreign background (4.91 compared with 3.55, p-value 0.000). The same assessment was made regarding the reliability of the suspect's statement (4.53 compared with 3.36, p-value 0.000). For the question of perceived discomfort, the conduct of the young suspect with a foreign background led to considerably greater discomfort than the conduct of the young suspect with a Swedish background (6.88 compared with 4.96, p-value 0.000).

The last question concerned whether the respondents would have convicted the young suspect. Fifty-nine per cent of the respondents stated that they would have convicted the young foreign-background suspect, while 29 per cent stated that they would have convicted the young Swedish-background suspect. A similar result was identified with regard to the answer 'no'; only 13 per cent of the respondents stated that they would not have convicted the young foreign-background suspect, while 38 per cent stated that they would not have convicted the young Swedish-background suspect. In other words, three times more respondents stated that they would have acquitted the young suspect with a Swedish background compared to the proportion who stated that they would have acquitted the young suspect with a foreign background.

4.3 *A Study of Swedish Court Decisions*

In the second study, all Swedish district court decisions concerning sexual harassment from the years 2013, 2015, and 2017 were examined, where the defendant was between the ages of 15 and 17 at the time of the criminal conduct.[46] In the light of the limited number of participating legally qualified judges in the experimental study presented above, the study of district court decisions provides an important insight into the actual evaluation of evidence in similar cases. The presentation below focuses mainly on the results from 2017, in the light of the previously mentioned shift in discourses regarding migration. It is interesting to note that the proportion of young newly arrived persons (under the age of 18) prosecuted in 2017 increased by 60 per cent compared to 2013 and 36 per cent compared to 2015.

Thirty-five per cent of the prosecuted cases in 2017 concerned young defendants with a Swedish background and 65 per cent concerned young defendants with a foreign background; 70 per cent of the latter involved newly arrived youths.[47] Of all examined cases, almost half concerned newly arrived youths (45 per cent).

Eighty-eight per cent of the prosecuted cases in 2017 led to a conviction and 12 per cent to an acquittal. Of the cases that led to a conviction, 29 per cent concerned young Swedish-background defendants and 71 per cent concerned young foreign-background defendants. Of the cases that led to an acquittal, 85 per cent concerned young Swedish-background defendants and 15 per cent concerned young foreign-background defendants. When studying the two youth groups separately, young defendants with a Swedish background were convicted in 72 per cent of the cases and acquitted in 28 per cent. Young defendants with a foreign background were convicted in 97 per cent of the cases and acquitted in only 3 per cent. In other words, a statistical relationship was identified between the factors of ethnic/cultural background and the assessment of guilt (p-value 0.001). Compared to 2015, the proportion of young defendants with foreign background who were acquitted decreased by 63 percentage points.

However, it is not enough merely to state that a statistical connection seems to exist between ethnic/cultural background and the assessment of guilt, as there may be evidentiary circumstances and evidentiary facts in the cases that could explain the connection. Therefore, a qualitative analysis was carried out, which considered all circumstances surrounding the alleged crimes and the evidentiary facts. The main results of this analysis showed that of the young

46 Lainpelto, K. 'Ett dömande eller ett fördömande rättsväsendet? – En fråga om integration' [*A judicial or condemning judiciary? – A question regarding integration?*], in Helander, K. and Leviner, P. (Eds.), *Barn, migration och integration i en utmanande tid* [*Children, migration and integration in a challenging time*] (Ragulka Press, 2019): 127–158.

47 'Newly arrived youth' refers to a young person under the age of 18 who has not resided in Sweden for more than three years at the time of the alleged crime.

defendants with a Swedish background, 28 per cent confessed to the crime. The corresponding number for young defendants with a foreign background was only 1 per cent. Therefore, the defendants' attitude to the charges does not seem to explain the statistical deviation. Rather, the deviation appears even more inexplicable in the light of the proportion of denials among young defendants with a foreign background.

5 The Scene of the Crime and the Relationship between the Defendant and the Victim

In the studied cases, a difference emerged between young Swedish-background and foreign-background defendants in terms of the relationship between the defendant and the victim and the scene of the crime. In only one case regarding young defendants with a Swedish background, the youth was previously unknown to the victim at the time of the alleged crime (3 per cent). In the other cases (97 per cent), the victim and the defendant knew each other before the alleged crime took place.

In a large proportion of the cases regarding young defendants with a Swedish background, the alleged crime had been committed via digital platforms for communication (40 per cent), at school (30 per cent), and at the victim's own house (20 per cent). In the case of young defendants with a foreign background, the defendant was previously unknown to the victim in 63 per cent of the cases and a majority of these cases concerned newly arrived youths. The majority of the charges against young defendants with a foreign background concerned alleged sexual harassment in public places. The most common locations were public music events, public swimming pools, and public transportation.

6 The Evidentiary Basis

As previously mentioned, in a majority of the cases studied involving young defendants with a Swedish background, the evidentiary basis was relatively strong. The main reason for this is that a large proportion of the cases concerned sexual harassment via digital platforms for communication; hence the prosecutors were able to present persuasive technical evidence. In addition, when the alleged crime had been committed at a school, the prosecutors could often present direct witnesses. The prevalence of strong evidence can also explain why young defendants with a Swedish background chose to confess in almost 30 per cent of the cases.

In the case of young defendants with a foreign background, not a single case concerned sexual harassment via digital platforms for communication; these cases lacked the strong evidentiary bases found in the cases regarding young Swedish-background defendants. In cases concerning young foreign-background defendants, the most common piece of evidence, especially in cases concerning newly arrived youths, was the victim's uncorroborated statement. A corresponding evidentiary basis occurred in only one of the studied cases concerning young defendants with a Swedish background. In this case the defendant was acquitted due to lack of corroborating evidence. However, newly arrived youth were often convicted on the basis of the victim's uncorroborated statement. It was also difficult to access the court's argumentation because the grounds for the decisions often were only briefly elaborated, despite an evidentiary basis that was frequently quite difficult to assess.

In several cases involving newly arrived youths, the victim had in some way identified the suspect. Nevertheless, photo array had been used in one only case. Instead, the identifications in the studied cases consisted of showups, i.e. when the witness is presented with a single suspect. According to current research, showups are associated with a number of risks, mainly because of the absence of line-up fillers. Showups are therefore recommended only for exceptional cases. Still, the district courts did accept this non-conventional method of identification in several cases concerning newly arrived youths.

Several identifications took place in locations where the young suspect had been in the company of other persons of the same age and of the same ethnic origin (e.g. when youths assigned to a residential care home for unaccompanied children visited a public swimming pool). In the light of the well-known phenomenon of own-race bias, the courts had several reasons to consider the risk of incorrect identifications. Several of the identifications were also based on extremely vague witness descriptions. Despite these circumstances, and the fact that the accused denied the allegations, the newly arrived youths were found guilty of sexual harassment in the majority of the cases based on uncorroborated victim accounts.

In addition, in several of the cases involving newly arrived youths, the charges were built on vague time frames – a circumstance that may limit the defendant's ability to properly respond to and challenge the accusations (equality of arms). The vague time frames are difficult to explain considering that most cases concerned sexual harassment on a single occasion by a suspect previously unknown to the victim. Furthermore, the youths were burdened by remarkably long investigation times. In some cases, a whole year had passed from the initial police report to the first interrogation with the young suspect. The defendants' counsels were not always given the opportunity to attend police interviews with child victims. Indeed, the counsels were given the opportunity to request additional interrogations, but many of these counsels refrained from requesting further investigation because it was not deemed to be meaningful to carry out in-depth interrogations with child witnesses such a long time after the alleged crime. Using recorded statements in evidence at the time of the interrogation or at a later stage of the process, when the defendant has not been given the opportunity to question and challenge the witness, is inconsistent with the right to a fair trial if the outcome of the case is entirely dependent on the credibility of the witness's statement.[48] However, because the counsels had been given the opportunity to ask for additional interrogation, but had refrained, the newly arrived youths' right to a fair trial was not formally violated. Still, it can be said that to a certain extent, the right to a fair trial was compromised as a consequence of the long investigation times.[49]

7 Discussion

The results of the two studies suggest that young foreign-background defendants, especially newly arrived defendants, are often found to be guilty on the basis of vague evidence. In addition, these youths are not ensured the right to a fair trial to the same extent as their Swedish counterparts.

The existence of discriminatory treatment due to an impartial court is difficult to study and substantiate. There also seems to be some resistance to acknowledging such a phenomenon. It can probably be perceived as offensive that the institution responsible for safeguarding everyone's equality before the law (and the courts) is not doing its job – especially when it comes to children and young persons. However, the fact that the phenomenon is difficult to study and substantiate does not mean that discriminatory treatment does not occur.

We already know that members of the court frequently fall victim to various sources of error when evaluating evidence. In addition, because Swedish law is based on the principle of free evaluation of evidence,[50] this process is inevitably characterized by a certain degree of subjectivity. One such source of error is the categorization of individuals – a categorization often based on generalizations and stereotypes conveyed in the media and in political and societal discourses.

---

48 See European Court of Justice Case of *S.N. v. Sweden*, 2 July 2002 (Application no. 34209/96) and the Supreme Court B 360-14 10 April 2015 (NJA 2015 p. 222).
49 Cf. Article 14(3) of the ICCPR.
50 Lainpelto, K., *Stödbevisning i brottmål* (Stockholm: Jure förlag AB, 2013).

Further, the risk of discriminatory treatment is greater when the members of the court enjoy greater freedom of action, which explains why the risk increases in cases involving less serious crimes and a vague evidentiary basis.[51] The risk also seems to increase when the crime in question is perceived as a threat to fundamental societal values and social order. In addition, association of a certain group with a crime that is perceived to threaten fundamental societal values can increase the tendency to prosecute the members of this group and result in more frequent sentencing and/or harsher punishments.

This tendency can be explained in the light of a perceived need to condemn the group and the group members' actions. Even if the condemnation is expressed at an isolated trial, the condemnation has a wider social function of particular importance at a time of heightened societal unease regarding a certain group. In this way, the condemnation becomes a justified practice of power that aims at compelling the group's members to internalize the societal values from which they are considered to have deviated.

Against this background, this treatment of newly arrived youths can be described as a 'disciplining activity' and establishment of examples designed to exert control and promote exclusion rather than inclusion and reintegration.[52]

The perceived need to condemn may possibly be strengthened by the fact that the majority of the studied cases involving newly arrived youths concerned sexual harassment in public places by previously unknown perpetrators. One consequence of the condemnation, though, is that the distance between 'us' and 'them' increases, as the cultural conflict is transformed into a question of who should and should not be included, thus creating a breeding ground for structural discrimination.

Another result worth noting is that in the majority of court decisions concerning newly arrived youths, the evidence consisted solely of the victim's uncorroborated statement. In such cases, the credibility of the defendant and the reliability of the defendant's statement become crucial. The construction of 'the evil other' may explain the results of the experimental study which showed that the young Swedish-background suspect was perceived as more credible than the young suspect with a foreign background. The same assessment was made regarding the reliability of the statement provided.

---

51 See for example Tittle, C. R. and Curran, D. A., 'Contingencies for Dispositional Disparities in Juvenile Justice', *Social Forces* 67, no. 1 (1988): 23–58; Rachlinski, J. J. and Wistrich, A.J., 'Judging the Judiciary by the Numbers – Empirical Research on Judges', *Annual Review of Law and Social Science* 13, no. 1 (2017): 203–229.

52 Littlechild, B., 'Young Offenders, Punitive Policies and the Rights of Children', *Critical Social Policy* 17, no. 53 (1997): 73–92, 86.

Furthermore, the antipathy identified in the same study, in the form of greater discomfort when the suspect was of foreign descent, is particularly interesting. A fundamental right in the CRC (and other human-rights instruments) is equality before the courts. However, the relevant question here is how newly arrived youths can respond to and challenge the court members' feelings of resentment and antipathy. The occurrence of such feelings should also be discussed in the light of the child's right to be presumed innocent until proven guilty (Article 40(1)(b)(i) of the CRC) and the requirement of an impartial court (Article 40(2)(b)(iii) of the CRC).

8 Concluding Remarks

The justice system plays an important role in ensuring that social norms are maintained (and created). In times of societal unease, the judicial process may be likened to a process of condemnation, which in the long run can lead to social exclusion for certain groups in the society. Although the results presented in this chapter offer only a snapshot, it is possible to discern a treatment that seems to make a distinction between two groups of youths. This treatment can be described in some cases as a violation of the very essence of the CRC and, in addition, could constitute a breeding ground for structural discrimination.

The vulnerability of newly arrived youths in particular is doubled; they are not ensured their rights during the criminal proceedings, nor are they offered the opportunities to which they are entitled once the proceedings are completed. In addition, association of a certain group with a crime that is perceived to threaten fundamental societal values can lead to an increased tendency to prosecute the members of this group, as well as more frequent sentencing and/or harsher sentences than for others.[53] Both conscious and non-conscious antipathies can transform the judicial process into a process of condemnation.[54] Parallels can be drawn to the perception that actions can be caused by either internal or external factors. Actions of persons belonging to minority

---

53 See Weenink, D., 'Explaining Ethnic Inequality in the Juvenile Justice System – An Analysis of the Outcomes of Cutch Prosecutorial Decision Making', *The British J of Criminology* 49, no. 2 (2009): 220–242, 220; Gur Arye, M., 'The Legitimacy of Judicial Responses to Moral Panic – Perceived vs. Normative Legitimacy', *Criminal Justice Ethics* 37, no. 2 (2018): 141–163. Youth groups are no exception, see for example, Pakes, F., 'A Panicky Debate – The State of Moroccan Youth in the Netherlands'. In Morgan, G., and Poynting, S. (Eds.), *Global Islamophobia – Muslims and Moral Panic in the West.* (London: Routledge, 2016): 47–58.

54 See for example, Gur Arye, M., (2018), 141; Dagistanli S., and Grewal, K., 'Perverse Muslim Masculinities in Contemporary Orientalist Discourse – The Vagaries of Muslim

groups are more often considered to be caused by internal and inherent factors, while actions of persons in the majority population are often considered to be caused by external factors. Actions caused by internal factors more often lead to stricter assessments and condemnation,[55] and this may explain why individuals of the minority population are more often perceived as a threat requiring strategies based on punishment and control.[56]

Furthermore, a successful reintegration is based on the premise that society is willing to accept and welcome the child back into society.[57] In other words, children's reintegration is about an interaction between the individual's autonomy and will to be reintegrated into society and the conditions in which society allows this autonomy to operate. A treatment that aims at condemnation and social exclusion can lead to limited opportunities for reintegration and participation for the group of 'newly arrived' youths that has been the focus of this chapter.

The studies presented in this chapter can be described as a starting point in terms of understanding the consequences of the discourses surrounding the group of foreign-background youths in Sweden, but significant knowledge gaps remain. More research is needed to identify particularly vulnerable groups of children and youths at both the individual and societal level. In such a quest for knowledge, it is particularly important that children and youths are involved and asked to relate their experiences – especially in terms of the impact of discrimination on continued life opportunities.

References

Adam, Emma K., Jennifer A. Heissel, Katharine H. Zeiders, Jennifer A. Richeson, Emily C. Ross, Katherine B. Ehrlich, Dorianne J. Levy, Margaret Kemeny, Amanda B. Brodish, Oksana Malanchuk, Stephen C. Peck, Thomas E. Fuller-Rowell, and Jacquelynne S. Eccles. 2015. "Developmental Histories of Perceived Racial

---

Immigration in the West'. In Morgan, G., and Poynting, S. (Eds.), *Global Islamophobia – Muslims and Moral Panic in the West* (New York: Routledge, 2016): 119–142.

55 See Rotter, J. B., 'Generalized Expectancies for Internal Versus External Control of Reinforcement', *Psychological Monographs* 80, no. 1 (1966): 1–28.

56 Bridges, G. S., and Steen, S., 'Racial Disparities in Official Assessments of Juvenile Offenders – Attributional Stereotypes as Mediating Mechanisms', *American Sociological Review* 63, no. 4 (1998): 554–570, 554, 556.

57 Cipriani, D., *Children's Rights and the Minimum Age of Criminal Responsibility – A Global Perspective* (New York: Routledge, 2009), 36f.

Discrimination and Diurnal Cortisol Profiles in Adulthood – A 20-Year Prospective Study", *Psychoneuroendocrinology* 62: 279–291.

Besson, Samantha. 2005. "The Principle of Non-Discrimination in the Convention on the Rights of the Child", *International Journal of Children's Rights* 13: 433–461.

Bisso, Ramil. 2017. *Fördomar mot utlandsfödda i brottmålsprocessen.* Stockholm: Stockholm University Press.

Bridges, George S., and Sara Steen. 1998. "Racial Disparities in Official Assessments of Juvenile Offenders – Attributional Stereotypes as Mediating Mechanisms", *American Sociological Review* 63(4): 554–570.

Cipriani, Don. 2009. *Children's Rights and the Minimum Age of Criminal Responsibility – A Global Perspective*. New York: Routledge.

Dagistanli, Selda, and Kiran Grewal. 2016. "Perverse Muslim Masculinities in Contemporary Orientalist Discourse – The Vagaries of Muslim Immigration in the West", in George Morgan, and Scott Poynting (Eds.), *Global Islamophobia – Muslims and Moral Panic in the West* 119–142. New York: Routledge.

De Genova, Nicholas. 2018. "The 'Migrant Crisis' as Racial Crisis – Do Black Lives Matter in Europe?", *Ethnic and Racial Studies* 41(10): 1765–1782.

European Court of Justice Case of *S.N. v. Sweden,* 2 July 2002 (Application no. 34209/96).

Gur Arye, Miriam. 2018. "The Legitimacy of Judicial Responses to Moral Panic – Perceived vs. Normative Legitimacy", *Criminal Justice Ethics* 37(2): 141–163.

Hestermann, Thomas. 2018. "Refugee and Migrants in the Media – The Black Hole", in Helmut Kury, and Sławomir Redo (Eds.), *Refugee and Migrants in Law and Policy – Challenges and Opportunities for Global Civic Education*, 125–136. Cham: Springer.

Klapp, Orrin E. 1959. "Notes Toward the Study of Vilification as a Social Process", *The Pacific Sociological Review* 2(2): 71–76.

Lainpelto, Katrin, 2013. *Stödbevisning i brottmål.* Stockholm: Jure förlag AB.

Lainpelto, Katrin. 2019. "Ett dömande eller ett fördömande rättsväsendet? – En fråga om integration" [*A judicial or condemning judiciary? – A question regarding integration?*], in Karin Helander, and Pernilla Leviner (Eds.), *Barn, migration och integration i en utmanande tid* [*Children, migration and integration in a challenging time*] 127–158. Ragulka Press.

Littlechild, Brian. 1997. "Young Offenders, Punitive Policies and the Rights of Children", *Critical Social Policy* 17(53): 73–92.

Manco, Eva. 2013. *The United Nation Convention on the Rights of the Child: Are Children 'In Conflict with the Law' Really Protected? A Case Study of Republic of Albania's Juvenile Justice System.* Sheffield: University of Sheffield Press.

Manco, Eva. 2016. "Protecting the Child's Right to Participate in Criminal Justice Proceedings", *Amsterdam Law Forum* 8(1): 48–77.

Melnyk, Iurii. 2017. "'Something is Immensely Rotten in the Media Republic' – The Information Dimension of the Refugee Crisis in Europe" *Social Communication* 3(1): 40–53.

Pakes, Francis. 2016. "A Panicky Debate – The State of Moroccan Youth in the Netherlands", in George Morgan, and Scott Poynting (Eds.), *Global Islamophobia – Muslims and Moral Panic in the West*, 47–58. Routledge.

Rachlinski, Jeffrey J., and Andrew J. Wistrich. 2017. "Judging the Judiciary by the Numbers – Empirical Research on Judges", *Annual Review of Law and Social Science* 13(1): 203–229.

Rotter, Julian B. 1966. "Generalized Expectancies for Internal Versus External Control of Reinforcement", *Psychological Monographs* 80(1): 1–28.

Shamir, Ronen. 2005. "Without Borders? Notes on Globalization as a Mobility Regime", *Sociological Theory*, 23(2): 197–217.

Sinram, Jana. 2017. "'I am not a Racist, but ...' – The Phenomenon of Hate Comments on Refugees in Germany and How to Deal with Them", in Annette Jünemann, Nikolas Scherer, and Nikolas Fromm (Eds.), *Fortress Europe? – Challenges and Failures of Migration and Asylum Policies*, 159–165. Wiesbaden: Springer.

Stephan, Walter G., and Cookie White Stephan. 2000. "An Integrated Threat Theory of Prejudice" in Stuart Oskamp (Ed.), *Reducing, Prejudice and Discrimination*, 23–45. Mahwah: Lawrence Erlbaum Associates Publishers.

Stephan, Walter G., Rolando Diaz-Loving, and Anne Duran. 2000. "Integrated Threat Theory and Intercultural Attitudes – Mexico and the United States", *Journal of Cross-Cultural Psychology* 31(2): 240–249.

Supreme Court NJA 2015 p. 222.

Sutherland, Elaine E. 2019. "Article 2 of the United Nations Convention on the Rights of the Child – Non-Discrimination and Children's Rights", in Marit Skivenes, and Karl Harald Søvig (Eds.), *Child Rights and International Discrimination Law – Implementing Article 2 of the UN Convention on the Rights of the child*, 23–41. New York: Routledge.

Tittle, Charles R., and Curran, Debra A. 1988. "Contingencies for Dispositional Disparities in Juvenile Justice", *Social Forces* 67(1): 23–58.

United Nations Committee on the Rights of the Child. *General comment No. 1 (2001), Article 29 (1), The aims of education*. CRC/GC/2001/1 (17 April 2001).

United Nations Committee on the Rights of the Child. *General comment No. 5 (2003). General measures of implementation of the Convention on the Rights of the Child*. CRC/GC/2003/5 (27 November 2003).

United Nations Committee on the Rights of the Child. *General comment No. 10 (2007). Children's Rights in Juvenile Justice*. CRC/C/GC/10 (25 April 2007).

United Nations Committee on the Rights of the Child. *General Comment No. 15 (2013). The Right of the Child to Enjoyment of the Highest Attainable Standard of Health.* CRC/C/GC/15 (13 April 2013).

United Nations Committee on the Rights of the Child. *General Comment No. 24* on Children's Rights in the Child Justice System. CRC/C/GC/24 (18 September 2019).

United Nations Office of the High Commissioner for Human Rights. *Manual on Human Rights Reporting Under Six Major International Human Rights Instruments* (HR/PUB/91/1 1997).

United Nations Committee on the Rights of the Child. *General comment No. 13 (2011), The right of the child to freedom from all forms of violence*, CRC/C/GC/13, 18 Apr. 2011.

United Nations Human Rights Committee. *General Comment No. 18, Non-discrimination*, CCPR, 10 November 1989.

United Nations Human Rights Committee. *General comment No. 32 (2007). Article 14, Right to equality before courts and tribunals and to fair trial.* CCPR/C/GC/32, 23 August 2007.

Van Bueren, Geraldine. 2006. "Article 40: Child Criminal Justice", in André Alen, Johan Vande Lanotte, Eugeen Verhellen, Fiona Ang, Eva Berghmans, and Mieke Verheyde (Eds.), *A Commentary on the United Nations Convention of the Rights of the Child, Article 40; Child Criminal Justice* (Leiden: Martinus Nijhoff Publishers).

Weenink, Don. 2009. "Explaining Ethnic Inequality in the Juvenile Justice System – An Analysis of the Outcomes of Cutch Prosecutorial Decision Making", *The British Journal of Criminology* 49(2): 220–242.

Witold, Klaus, Miklós Lévay, Irena Rzeplińska, and Miroslav Scheinost. 2018. "Refugees and Asylum Seeks in Central European Countries – Reality, Politics and the Creation of Fear in Societies", in Helmut Kury, and Sławomir Redo (Eds.), *Refugees and Migrants in Law and Policy – Challenges and Opportunities for Global Civic Education*, 457–494. Cham: Springer.

A Response to Katrin Lainpelto

Rebecca Adami

In her chapter on the right to non-discrimination for youth with migrant backgrounds, Lainpelto explores the legal example where children with immigration backgrounds appear to receive unequal treatment before the courts when compared to how judges' reason in similar cases where the child has a Swedish background. Critical perspectives that consider only racial inequality will not capture the complexity in the legal problematization that Lainpelto raises in her chapter, namely – in my reading – how children's rights become trapped between several discriminatory discourses, prejudices, and political interests, and where racism intersects with other oppressive structures. This is not explicitly addressed in the chapter but similar problematisations could be explored further by studying the rights of the child from intersectional understandings of how the child is discriminated against due to racist, sexist, ableist, and childist attitudes and sentiments in any given case.

The legal cases studied in Lainpelto's chapter concern allegations of sexual harassment, in which courts seem to reflect racial bias and where less legal evidence is asked for in cases that involve Swedish youth compared to cases of youth with immigrant backgrounds. How racist stereotypes and sexist prejudice against boys from marginalized groups in society play a part in such allegations would greatly benefit from further study. Lainpelto notes how the allegations of sexual harassment against youth with immigrant backgrounds relate to instances in public places, involving 'he-said-she-said' situations without due evidence. In contrast, notes Lainpelto, such necessary evidence was available in several of the cases involving Swedish youth.

To deepen this understanding even more, we need to explore the unequal status of children in courts through intersectionality with the added layer of childism, for an analysis of how children are discriminated against in relation to overlapping prejudice structures – in this case, racism, sexism, and childism. Childism, as explored in my chapter, consists of prejudice, discrimination, or antagonism directed against someone who is zero to 18 years old, based on the belief that adults are superior. Childism characterizes persons as defined by their lack of adult abilities and as inferior to adults who possess such abilities. On this basis, children are assigned or denied certain perceived abilities, skills, or character traits.

We see in Lainpelto's chapter that through the formulations in the CRC of non-discrimination regarding children, the wording has been limited: the provision excludes mention of how children can be discriminated against due to their own belonging, as individuals, and how different types of discrimination are directed against children of colour, for example.

A child accused of a crime may lack proper legal representation, and risk being judged by a court that exhibits unreflected forms of bias as not only racial but adult bias as well. Harmful stereotypes and negative attitudes about youth and about children with migrant backgrounds – that they are untrustworthy, prone to mischief, and that they can be overly sexual – risk derogating a process of due neutrality and influencing the outcome of the court proceedings.

The power structures that intersect for children before the law in the cases mentioned by Lainpelto will not be framed within current discrimination grounds that exclude age-based, gender-based, and racial discrimination against children. The attitudes held by the adult community about children and their characteristics, including adult perspectives regarding which rights and interests will trump children's rights and interests, may hinder the full realization of the child's rights because, as a heterogenous group – consisting of all other minority groups – children are nonetheless marginalized within every minority group as a result of childism.

Following the example of Lainpelto on children's right to equality discerning and describing current inequality and discrimination against children deserve greater attention in law and forensic studies. How do prejudices in society against children in general and against children with migration backgrounds influence children's access to justice? Addressing age-based and racialized prejudice against children is imperative in advancing social justice for children and in realizing their rights as set forth in the CRC. It is important that childism is not treated as just another aspect of a feminist or multicultural approach. As noted by Susan Moller Okin,[1] there could be inherent tensions between multiculturalist and feminist rights discourses. An additional layer in need of further discernment is the set of rights tensions between anti-racist, anti-sexist, and anti-childist efforts to address social injustices against children.

1 Okin, S. M.,'Is Multiculturalism Bad for Women?'. In Okin, S. M., Cohen, J., Howard, M., Nussbaum M.C. (Eds.), *Is Multiculturalism Bad for Women?* (New Jersey: Princeton University Press, 1999): 9–24.

Reference

Okin, Susan Moller. 1999. "Is Multiculturalism Bad for Women?", in Susan Moller Okin, Joshua Cohen, Matthew Howard, Martha C. Nussbaum (Eds.), *Is Multiculturalism Bad for Women?* 9–24. New Jersey: Princeton University Press.

CHAPTER 5

Children's Right to Health(Care) – in Light of Medical Advancements and Developments in Paediatric Care

Kavot Zillén

1 Introduction

Good health and living conditions enable people to achieve their full potential and are fundamental for the development of every human being. This is especially true for children, given their rapid physical, cognitive, and other evolving capacities. The enjoyment of the highest attainable standard of health (the right to health) is a core human right recognized in numerous international instruments, for example in Article 12 in the UN Convention on Economic, Social and Cultural Rights (CESCR). Specifically, children's right to health is enshrined in Article 24 of the UN Convention on the Rights of the Child (CRC), which addresses states' responsibilities in ensuring all children their right to health, including access to quality healthcare services.

The realization of the right to health can be pursued through a number of approaches; these include establishment of methods to develop adequate healthcare that is safe, scientifically and medically appropriate, of good quality, and respectful of medical ethics. Biomedical research, epidemiological studies, and healthcare research have all contributed to healthcare advancements that benefit children in various ways, enabling children with rare diseases, chronic diseases, and disabilities to live healthier, longer, and more active lives. Nevertheless, new and innovative interventions designed for children can also cause or contribute to adverse health consequences and create negative outcomes in terms of their fundamental rights.

The aim of this chapter is to analyse children's right to health, with particular focus on the right to access quality care in light of medical advances and developments in paediatrics.[1] The realization of a child's right to health

1 The article is related to a research project on decision-making for children in a state of medical indeterminacy ('Beslutsfattande för barn vid medicinsk behandling med ovissa resultat') with financial support from the Swedish Research Council (Vetenskapsrådet), project id. 2017-02992.

includes the wide range of rights and freedoms that are determinate to children's health, such as the rights to non-discrimination, right to life, survival and development, and right to be heard and to participate. Because children rely on adults for their growth and development, they have historically been treated as passive beings requiring parents to provide appropriate direction and guidance. The question that remains however is in what way this may undermine the ability of the child to exercise his or her rights in different settings, such as when it comes to participation and decisions-making in health related matters. Ensuring the right to health for children requires a general understanding of the health risks children face; these risks often vary at different stages of development. These developmental phases can also affect the way children understand and recognize their rights, as well as their abilities to exercise them. The chapter therefore starts with a description of children's possibilities to exercise their rights in relation to different phases of their development.

2 Exercise of Rights in Relation to Different Stages of Childhood Development

The CRC requires states to respect and recognize all children as persons in their own right and to treat them as independent right holders – from early childhood to adolescence. However, the exercise of children's rights is a complex process that depends on the child's evolving capacity. For example, children are not always considered to be competent to consent to or refuse medical care. Instead, the child's parents or legal guardians will act on the child's behalf in order to safeguard the child's interests. It would therefore be more accurate to describe the realization of children's rights as a process in which children exercise their rights through support and assistance from others (often parents).[2] This process varies relative to the age and maturity of the child, in terms of development phases during childhood. An understanding of the complexities of child development can shed light on some of the challenges involved in realizing children's rights in healthcare.

Early childhood is defined differently depending on the context, but on an international human rights level, early childhood is described as the period

2 See for example Zillén, K., 'Barnets bästa i hälso- och sjukvården'. In Åhman, K., Leviner, P., and, Zillén, K. (Eds.), *Barnkonventionen i praktiken. Rättsliga utmaningar och möjligheter* (Stockholm: Norstedts Juridik, 2020): 255–279.

from birth to the age of 8 years.[3] In practice, this covers the time throughout infancy, the preschool years, and the transition to school. Early childhood is generally characterized as a period of rapid growth and development, including increasing mobility, communication skills, intellectual capacities, and emotional and cultural skills. The earliest years of a child's life are also regarded as the foundation for good physical and mental health throughout life. The UN Committee on the Rights of the Child has described early childhood as a critical period for realizing children's rights. The health of young children is at particular risk from (among other things) malnutrition, disease, poverty, and neglect.[4] The Committee has highlighted that young children have special requirements regarding physical nurturance, emotional care, and sensitive guidance, as well sufficient time and space for social play, exploration, and learning.[5] Thus, proper intervention strategies during early childhood have the potential for significant positive effects on young children's current health and future health prospects.

The period between childhood and adulthood (from age 10 to 19), also known as adolescence, is another important time for laying the foundations of good health.[6] Although young adolescents aged 10–14 years have the lowest risk of death of all age groups, half of all mental health disorders in adulthood start by age 14, and suicide is one of the three leading causes of death among adolescents.[7] The WHO Report on Global Standards for Quality HealthCare Services for Adolescents states that mental health problems are often neglected among youth, even though these problems are the main cause of illness and disabilities among adolescents.[8] In addition to the significant burden of neuropsychiatric disorders, other phenomena such as violence, accidents, and infectious disease constitute risks for adolescent health.

The Committee on the Rights of the Child has raised concerns that States parties have not given sufficient attention to the specific challenges involving children (both young children and adolescents) as rights holders and the

3 UN Committee on the Rights of the Child. General *comment No. 7. Implementing child rights in early childhood* (2005), CRC/C/GC/7/Rev.1, para. 4.

4 Regarding continued problems with child mortality, see UN Inter-agency Group for Child Mortality Estimation, *Levels and Trends in Child Mortality, Report 2020 Child mortality* (United Nations Children's Fund 2020), 4.

5 UN Committee on the Rights of the Child. *General comment No. 7*. (2005), para. 5.

6 WHO, *The second decade: Improving adolescent health and development* (2001), 2.

7 WHO, *Guidelines on mental health promotive and preventive interventions for adolescence: helping adolescence thrive* (Geneva, 2020), 1.

8 WHO, *Global standards for quality health care services for adolescents* (Geneva, 2015), para. 7.

promotion of child health and development.[9] One challenge in the realization of children's rights in healthcare – particularly during adolescence – is to involve children in decision-making processes about their health.[10] This is a requirement enshrined in Article 12 of the Convention.[11] It gives children the chance to express their views freely and to have those views taken into account in accordance with their age and level of maturity. In addition, the Committee has highlighted the need for states to consider allowing children to consent to certain medical treatments and interventions without the permission of a parent,[12] thus indicating children's status as independent right holders.

When age thresholds such as evidence of sufficient maturity and mental capacity are used as requirements for the child's right to participation in matters such as healthcare, adolescents may find their maturity tested and cognitive development questioned by medical personnel.[13] This may result in a lack of respect for the child's abilities to participate actively in the promotion of their own health.[14] Consequently, respect for children's views may be overlooked or rejected on the grounds of insufficient age and immaturity.[15] This may result from the idea and presumption that young people lack certain capacities or abilities – such as cognitive capacity and psychosocial maturity – that are necessary for decision-making. As elaborated in Chapter 6 of this volume, regarding the theory of childism, these assumptions regarding children

---

9 UN Committee on the Rights of the Child. *General comment No. 7* (2005) para. 6; UN Committee on the Rights of the Child. *General comment No. 4, Adolescent Health and Development in the Context of the Convention on the Rights of the Child* (2003), CRC/GC/2003/4.

10 When it comes to recent literature on medical decision-making regarding children from a Swedish legal perspective, see for example Slokenberga, S., 'The standards of care and implications for paediatric decision-making. The Swedish viewpoint'. In Néill, C. Ó et al., (Eds.), *Routledge handbook on global health rights* (Abingdon: Routledge, 2021): 122–151; Holmqvist, A., *Integritet på undantag?: En studie av barns röst i patientlagen och patientorganisationer* (Stockholm: Ersta Sköndal Bräcke högskola, 2019); Zillén, K. (2020).

11 See Lindkvist, L., Chapter 7 in this volume.

12 UN Committee on the Rights of the Child. *General Comment No. 15. The Right of the Child to the Enjoyment of the Highest Attainable Standard of Health*, (2013) CRC/C/GC/15, para. 31.

13 Zillén, K., Garland, J., and Slokenberga, S., *The Rights of Children in Biomedicine: Challenges posed by scientific advances and uncertainties* (The Committee on Bioethics of the Council of Europé, 2017), 15.

14 See Aldersson, P., Bellsham-Revell, H. and Brierley, J., et al., '*Children's informed signified and voluntary consent to heart surgery: Professionals' practical perspectives*' *Nurs Ethics* 0, no. 0 (2022): 1–13.

15 See Daly, A, 'Assessing Children's Capacities', *International Journal of Children's Rights* 28, no. 3 (2020): 471–499.

are seemingly based on a preconceived notion: children lack certain abilities and therefore are inferior to adults.[16] It can also be the result of viewing children as 'future adults', making it morally acceptable to treat children differently from adults.[17] These seemingly paternalistic values[18] can even be detected in the science regarding the cognitive and psychosocial development of children. Primary evidentiary support in the medical literature presents the claim that most minors are not mature enough to make serious medical decisions.[19] This is often drawn from neuroscientific and psychological studies, which show that individuals under age 21 tend to downplay long-term consequences, and that humans do not acquire psychosocial maturity before the age of 20. These studies, however, are rarely based on clinical analysis of children's consent in a healthcare context, where cognitive capacity might vary depending on individual features, diagnoses, and treatments.[20]

The natural variation in children's development always needs to be taken into consideration when assessing their capacity. The development of children's cognitive capacities as well as their psychosocial maturity may vary according to their individual nature, as well as their gender, living conditions, family organization, care, etc. It is therefore important to emphasize that children are subject to developmental differences and vulnerabilities at different phases of life. While a young child generally requires more parental guidance and support than an older child, it is important to consider individual variations in the capacities of children of the same age, along with their methods for making choices and communicating their wishes and desires. Therefore, understanding children's different developmental phases and the diversities that exist among children is essential to safeguarding children's exercise of rights as their capacity develops.

3 Children's Right to the Highest Attainable Standard of Health

3.1 *What Is Meant by 'the Right to Health'?*

The child's right to the highest attainable standard of health is considered a fundamental human right that embraces a wide range of socioeconomic factors. Contracting states are required to provide healthcare to the entire population

16 See Adami, R., Chapter 6 in this volume.
17 See Lindblom, L., Chapter 8 in this volume.
18 See Peleg, N., Introductory note in this volume.
19 Zillén, K., Garland, J., and Slokenberga, S. (2017), 19.
20 Ibid. 19.

and to prevent diseases. As noted by the UN Committee on Economic, Social and Cultural Rights, the right to health is not to be understood as a right to be 'healthy'; rather, it includes a right to access a system of health promotion that gives equal opportunities for people to enjoy the highest attainable level of health.[21] Consequently, the right to health must be understood as a right to the enjoyment of a variety of facilities, goods, services, and conditions necessary for the realization of the highest attainable standard of health.[22] Particularly in the case of children, international human rights committees have highlighted states' obligations in ensuring children equal access to physical and mental health services, as well as adequate nutrition, safe environments, etc.[23]

3.2 *The AAAQ Framework – Four Standards for Healthcare Services*

In order for the state to meet the requirements for providing the highest attainable standard of health, the medical standards must be consistent with the UN 'AAAQ' Framework: Availability, Accessibility, Acceptability, and Quality. These criteria were first developed by the UN Committee on Economic, Social and Cultural Rights and have been reused and shaped from a child-rights perspective by the Committee on the Rights of the Child. The Committee has described the AAAQ criteria as performance and implementation obligations to fulfil the requirements for the right to health.[24] The realization of the child's right to health requires the *availability* of the necessary quantities of functioning children's health facilities, goods, services, and programmes. This includes sufficient hospitals, clinics, health practitioners, mobile teams and facilities, community health workers, equipment, and essential drugs to provide healthcare to all children, pregnant women, and mothers within the State. However, sufficient quantities of health-related facilities, goods, and services, etc. are not enough to ensure the highest attainable standard of health for children. These must also be *accessible* to all children, without discrimination of any kind. Consequently, the accessibility criterion incudes a non-discrimination dimension that focuses on three aspects of accessibility: physical accessibility to meet the needs of children with disabilities; economic accessibility that makes the service available for all, irrespective of their ability to pay; and

---

21 UN Committee on Economic, Social and Cultural Rights, *General Comment No. 14: The Right to the Highest Attainable Standards of Health*, (2000) (art. 12), E/C.12/2000/4, para. 8.

22 UN Committee on Economic, Social and Cultural Rights, *General Comment No. 14*, para. 4 and 9.

23 Ibid., and UN Committee on the Rights of the Child. *General Comment No. 15* (2013), para. 7 and 18.

24 UN Committee on the Rights of the Child. *General Comment No. 15*. (2013), para. 2.

information accessibility, i.e. making health-related information understandable. In addition, the third criterion of the right to health: *acceptability* entails that all health-related facilities, goods, and services should adhere to medical ethics standards as well as the child's needs, culture, and language.

Perhaps the most central and relevant criterion for this chapter is *quality*. It places obligations on the state to ensure that health-related facilities, goods, and services are scientifically and medically appropriate and of sufficient quality. Treatments, interventions, and medicine for children must be based on the 'best available evidence'; drugs must be scientifically approved and appropriate for children and monitored for adverse reactions, etc.[25] Safety is the foundation – and a critical element – for delivering quality healthcare, in order to minimize risks and harm to service users.[26] Another feature of quality care is effectiveness; hence, the care is evidence-based and in accordance with current professional knowledge and results in improved health outcomes for patients. Consequently, good quality care interrelates strongly to both patient safety and efficiency. As will be described below, when no clear and validated evidence of the effectiveness and safety exists regarding innovative therapies in paediatric care, these two dimensions of quality care can challenge children's right to healthcare.

4 Advances in Paediatric Care – Benefits and/or Harm?

As indicated earlier in this chapter, the right to health includes a legal obligation on the state to make medical treatment and care available in order to meet children's special health needs. Children's health needs are often, but not always, handled in a paediatric setting that is focused on medical science related to the children's physical, mental, and social health from birth to adolescence. Paediatric care also embraces proper health prevention and intervention strategies during early childhood that can improve the physical health of infants and children. States' obligation to ensure children's right to health

25 For a legal analysis about evidence-based medicine and science, and proven experience from a Swedish perspective, see for example Garland, J., *On Science, Law, and Medicine: The Case of Gender-'Normalizing' Interventions on Children Who Are Diagnosed as Different in Sex Development* (Uppsala: Uppsala University, 2016); Wahlberg, L. and Sahlin, N-E, 'Om icke vedertagna behandlingsmetoder och kravet på vetenskap och beprövad erfarenhet', *Förvaltningsrättslig tidskrift*, no. 1 (2017): 45–66; Wahlberg, L., 'Rätten till ersättning för gränsöverskridande vård och kravet på vetenskap och beprövad erfarenhet' *Förvaltningsrättlig tidskrift*, no. 4 (2018): 789–818.

26 WHO, *Quality of care: a process for making strategic choices in health systems* (Geneva, 2006).

therefore includes preventive measures that may have a positive impact on children's wellbeing and future health prospects. This aspect includes making new technologies and medication available in paediatric care in ways that can make healthcare more efficient and improve the health and lives of children. Accordingly, the Committee on the Right of the Child has stressed that development of technology, medications, equipment, interventions, and processes can contribute to significant advances in children's health in different areas.[27] An essential part of paediatric care is therefore the application of new and advanced technologies, including medication, equipment, and interventions that can improve the care. However, applying these interventions in paediatric care can be considered beneficial only when they are effective and safe; this caveat relates to the abovementioned quality assurance dimension as a key component of the right to health.[28]

One of the problems generated by the use of innovations in paediatric medicine is that unknown variables can create adverse outcomes for children. As an example, medical intervention in the earliest stages of children's lives, such as in neonatology (care for new-borns), sometimes lacks information about mid- or long-term effects on children's health.[29] Despite the many advancements in neonatal medicine, the long-term risks of care interventions for premature infants – such as risks for future mental health problems – are poorly understood. There are also examples of interventions that have been shown to have adverse effects, but that are still in use, such as antibiotic treatment in the neonatal period that can impair growth during the first six years of life.[30] Such risks exist for older children and adolescents as well, such as the development of various medications for mental-health and behavioural problems. One example concerns the use of pharmacological interventions for children with ADHD (Attention-Deficit/Hyperactivity Disorder). ADHD is classified as one of the most common mental-health problems among children, and the use of stimulant medications prescribed for ADHD has grown significantly in recent years.[31] Side effects and risks include cardiovascular risks, decreased

27 UN Committee on the Rights of the Child. *General Comment No. 15* (2013), para. 41.

28 Regarding the legal content of the quality criteria in a pediatric context, see for example Slokenberga, S. (2021).

29 Caffarelli, C. et al., 'Best practices, challenges and innovations in pediatrics in 2019', *Italian Journal of Pediatrics* 46, no. 176 (2020): 1–12.

30 Uzan-Yulzari, A. et al., 'Neonatal antibiotic exposure impairs child growth during the first six years of life by perturbing intestinal microbial colonization', *Nature Communications* 12, no. 443 (2021): 1–12.

31 Boudreau, A. and Mah, J., 'Predicting Use of Medications for Children with ADHD: The Contribution of Parent Social Cognitions', *Journal of the Canadian Academy of Child and*

appetite, insomnia, headache, dizziness, and mood changes including anxiety and depression.[32] There is also lack of evidence regarding long-term benefits of these stimulant medications. Likewise, questions have been raised concerning the use of so-called 'smart pills' for children in order to increase their cognitive ability; the immediate and long-term risks for these medications remain unknown.[33]

Scientific advances and risk-laden practices in paediatric care are many, and the examples here are but a few illustrations of problems generated by these advances and innovative therapies. These challenges give rise to central and still unresolved questions as to whether the usage of scientific advancements and developments that aim to improve children's health and lives can in fact jeopardize children's right to health, particularly when scientific efficacy and safety aspects are not fully validated.[34]

Nevertheless, children should benefit from the use of new technologies that can improve their health and or save their lives. In this regard, why should children be treated less favourably than adults? This reconnects to theories of justice as addressed in Chapter 8 of this volume. The European Commission, for example, has stressed that approvals of paediatric drugs are often delayed when compared to adult medications, and that there is a great demand for child-specific treatments for diseases that affect only children or that manifest differently in adults and children.[35] Consequently, withholding children from the opportunities to undergo innovative therapies and medical interventions can in fact lead to injustice and unequal access to medicine and the benefits of

---

Adolescent Psychiatry 29, no. 1 (2020): 26–32; Kollins, S. et al., 'Effectiveness of a digital therapeutic as adjunct to treatment with medication in pediatric ADHD' *Npj Digital Medicine*, 4, no. 58 (2021): 1–8.

32 Currie, J., Stabile, M., and Jones, L., 'Do stimulant medications improve educational and behavioral outcomes for children with ADHD?', *Journal of Health Economics* 37 (2014): 58–69; Kollins, S. et al. (2021).

33 Nicholson, P., and Wilson, N., 'Smart drugs: implications for general practice', *The British journal of general practice: the journal of the Royal College of General Practitioners* 67 (2017): 100–101.

34 See Leviner, P., 'Who has the Final Word? On Trust and Legal Uncertainty within the Swedish Healthcare System'. In Goold, I., Auckland, C. and Herring, J. (Eds.), *Medical decision-making on behalf of young children: a comparative perspective* (Oxford: Hart Publishing Ltd, 2020): 155–166.

35 Report from the Health and Food Safety Commission to the European Parliament and the Council. *State of Paediatric Medicines in the EU – 10 years of the EU Paediatric Regulation* (COM (2017) 626). Accessed 22 June, 2021. https://ec.europa.eu/health/sites/health/files/files/paediatrics/docs/2017_childrensmedicines_report_en.pdf.

scientific progress as compared to adults, which in turn can constitute a breach of children's right to health without discrimination.

5 Conclusions

As with all care, it is not always possible to predict all the consequences and side effects of a treatment. Nevertheless, some of the interventions in use in paediatric settings can have both ethical and legal implications and affect children's right to health in serious ways. The most pressing concern regarding these advances in relation to the child's right to health is the lack of sufficient scientific support regarding treatment safety and efficacy. Given the states' obligations to promote the health of children and protect them from harm, it is clear that harmful practices should not be tolerated. A prerequisite for states to fulfil children's right to health is first and foremost to ensure access to good health care. But what if standard care in a particular situation concerning critically ill children is not enough to cure or save a child's life, and the only alternative is to use innovative therapy with unproven effectiveness and unknown adverse effects?

The truth is that risks are involved in using innovative therapies in paediatric practice, and it is likely that such risks will always exist to some degree. Some innovations have even been proven to cause direct harm to children.[36] Still, this uncertainty should not stand in the way of children receiving potentially life-saving innovative treatments. The challenges that advancements in the area of paediatrics pose to children's right to health are complex and require a nuanced discourse about the validity of such practices. On the one hand, these innovations can be used to improve health and survival for many critical paediatric diseases, but on the other hand they may be harmful and pose risks to children's health and wellbeing, especially when these methods lack sufficient scientific support. It should be clear by now that while these technologies potentially enable different ways to improve children's health and save their lives, they also introduce challenges in relation to the child's right to health, and more specifically, children's right to access quality care that is safe and effective.

A careful approach, but not a barrier, therefore, is recommended in the introduction of all new technologies in paediatric care. In this regard it is

---

36 Zimmerman, J. et.al., 'Research as a Standard of Care in the PICU', *Pediatric Critical Care Medicine* 17, no. 1 (2016): 13–21.

essential that caregivers, healthcare personnel, and parents safeguard the child's rights to participate in these healthcare decisions.[37] Medical paternalism towards children is widely justified based on children having insufficient capacities to make appropriate choices. However, in situations where children are the subject of treatments that may be invasive, lacking in scientific support, or used in practice without confirmation through long-term data, the child's views and interests should be given due weight. In these cases, children may have first-hand experience of the treatment and may be in a better position to know whether they want to continue the therapy, particularly if the illness recurs. The paternalistic presumption in paediatric care – which holds that parents and physicians are better positioned to determine treatment options for a child – is not always justified. Children with critical illnesses and a shorter life expectancy may have more relevant experience regarding their own conditions and may have very mature views of their own lives, thus justifying their right to make their own decisions regarding their care.[38] In the end, paternalistic management should always be kept to a minimum, so that children can express their views and participate in their own development wherever and whenever possible.

References

Alderson, Priscilla, 2007. "Competent Children? Minors' Consent to Health Care Treatment and Research", *Social Science Medicine* 65(11): 2272–2283.

Alderson, Priscilla, Hannah Bellsham-Revell, Joe Brierley, Nathalie Dedieu, Joanna Heath, Mae Johnson, Samantha Johnson, Alexia Katsatis, Romana Kazmi, Liz King, Rosa Mendizabal, Katy Sutcliffe, Judith Trowell, Trisha Vigneswaren, Hugo Welleslay, and Jo Wray. 2022. "Children's informed signified and voluntary consent to heart surgery: Professionals' practical perspectives", *Nursing Ethics* 0(0): 1–13.

Boudreau, Ainsley, and Janet Mah. 2020. "Predicting Use of Medications for Children with ADHD: The Contribution of Parent Social Cognitions", *Journal of the Canadian Academy of Child and Adolescent Psychiatry* 29(1): 26–32.

Caffarelli, Carlo, Francesca Santamaria, and Angelica Santoro. 2020. "Best practices, challenges and innovations in pediatrics in 2019", *Italian Journal of Pediatrics* 46(176): 1–12.

37 C.f. Lindkvist, L., Chapter 7 in this volume.

38 See Alderson, P, 'Competent Children? Minors' Consent to Health Care Treatment and Research', *Soc Sci Med* 65, no. 11 (2007): 2272–2283.

Currie, Janet, Stabile Mark, and Jones Laurent. 2014. "Do stimulant medications improve educational and behavioral outcomes for children with ADHD?", *Journal of health economics* 37: 58–69.

Daly, Aoife. 2020. "Assessing Children's Capacity", *The International Journal of Children's Rights* 28(3): 471–499.

Garland, Jameson. 2016. *On Science, Law, and Medicine: The Case of Gender-'Normalizing' Interventions on Children Who Are Diagnosed as Different in Sex Development.* Uppsala: Uppsala University Press.

Health and Food Safety Commission to the European Parliament and the Council (report). *State of Paediatric Medicines in the EU – 10 years of the EU Paediatric Regulation* (COM (2017) 626). Available at: https://ec.europa.eu/health/sites/health/files/files/paediatrics/docs/2017_childrensmedicines_report_en.pdf accessed January, 2022.

Holmqvist, Anna. 2019. *Integritet på undantag?: En studie av barns röst i patientlagen och patientorganisationer*. Ersta Sköndal Bräcke högskola: University Press.

Kollins, Scott H., Ann Childress, Andrew C. Heusser, and Jacqueline Lutz. 2021."Effectiveness of a digital therapeutic as adjunct to treatment with medication in pediatric ADHD", *Npj Digital Medicine* 4(58): 1–8.

Leviner, Pernilla. 2020. "Who has the Final Word? On Trust and Legal Uncertainty within the Swedish Healthcare System", in Imogen Goold, Cressida Auckland, and Jonathan Herring (Eds.), *Medical decision-making on behalf of young children: a comparative perspective,* 155–166. Oxford: Hart Publishing Ltd.

Nicholson, Paul, and Nigel Wilson. 2017. "Smart drugs: implications for general practice", *The British journal of general practice* 67(656): 100–101.

Slokenberga, Santa. 2021. "The standards of care and implications for paediatric decision-making. The Swedish viewpoint", in Clayton Ó Néill, Charles Foster, Jonathan Herring, and John Tingle (Eds.), *Routledge handbook on global health rights,* 122–151. New York: Routledge.

United Nations Committee on Economic, Social and Cultural Rights. *General Comment No. 14 (2000) The Right to the Highest Attainable Standards of Health* (*art. 12*). E/C.12/2000/4.

United Nations Committee on the Rights of the Child. *General comment No. 4 (2003) Adolescent Health and Development in the Context of the Convention on the Rights of the Child.* CRC/GC/2003/4, 1 July 2003.

United Nations Committee on the Rights of the Child. *General comment No. 7 (2005): Implementing child rights in early childhood,* CRC/C/GC/7/Rev.1, 20 Sept. 2006.

United Nations Committee on the Rights of the Child. *General Comment No. 15 (2013): The right of the child to the enjoyment of the highest attainable standard of health* (*art. 24*). CRC/C/GC/15, 17 April 2013.

United Nations Inter-agency Group for Child Mortality Estimation. 2020. *Levels and Trends in Child Mortality, Report 2020 Child mortality.* United Nations Children's Fund.

Uzan-Yulzari, Atara, Olli Turta, and Anna Belogolovski. 2021. "Neonatal antibiotic exposure impairs child growth during the first six years of life by perturbing intestinal microbial colonization", *Nature Communications* 12(443): 1–12.

Wahlberg, Lena. 2018. "Rätten till ersättning för gränsöverskridande vård och kravet på vetenskap och beprövad erfarenhet", *Förvaltningsrättlig tidskrift* (4): 789–818.

Wahlberg, Lena, and Nils-Eric Sahlin. 2017. "Om icke vedertagna behandlingsmetoder och kravet på vetenskap och beprövad erfarenhet", *Förvaltningsrättslig tidskrift* (1): 45–66.

World Health Organization, WHO. 2001. *The second decade: Improving adolescent health and development.* Department of Child and Adolescent Health and Development Family and Community Health.

World Health Organization WHO. 2006. *Quality of care: a process for making strategic choices in health systems*. Geneva.

World Health Organization WHO. 2015. *Global standards for quality health care services for adolescents*. Geneva.

World Health Organization WHO. 2020. *Guidelines on mental health promotive and preventive interventions for adolesence: helping adolescence thrive*. Geneva.

Zimmerman, Jerry, Kanwaljeet J. S. Anand, Kathleen L. Meert, Douglas F. Willson, Christopher J. L. Newth, Rick Harrison, Joseph A. Carcillo, John Berger, Tammara L. Jenkins, Carol Nicholson, and Michael Dean. 2016. "Research as a Standard of Care in the PICU", *Pediatric Critical Care Medicine* 17(1):13–21.

Zillén, Kavot. 2020. "Barnets bästa i hälso- och sjukvården", in Karin Åhman, Pernilla Leviner and Kavot Zillén (Eds.), *Barnkonventionen i praktiken. Rättsliga utmaningar och möjligheter,* 255–278. Stockholm: Nordstedts Juridik.

Zillén, Kavot, Jameson Garland, and Santa Slokenberga. 2017. *The Rights of Children in Biomedicine: Challenges posed by scientific advances and uncertainties.* Strasbourg: Council of Europe.

A Response to Kavot Zillén

Margareta Aspán

The chapter on children's right to health(care) actualizes a number of important concepts on both a structural and individual level for theorizing children's rights and lives regarding paediatric care, but also concerning the meaning of having the right to health. The UN 'AAAQ' framework distinguishes the need of standards for *Availability, Accessibility, Acceptability, and Quality*, and Zillén argues that the quality and safety in healthcare cannot be overemphasized. She also asks the important question of how to improve and develop treatments for children without risks.

The need to advance healthcare and medical treatments for children requires testing and evaluations from within the target group. The development of life-saving or life-improving efforts can imply unforeseen consequences, as innovative methods may not be fully validated.

Paediatric care and other interventions for children's well-being are directed towards all children, but Zillén reminds us of the significant differences among children, due not only to age but also in terms of individual capacity, maturity, and needs. Further exploration of the ethical aspect of consent discussed here is of utmost importance.

As childhood sociologists Priscilla Alderson, Katy Sutcliffe, and Katherine Curtis state, the 'age of consent' is not static, but varies over time and between countries, as do views on what it means to be competent. Is competence an *outcome* as in being the decision-maker, or can competence be – as these sociologists suggest – a *process* in which the methods preceding the decision must be 'justifiable'?[1] A view in which age sets the criterion for maturity and consent is based on what they see as 'out-dated' age-stage theories.[2] In addition, a process view of consent, and not consent as an event in which the child's maturity is measured, might strengthen the child's possibilities to better understand the situation and consequently enhance the child's trust and involvement in the treatment. Being informed can reduce anxiety and, as noted by Priscilla

1 Alderson, P., Sutcliffe, K., and Curtis, K., 'Children's Competence to Consent to Medical Treatment', *Hastings Center Report* 36, no. 6 (2006): 25–34, 31.

2 Ibid., 25.

Alderson, can support the child as he or she attempts to 'make sense of the experience'.[3]

Zillén's chapter calls to mind the work of Janusz Korczak (1878–1942), a Polish pioneer of children's rights and also a paediatrician, pedagogue, author of children's literature, and director of orphanages in Warsaw during the 1920s and up until his death 1942. His Magna Charta for Children's Rights – written during the first World War and seemingly strange at first glance – reads as follows:

> 1) The right of a child to his/her own death, 2) The right of a child to the present day, 3) The right of a child to be what he/she is.[4]

The first right could be interpreted in several ways, but supposedly Korczak meant that it is harmful to overprotect children, lock them up, or rescue them from the risky world. A child must be a part of its surroundings to develop a sense of 'what he/she is'. The child's right to its own death can also point to the adult's responsibility to provide a dying child with adequate information – not an altogether unusual situation in Poland a hundred years ago. The right to one's own death could also entail the child's right to the 'present day', as adults must care about and support what a child experiences at any and all times of its life.

This reveals an understanding of children as competent, contrasting what John Tobin, Australian professor of law, describes as a common view on children: as 'victims and passive recipients of assistance'.[5] A rights-based view would instead acknowledge how children are 'victims of human rights violations but also potential agents and collaborators', indeed in need of protection but with capacity for 'supported decision-making' within its evolving capacities.[6] Even if a child does not have a lot of experiences, he or she is the one who receives medical treatments in periods of illness, and who experiences the pain and fear as well as the recovery and comfort. Such feelings do not correspond to levels of maturity. It is only the conceptualization and the handling

3 Tobin, J., 'Children's Right to Health'. In Kilkelly, U. and Liefaard, T. (Eds.), *International Human Rights of Children, International Human Rights*. (Singapore: Springer Nature Singapore Pte Ltd, 2018): 1–22. https://doi.org/10.1007/978-981-10-3182-3_12-1 (Tobin refers to Alderson, P., 'Children's consent to surgery' (1993) in Didcock, E., 'Issues of consent and competency in children and young people', *Current Pediatrics* 16: 91 (2006)).

4 Korczak, J., *How to love a child* (1920), 123.

5 Tobin, J. (2018), 17.

6 Ibid., 17.

of the emotional state that differ in terms of age, earlier experiences, and life situation of an individual.

Living conditions for children still vary worldwide in terms of education and healthcare, and standards seem to depend on continuous shifts in discourses regarding needs and priorities. UNICEF reported that in 2020, after the pandemic's first year that the health coverage for children declined in one third of the survey's 140 countries.[7] As Zillén concludes in her chapter, healthcare and health innovations must respond to important aspects of quality. One could also add that, in light of the reported decreasing access to healthcare during crises, comprehensive initiatives must be put in place to maintain standards, even in such trying times. As Janusz Korczak insisted: children do not need charity; they need the possibility to exercise their rights as human beings.

References

Alderson, Priscilla, Katy Sutcliffe, and Katherine Curtis. 2006. "Children's Competence to Consent to Medical Treatment", *Hastings Center Report* 36(6): 25–34.

Korczak, Janusz, 1920. *How to love a child.* http://www.januszkorczak.ca/legacy/3_How%20to%20Love%20a%20Child.pdf accessed June 2021.

Tobin, John. 2018. "Children's Right to Health", in Ursula Kilkelly, and Ton Liefaard, (Eds.), *International Human Rights of Children, International Human Rights,* 1–22. Singapore: Springer Nature Singapore Pte Ltd. https://doi.org/10.1007/978-981-10-3182-3_12-1.

UNICEF. 2020. *Averting a lost COVID generation. A six-point plan to respond, recover and reimagine a post-pandemic world for every child,* https://www.unicef.org/media/86881/file/Averting-a-lost-covid-generation-world-childrens-day-data-and-advocacy-brief-2020.pdf accessed 19 September 2021.

7 UNICEF, *Averting a lost COVID generation. A six-point plan to respond, recover and reimagine a post-pandemic world for every child* (2020).

PART 2

Conceptualizing the Rights of the Child: Political, Ethical, and Moral Dimensions

CHAPTER 6

Childism – on Adult Resistance to Children's Rights

Rebecca Adami

1 Introduction

Children's rights theory emanating from childhood studies has dealt extensively with child rights-infused research ethics, exploring questions concerning how to conduct ethically sensitive[1] and agency-oriented research in studies with children.[2] Such questions concern how to 'give voice' to children's own lived experiences, and how to ensure active participation, influence, and consent in the production of knowledge *with* children.[3] If child rights theory is to add an important layer to earlier philosophical, sociological, and anthropological works on children's experiences of their rights, this must be achieved by invoking questions regarding the prevailing lack of social justice for children. This lack of social justice can be analysed through the concept of childism, which according to Elisabeth Young-Bruehl refers to prejudice against children that leads to structural discrimination and oppression against children. Analysing childism addresses aspects of power, discrimination, and marginalizing structures concerning children. The aim of this chapter is to explore resistance to the realization of children's international human rights by arguing that these can be recognized as examples of age-based discrimination against children that disadvantage children, stemming from overlapping childist, racist, sexist, and ableist prejudice against children.

---

1 See Christensen, P., and Prout, A., 'Working with Ethical Symmetry in Social Research with Children', *Childhood* 9 (2002): 477–97.

2 See Bessell, S., 'Rights-Based Research with Children: Principles and Practice'. In Skelton, T., Evans, R., and Holt, V. (Ed.), *Methodological Approaches Geographies of Children and Young People, vol. 2* (Singapore: Springer, 2017): 223–40.

3 Aitken, S., Lund, R., and Kjornholt, A., 'Why Children? Why Now?', *Children's Geographies* 1–2, no. 3 (2007): 3–14; Punch, S., 'Research with Children: The Same or Different from Research with Adults?', *Childhood* 9, no. 3 (2002): 321–41; Tisdall, K. and Punch, S., 'Not so New? Looking Critically at Childhood Studies', *Children's Geographies* 10, no. 3 (2012): 249–64; Reynolds, P., Nieuwenhuys, O., and Hanson, K., 'Refractions of Children's Rights in Development Practice: A View from Anthropology', *Childhood* 13, no. 3 (2006): 291–302. See also Karlsson, Chapter 10 in this volume.

DOI:10.1163/9789004511163_014

Childism characterizes children as defined by their lack of adult abilities and, therefore, as inferior to adults. On this basis, children are assigned or denied certain perceived abilities, skills, or character traits. In childist[4] societies children are perceived as lacking abilities and are viewed as less valuable, or even less than human. Children in this scenario are described, for example, as lacking any capacity for rationality, logical thinking, or empathy, and orphans and street children are treated without due respect for them as human individuals. The manifestations of childism, drawing on Young-Bruehl's work on earlier prejudice studies, are comparable to racist, sexist, and ableist attitudes and beliefs.[5] By studying expressions and enactments of childism, we may better understand the prevalence of violence and abuse against children. It is by addressing adult's prejudice about children that reasons and arguments for denying children basic rights and freedoms can be systematically examined. Age discrimination against children is a type of discrimination which is based on the age of the person (below 18 years) and occurs when a person is treated less favourably because of age (0–18), including age stereotyping.

In recent years, childism has become firmly grounded in John Wall's conceptualization, through which childism finds a parallel in feminism.[6] Wall provides several arguments for not defining childism in relation to prejudice studies, as was done in earlier work by Elisabeth Young-Bruehl. While seemingly motivated by ambitions similar to those of this chapter – to challenge theories and research treating children as mere objects of adult agency when discussing their rights – Wall states that childism as conceptualized by Young-Bruehl 'offers only a negative, deficit-oriented lens for studying childhoods, and not a positive, agentic one'.[7] He further states that by defining childism as age-based prejudice and discrimination against children, 'children are primarily framed as passive objects of adult socialization or harm'.[8] Finally, Wall argues that 'this deficit concept of childism likely deepens their oppression' as it 'assumes that only adults can act in child-empowering ways'.[9]

4 One can find parallels between childist, racist, sexist and ableist prejudice that disadvantage children.

5 Young-Bruehl, E. *The Anatomy of Prejudices* (Cambridge, Mass.: Harvard University Press, 1996); *Childism: Confronting Prejudice against Children* (New Haven: Yale University Press, 2012).

6 Wall, J., 'From Childhood Studies to Childism: Reconstructing the Scholarly and Social Imaginations', *Children's Geographies* 20, no. 83 (2022): 257–270.

7 Wall, J. (2022), 7.

8 Ibid., 7.

9 Ibid., 7.

The intentions of the abovementioned two uses of the concept might not be in as much opposition as Wall initially stated, since the ambitions speak of the need to generate more justice-oriented theory, methodology, and epistemology concerning children as rights subjects. I intend to use childism to explore structures of discrimination and systematic notions of injustice. In this way, my use of childism extends its initial focus on adults' prejudice against children; while prejudice serves to uphold inequality, childism – like sexism, racism, and ableism – can help us discern the *structures* that put children at a disadvantage as a heterogenous, marginalized group. Firstly, as it has been important to address sexism leading to gender-based discrimination, naming childism helps us address human rights violations against children in terms of discrimination. 'Women' are not turned into passive objects of male agency through such critical work, but through unaddressed sexist reasoning. Addressing childism that already exists in daily conversations and in various forms of communication and media would not turn children into passive objects of adult agency, but the treatment of children stemming from unaddressed prejudice and discrimination in such discourses in societies will. If children's agency is to be taken seriously by adults – irrespective of children's physical abilities relative to those of adults – existing negative beliefs about children must be named and challenged.

The aim and intentions of the two uses of childism seem aligned – to contribute to anti-racist and anti-sexist work – but the definitions of the concept differ. Scholars using childism as an equivalent to feminism might argue that childism is the start of a child rights movement. The flaw with that ideal, however, is how (adult) researchers may overlook the need to first address the structures of power and discrimination fed by potentially unreflected adult biases and prejudice against children. Just as critical-race theorists would problematize engaging in work on the Civil Rights Movement without naming racism, white ignorance, or white privilege, childism as an equivalent with sexism, racism, and ableism helps us problematize unaddressed forms of discrimination against children, adult ignorance, and adult privilege.

In parallel with using a critical conceptualization of childism, I need to refrain here from defining a 'child' (assigning particular abilities or characteristics to children or denying them certain capacities through such definitions). Additionally, in contrast to adult claims of empowering children's voices, I employ childism to problematize the structures that risk hindering children from being heard and limiting their subjectivity. This work thus harmonizes with earlier child rights theory that seeks to reconceptualize the legal capacity of children.[10] What is gained is a new discursive space in which to negotiate adults' domination – exploring questions concerning social justice, age equality, and non-discrimination of children – when assumptions about children are no longer taken for granted as solid facts but examined as contaminated by prejudice.

What, then, is the relation between the concepts of childism and adultism? Adultism refers to oppressive forms of adults' power over children, while childism refers to the discursive practices that uphold adult norms and supremacy in society.[11] We can see a similar distinction in how sexism supports male supremacy and hegemonic masculinity, as well as in the ways in which racist discourses sustain white supremacy.

If adults are not aware of their own complicity in a discriminatory system of limiting structures and beliefs against children, these structures and beliefs are left unproblematized. For example, not admitting that children face structural discrimination due to age means that adults can ignore the fact that children can be denied the most basic right to healthcare and mental healthcare, while hospitals and health institutions will generally require guardians' consent – without which a child has no right to receive care.

Childism consists of prejudice, discrimination, or antagonism directed against someone who is between 0–18 years old, based on the belief that adults are superior. Childism defines persons by their lack of adult abilities and as inferior to adults with such abilities. On this basis, children are assigned or denied certain perceived abilities, skills, or character traits. Childist discourses work to keep children subordinate to adults through various forms of violence.[12] Conceptualizing childism as a form of discrimination against children is meaningful in human rights theory because it speaks to how earlier critical

---

10 See Bach, M., and Kerzner, L., *A New Paradigm for Protecting Autonomy and the Right to Legal Capacity: Advancing Substantive Equality for Persons with Disabilties through Law, Policy and Practice* (Law Commission of Ontario, October 2010); Federle, K., 'On the Road to Reconceiving Rights for Children: A Postfeminist Analysis of the Capacity Principle', *DePaul Law Review* 42, no. 3 (1993): 983–1028.

11 Adultism is here referred to as the order of power of adult supremacy whereby adults hold privileges, status and primary power of moral authority, property and social privilege. Childism consists of the prejudice and discriminatory structures that serve to uphold adult order of power, as sexism serves to uphold the power of male supremacy and racism serves to uphold the power of white supremacy.

12 Violence here includes epistemic violence which concerns the harm caused children due to how adults speak about them in belittling and negative and stereotypical ways. Epistemic injustice refers to how some people, children for example, are not seen as valid sources of knowledge, giving testimony of injustices, drawing on Fricker, M. *Epistemic injustice: Power and the ethics of knowing*. (Oxford: Oxford University Press, 2007).

theories addressing racism, sexism, and ableism have pushed the human-rights framework to become more inclusive through definition of different forms of discrimination. Hatred against women and racialized hatred have been named in critical work and covered in articles in international conventions on human rights.[13] Like racism, sexism, and ableism, childism is based on prejudice, ignorance, and even hatred against a group of people.

The use of the theory of intersectionality, according to Karl Hanson and Noam Peleg, 'enables us to move beyond thinking about children's minority status based on their age or assumed lack of or insufficient capacities', and to include 'the variations in children's experiences relating to identity, personality, poverty, ethnicity, race, religion, gender, sexuality and social background, as well as the intersections of these elements'.[14]

The contribution of childism in this chapter adds to human rights theory and child rights theory in terms of the need to add the additional layer of age-based discrimination against children and children's subordination to an intersectional lens on children's rights. Its contribution could be measured by the extent to which childism will disrupt taken-for-granted assumptions in earlier work, where prejudice and negative attitudes towards children have not yet been unveiled.[15]

The aim of this chapter is to explore identified obstacles to the realization of children's international human rights by arguing that such obstacles can be recognized as examples of age-based discrimination against children, stemming from overlapping childist, racist, sexist, and ableist prejudice against children. How may we understand the logic behind social obstacles to children's human rights by naming childism as a system of prejudice and discrimination against children, and how could such understandings inform processes for a strengthened discourse on children's rights?

---

13 See Article 1 in the Convention on the Elimination of All Forms of Discrimination against Women, CEDAW, and Article 1 in the Convention on the Elimination of Racial Discrimination, CERD.

14 Hanson, K. and Peleg, N., 'Waiting for Children's Rights Theory', *The International Journal of Children's Rights* 28, no. 1 (2020): 15–35, 23.

15 Contrarily, one could claim that labelling children as a minority group and naming stereotypes against children reinforce such categorizations that we might want to move beyond through notions of uniqueness. However, not acknowledging how children are already treated unfairly due to prejudice and stereotyping would be expressing adult ignorance about children's subordination. Discussions about adult-child relationality that neglect power, and when faced with questions concerning social justice, thus risk obscuring privilege.

2 Resistance against Children's Rights: The Need for Theory on Childism

Michael Freeman[16] argues that in order to take children's rights seriously, a cultural revolution is needed in terms of adults' attitudes toward children. Laura Lundy similarly notes the resistance to taking children's rights seriously, in terms of how children could be rights-holders as 'indicative of a wider problem: it appears to be perfectly acceptable to deny that children are, should or can be rights-holders when there are very few who would publicly assert that they do not 'believe' in human rights'.[17]

It is not enough merely to acknowledge a poor realization of children's rights; as Lundy and Peleg note in the introduction to this volume, we need a conceptual framework to analyse why discursive negations of children's rights persist.[18] This chapter will not consider theories *justifying* the idea of children's moral and legal rights – which for example have called for shifts in perspective from arguments of children's capacity to their interests[19] – or theories that *base justification* on the kind of rights that should be given to children.[20] A conceptualization of childism is thus not a theory for justification, but rather a critical approach for analysing resistance among adults to the moral and legal rights of children. A theory that addresses systemic inequality and legislation against discrimination could generate a needed change in attitudes and beliefs in relation to children's rights, for example making the violence against and oppressions of children visible as a form of discrimination. As noted, childism refers to prejudice against children that leads to structural discrimination, and through childist discourse, children are characterized as defined by their lack of adult abilities and, therefore, as inferior to adults.

The human-rights discourse has been informed by adult bias: ideas of the rights-holder have been defined according to adult normativity, human rights violations have been systematically analysed according to adult definitions,

16 Freeman, M. *Children's Rights*, vol. I, 2 vols. (Wiltshire: Ashgate Darmouth, 2004).

17 Laura Lundy, 'Editorial: A Lexicon for Research on International Children's Rights in Troubled Times', *International Journal of Children's Rights*, no. 27 (2019): 595.

18 See Laura Lundy and Noam Peleg in this volume.

19 See Tobin, J., Justifying Children's Rights', *The International Journal of Children's Rights* 21, no. 3 (2013): 395–441.

20 See Wald, M., 'Children's Rights: A Framework for Analysis'. In Freeman, M. (Ed.), *Children's Rights*, vol. I, 2 vols. (USA: Ashgate Darmouth, 2004): 113–140; Freeman, M. (2004).

and violence against children has not been properly legislated against in a majority of Member States to the UN.[21]

In contrast to the UN Convention on the Elimination of All forms of Discrimination Against Women (CEDAW) and the UN Convention on the Elimination of Racial Discrimination (CERD), the CRC – at least not explicitly – does not aim towards the elimination of all forms of discrimination against children.[22] Inadequacy of addressing age-based discrimination against children in the CRC and when implementing human rights for children is a primary weakness in how we have thus far made meaning of children's rights.

The Committee on the Rights of the Child has regarded children's rights as a major challenge for all states and actors concerned, and ten years after the adoption of the CRC, Paulo David lists six obstacles to its realization: 1) the idea of children's rights rather than charity towards children challenges existing beliefs and attitudes held about children, 2) there is a lack of cooperation among the stakeholders responsible for realizing the rights of the child, 3) the child's right to participation challenges traditional adult behaviour and parental values, 4) the right to education has not been adequately addressed in terms of how it encompasses discrimination in school, including protection against corporal punishment and harassment, 5) children's civil rights are regarded by the adult community as a potential threat to adults' rights, and 6) Member States have undermined the international acceptance of the CRC through major reservations to the Convention.[23] These obstacles are discussed further under the following six sub-headings in relation to childism. I give different examples of the reasons listed above and show that these obstacles are still relevant for unveiling possible instances of age-based discrimination against children, and thus illustrate the associated difficulties of realizing the CRC.

2.1 *Challenging Childist Views about Children*

There is a need for a fundamental change of attitudes towards and beliefs about children in order to strengthen the discourse on children's rights. Childist beliefs consist of ideas that children are inferior to adults and should

---

21 See https://endcorporalpunishment.org/ for current statistics on legislation against corporal punishment.

22 See Daly, A., Thorburn Stern, R. & Leviner, P., *UN Convention on the Rights of the Child, Article 2 and Discrimination on the basis of Childhood: The CRC Paradox?*, Nordic Journal of International Law, Volume 91, 2022, s. 419–452.

23 David, P., 'Implementing the Rights of the Child: Six Reasons Why the Human Rights of Children Remain a Constant Challenge', *International Review of Education* 48, no. 3–4 (2002): 259–263.

know their place; children should not ask for too much, since their age-related differences relative to the ones of adults are said to justify children's inequality (thus disclaiming any argument for social justice for children). The child's perceived lack of ability or capacity relative to that of adults, risks leading to a poor realization of their rights as set forth in the CRC. An illustration of this problem – addressing violations of children's rights when prejudice and discrimination against children are not named in the first place – is found in a study on 'the practice of interpreting the law and physical child abuse in Sweden'.[24] Sköld, Sandin, and Schiratzki explore the potential tensions between governmental redress schemes to acknowledge past child abuse and interpretations of criteria for what is deemed 'normal child-rearing' or part of 'normal childhoods' in terms of physical abuse, sexual abuse, work exploitation, detention, discrimination, violation, and neglect of children in Swedish out-of-home-care between 1920 and 1980.[25] In their study of 1,225 decisions by the Swedish redress board on the severity of child abuse, Sköld et al. find a clear discrepancy between victims' sufferings and the 'implementation of an administrative legal system'[26] in which issues of justice through economic compensation are 'determined by what kind of past child abuse is recognized as wrongful today and/or what kind of past child abuse is assumed to have been recognized as wrongful in the past'.[27] As with other types of discriminatory forms of violence, the normalization of violence against children rests on established assumptions about children's inferiority – long-held assumptions that serve to maintain inequality, which results in unaddressed human rights violations and a 'silent pandemic'[28] of degrading treatment of children as a marginalized group. Prejudiced discourses on childhoods limit the respect for and the realization of children's rights, but are also open to change over time.

Within the human rights discourse, tensions between different minority groups and their rights claims can be further explored by studying the intersections of childism, racism, sexism, and ableism, in terms of how children's rights are compromised due to these overlapping systems. In a study on sexual abuse and children with neuropsychiatric disorders, Lindblad and Lainpelto

24 Sköld, J., Sandin, B., and Schiratzki, J., 'Historical Justice through Redress Schemes?', *Scandinavian Journal of History* 45, no. 2 (2020): 178–201.

25 Sköld, Sandin, and Schiratzki (2020), 182.

26 Ibid., 179.

27 Ibid., 180.

28 Adami, R. and Dineen, K., 'Discourses of Childism: How COVID-19 Has Unveiled Prejudice, Discrimination and Social Injustice against Children in the Everyday', *The International Journal of Children's Rights* 29 (2021): 353–370.

note the 'forensic complication' in 'overlap of symptoms between ADHD and post-traumatic stress disorder' and the 'comorbidity between these disorders', a dilemma 'reflected in the increased risk of ADHD in sexual abuse victims'.[29] They further note that children with disabilities are less easily recognized in the medical care system and are exposed to 'focused rather than open-ended questions, which increase the risk of eliciting non-accurate information'.[30] With an increased understanding of the commonality of prejudice, and hostility toward children and the overlapping prejudices against children with disabilities, we can examine how social inequality between adults and children is explained through childist and ableist discourses. The ways in which racist, sexist, and ableist prejudices become interwoven into childist attitudes about children calls for an intersectional lens for studying the discrimination that children face. It is not the actual or perceived differences between groups of people – between adults and children – that constitute a problem as such. The idea of equality and human rights for all encompass diversity. However, racist, sexist, ableist, and childist discrimination is based on connecting ideas of inferiority, along with a notion of superiority to such perceived differences and social myths of race and natural correlation between sex and assigned gender. By adding childism to intersectional analysis of discrimination that disadvantage children, we may better understand how negative beliefs and attitudes against children, as mentioned by David, still interfere with implementation of the CRC.

2.2 *Child Equity: The Need for Cooperation between Institutions*[31]

The enforcement of children's rights rests on the need and achievement of cross-sectional cooperation. Children's rights are relevant to a wide range of professionals working with social services, education, healthcare, police departments, courts, media, housing services, recreational activities, sports, and many more fields. What is actualized in such cooperation are conflicting interpretations of child equality. Thus far overlooked, and something that would constitute a major focus in this cross-sectional realization of children's

29 Lindblad, F. and Lainpelto, K., 'Sexual Abuse Allegations by Children with Neuropsychiatric Disorders', *Journal of Child Sexual Abuse*, no. 20 (2011): 182–195, 183.

30 Lindblad, F. and Lainpelto, K. (2011), 183.

31 Child equity is a structural and systemic concept that focuses the process for reaching equality when a system or structure in itself is unfair, biased, and discriminatory. See similar distinctions in relation to other forms of discrimination such as racial equity and gender equity; https://www.aecf.org/blog/racial-justice-definitions.

rights, is the importance of a clear definition of *the kind of equality* these various social institutions should strive for when it comes to children's rights. Are children's rights to physical health, mental health, quality education, and access to justice fulfilled according to the specific circumstances of each individual child, or are children regarded as appendages to families, for whom adults set the standards of 'best practice', 'best interests', and 'child-friendly' principles?[32]

A notion of formal equality for children would presume children to be treated 'as adults' where ideas of corresponding duties to rights exist. Age-based discrimination against children cannot be adequately addressed in demands for *formal equality*, but instead through *substantial equality*, by which children are not treated 'as adults' but their child-specific differences are respected. Adult normative assumptions about who is seen as a rights subject do not work well in discussions concerning children's rights because childhoods require additional rights related to children's dependency on adults, and the fact that children cannot be required to act as duty bearers in light of their lack of social, physical, and economic resources. In comparable situations, children are not as 'free' as adults to act in a variety of instances where their rights might be actualized. Through childism, we acknowledge that there is widespread discrimination against children, and that they might be treated unfairly and unjustly because they are children – as individuals who are not listened to, not taken into consideration in matters that affect them, and not spoken with but informed of decisions already taken by concerned adults according to adult and parental interests and ideas. Children's social conditions differ in crucial ways from that of the adult norm, and discussions on formal equality demand that children be treated 'as adults', ultimately leading (as we can see in the treatment of children as adults in court systems, and countless other examples) to their increased suffering.[33]

Courts would need to find ways to become more child equitable (fair and impartial), with the ambition of attaining fairness of treatment for children according to their specific condition. This may include equal or different treatment according to what would be considered equivalent in terms of children's rights and in refraining from reifying childist stereotypes of children and their needs; it would also require questioning adultist norms of standardized

---

32 See Zillén, K., Chapter 5 in this volume; Leviner, P., and Holappa T. Chapter 2 in this volume; Holmqvist, A. 'The Rights to Physical Integrity for Child Patients Jeopardized in Health and Medical Care?: A Blind Spot in the Patient Act and a Non-Issue for Patient Organisations in Sweden', *The International Journal of Children's Rights* 30, no.1 (2022): 98–119.

33 See https://jlc.org/issues/youth-tried-adults.

processes that hitherto may have overlooked the specific circumstances in which children may find themselves.

A conceptual shift from notions of formal equality toward a notion of *child equity*, I argue, is needed to take into consideration children's social condition in society. Child equity is defined here as fairness of treatment for children according to their needs. This may include equal or different treatment according to what would be considered equivalent in terms of children's rights and in avoiding reifying childist stereotypes and adultist norms. Child equity is thus based on ideas about substantive equality for children, which means that their social condition is taken into consideration when determining what is needed in order for their rights to be realized in different instances (conditions that may differ from those of adults – but not all adults – that may demand different treatment to acknowledge a child's disadvantaged position).

Child equity in cases of child abuse and violence against children could mean involving the family and guardians of a child in preventative and/or rehabilitation measures instead of applying the adult framework of criminal law on children.[34] In terms of legal justice, child equity would reflect children's rights that ensure support for a child in risk environments to seek counselling for abusive communication and violent patterns at home. The dependency of a child, along with the pervasive influence on a child's reasoning and actions that adults in their environment exercise, risk being overlooked as long as courts apply reasoning for criminal responsibility to children that is similar to the reasoning that applies to adults. In the UK and the US, for example, minors charged with serious crimes can be tried as adults before the law.[35] Child equity in terms of the 'best interests' of the child could shift the focus in legal reasoning, from an individualistic to a more relational and community-based approach to rehabilitation. Imprisonment or fines are based on adult ideas about corrective justice that may not be as easily applicable when children are affected by the legal system, either in conflict with the law or as victims of crimes. Rehabilitation and supportive structures in society – connecting family counselling, trauma, and crisis management for victims and abusers,

34 For further moral discussions on similar issues of taking into consideration the rights of the child in legal penalties, see Bülow, W., 'The Harms Beyond Imprisonment: Do We Have Special Moral Obligations towards the Families and Children of Prisoners?', *Ethical Theory and Moral Practice* 17, no.4 (2014): 775–789. On the importance of including moral considerations in terms of social justice other than imprisonment and punishment, see Vedananda, N., 'Learning to Heal: Integrating Restorative Justice into Legal Education', *New York Law School Law Review* 64 (2019/20): 95–114.

35 See the Juvenile Law Center, https://jlc.org/issues/youth-tried-adults.

parenting support, treatment for parents caught in alcohol or drug abuse, economic support, and therapy sessions – may be more aligned with child equity (fairness is relation to a child's specific condition) instead of conventional views of punishment and imprisonment.[36] Realizing children's rights based on more substantive forms of non-discrimination and equality demands that the process of cooperation between several social institutions is equitable in itself.

2.3 *Right to Participation: Challenging Prejudice against the Youngest Children*

Children's right to participation requires 'deep social changes in attitudes, behaviour, and values' of adults.[37] When studying obstacles to implementing Article 12 on children's right to participation, Rebecca Stern looks at 'traditional attitudes' when Member States explain inaction, and she comes to the conclusion that a focus on cultural attitudes overshadows 'the existing attitudes toward children in Western states'.[38] I find this problematization interesting, as here Stern addresses the way in which Western states may overlook their own attitudes toward children that hinder children's realization of their rights in their own states.

Prevailing arguments that Article 12 of the CRC applies solely to older children, and which cannot be enforced for younger children and infants, rest on childist attitudes and beliefs connected to children's abilities at different ages. How are children supposed to be heard in issues affecting them when prejudices about children – that they cannot reason, do not know what is best for them, are not to be trusted, and change their mind constantly – risk being left unchallenged?[39]

The child according to the UN Committee on the Rights of the Child, is 'able to form views from the youngest age, even when she or he may be unable to express them verbally'; thus a full implementation of Article 12

36 For a legal discussion about the best interests of the child and the limitations thereof in criminal proceedings, see Kaldal, A., 'Barnets Bästa Vid Våld Mot Barn – Kan Eller Bör En Förälder Ges Behandling i Stället För Straff?'. In Åhman, K., Leviner, P., and, Zillén, K. (Eds.), *Barnkonventionen i praktiken. Rättsliga utmaningar och möjligheter* (Stockholm: Norstedts Juridik, 2020): 331–356.

37 David, P. (2002), 260.

38 Thorburn Stern, R., *Implementing Article 12 of the UN Convention on the Rights of the Child: Participation, Power and Attitudes*, vol. 2, Stockholm Studies in Child Law and Children's Rights (Leiden: Brill, 2017), 163.

39 See similar arguments by Kaldal, A., Chapter 3 in this volume.

'requires recognition of, and respect for, non-verbal forms of communication including play, body language, facial expressions, and drawing and painting'.[40]

The enforcement of Article 12 – on the right for the child to be included and to be heard – requires adults to adjust their communication and attentive listening to individuals who do not excel in oralism. Appreciating diversity in abilities requires changed attitudes and beliefs about children who deviate from the adult norm and about children with disabilities. Interpreting the responsibility of adults to realize Article 12 in the CRC by developing knowledge on age-based discrimination could enhance the child's right to be heard, especially in securing the ability of individuals below the age of 12 to be listened to on their own terms.

The idea that children are not interested in social justice issues may lead adults to neglect to inform children about their rights.[41] In what ways do such beliefs prevent adults from engaging children in conversations about discrimination and social injustice? Reflecting on how prejudice challenges the implementation of children's rights can lead to more ethically sensitive relations between adults and children and to increased instances of using expert groups of children in politics and legislation, which in turn can lead to interventions other than those that adults may have thought of. Reflection on how prejudice against children leads to undue power imbalance in institutions that deal with children's rights can create venues for more resources in the field of implementing children's rights and freedoms. This progress could be achieved if children themselves take part in the process.

2.4 *The Right to Education as Including Protection against Age-Based Harassment and Assault*

Another obstacle to the realization of children's rights is the way in which rights *to something* might foreclose the rights of a child in the *exercise* of that same right. Children's right to cost-free education is one of their fundamental rights, but while the right to education is stated in the CRC, the discrimination and prejudice children face *in* education is not addressed in the Convention.[42]

---

40 UN Committee on the Rights of the Child. *General comment No.12 (2009): The right of the child to be heard.* CRC/C/GC/12, para. 9.

41 See for example the empirical study by Klara Dolk about adult-steered child influence in preschool settings, and how child participation was limited to deciding on which transport to take for school trips, not on issues concerning social justice and discrimination; Dolk, *Bångstyriga Barn: Makt, Normer Och Delaktighet i Förskolan* [*Unruly Children: Power, Norms and Participation in the Preeschool*] (Stockholm: Ordfront, 2013).

42 If we read Article 2 CRC together with Article 29 CRC, discrimination facing children due to their own position (unrelated to their family, such as sexuality) and age-based

It is not primarily formal curricula, but the hidden curricula – what is done by teachers in their daily interactions with children – that impacts children's subjectification and becoming a rights subject, according to Lisa Isenström. She notes that in her studies in Swedish schools, the actions of teachers in the school have a significant effect on children's learning about human rights, and also on their becoming rights subjects.[43]

When exploring children's experiences as rights subjects in education, the existence of corporal punishment, bullying, and inattentiveness to children's mental health should be reformulated as different forms of discrimination against children in need of more structural and systemic analysis. *Age-based violence* includes violent acts where children are primarily or exclusively the victims, and violence against children and youths connected to normative understandings of their age.

The right to education encompasses not only access *to*, but quality *of* education, and rights *in* education. Access may be hindered along socio-economic lines, quality may be compromised, and rights in education overlooked. The negative belief that children do not know what they need or what is best for them risks undermining children's own influence during their time in school.

Protection for children against *direct* and *indirect age discrimination* 'applied in education and children's services would ensure that the views and experiences of children are taken into account during the development of these'[44] and emphasizes the need for 'reasonable adjustments to enable equal access to public buildings and public transport'.[45] Direct age discrimination against children refers to when a child is treated less favourably – differently and worse – due to age, for example by being denied services. Indirect discrimination against children includes instances where a child is treated in the same way as everyone else, but still suffers unequal opportunities due to age, gender,

discrimination is still not covered in the CRC. For a more progressive reading of the CRC, we can turn to the Committee on the Rights of the Child. *General Comment No.1 (2001)* Article 29 (1): The aims of education CRC/GC/2001/1 17April 2001 which states that 'Discrimination on the basis of any of the grounds listed in article 2 of the Convention, whether it is overt or hidden, offends the human dignity of the child and is capable of undermining or even destroying the capacity of the child to benefit from educational opportunities'.

43 Isenström, L., 'Children as Growing Rights Subjects – The Significance of Teachers' Actions', *The International Journal of Children's Rights* 28, no. 2 (2020): 258–287.

44 Young Equals, *Making the Case: Why Children Should Be Protected from Age Discrimination and How It Can Be Done, Proposals for the Equality Bill* (UK: Children's Rights Alliance for England, 2009), 6.

45 Young Equals, 7.

disability, or race. Identifying instances of direct and indirect age discrimination against children by public institutions calls for a shift through childism and intersectional lenses from talking about children's needs to a discussion about the power structures that deny children's rights.

2.5 *Children's Rights Threatening Adult Rights? An Anti-childist Lens on Adult Power*

While there might be general support for the *idea* of children's rights, 'political parties, religious groups, teacher's organizations, parents associations' are groups that may feel 'that recognizing rights of children will infringe on their own rights'.[46] As noted by Susan Moller Okin,[47] there could be inherent tensions between different rights claims, and she discusses tensions between multiculturalist and feminist rights discourses. An additional layer that requires further discernment is the matter of rights tensions between anti-racist, anti-sexist, and anti-childist efforts to address social injustices.

As sex, race, ethnicity, language, religion, and other areas are mentioned as grounds for discrimination in international conventions on human rights, and as age – usually referring to the elderly – has not included age discrimination against children, these grounds are more likely to be taken into consideration in circumstances that might also affect the rights of the child. Special protection against discrimination for indigenous people, migrants, women, and persons with disabilities are all covered in UN conventions. Due to adultism – that is, adults being in power over children in degrading ways – these discrimination grounds risk being read as applicable only to adults in relation to services and rights. As noted earlier, the CRC contains no definition of age discrimination against children.

It is important for childism not to be treated as just another aspect of a feminist or multicultural approach. Issues that may benefit gender equality do not necessarily harmonize with respect for the individual child. Anti-sexist discourses in custody cases, for example, do not necessarily represent the rights of the child. *Adult perspective* in courts – regarding the rights, interests, and needs of adults primarily – would give precedence to concerned adults' ideas of what would be in the best interest of the child. Anti-childist lenses on *adultist norms* – norms that assign adults the status of being powerful and authoritative while disregarding children's voices, experiences, and different conditions – may question the interests of a parent, even though such an approach

46 David, P. (2002), 261.

47 Moller Okin, S., *Is Multiculturalism Bad for Women?* (Princeton: Princeton University Press, 1999).

may counter the traditional gender-based inequality or sexist reasoning found in national legislation and application of laws concerning custody.

Acknowledging that a minority group may be limited in the exercise of cultural and religious rights calls for special protection, but the flip side of such protection could lead adults to force children who are unable to provide 'full, free and informed consent' to undergo traditions harmful to their dignity.[48] When examining legislation and policies that may discriminate against children, the heterogeneity of children and their double (and sometimes multiple) marginalization must be acknowledged. Should a girl have the right to be heard and challenge adult women's expectations on her? Should a boy have the right to do the same against hegemonic masculinity? These are questions that anti-childist lenses on the rights of the child actualize when rights claims are viewed solely through the perspective of the right to culture, religion, or tradition. The attitudes of the adult community, including adult perspectives on marginalized groups, may hinder the full realization of the rights of the child because due to childism, children as a heterogenous group – consisting of all other minority groups – are nonetheless marginalized within every minority group.

Adult authority over children can have violating consequences when serving childist interests and beliefs of children. Anna Kaldal and Pernilla Leviner argue in a study from 2007 that it is important to recognize that parental rights and children's rights may conflict in both public and civil law, and they emphasize the importance of allowing social services to interview children without the presence or consent of the parents in such procedures.[49]

48 'Harmful practices are persistent practices and behaviours that are grounded on discrimination on the basis of sex, gender, age and other grounds as well as multiple and/or intersecting forms of discrimination that often involve violence and cause physical and/or psychological harm or suffering'. UN Committee on the Elimination of Discrimination against Women and UN Committee on the Rights of the Child. *Joint general comment No.31 of the Committee on the Elimination of Discrimination against Women and No.18 of the Committee on the Rights of the Child on harmful practices,* 4 November 2014, CEDAW/C/GC/31-CRC/C/GC/18, 6.

49 We have seen a strengthening of the child's right to be heard individually in the Swedish legislation the last decade, which may align with changes in beliefs and attitudes towards children over time. How the child's right to participation is to be understood is continuously debated and the potential conflict of parental rights and interests versus children's rights in such instances is still important to note. Kaldal and Leviner (2007). 'Silencing the conflict of interests between parental rights and the rights of the child – legal requirements for the social services to interview children', *Scandinavian Studies in Law* 50, (2007): 381–392. See Kaldal chapter 3 in this volume.

I argue that the well-established notion of *patriarchy* can be used as a basic concept to refer to both the structure of male domination over women and parental power over children.[50] The etymology of the term 'patriarchy' stems from Greek. It consists of the two words 'father' and 'ruler'. 'Father' implies having power over children in a family or demonstrating supremacy by being a parent and head of the household – traditionally a position bestowed upon men. Hence, two power structures intersect under patriarchy: the male/female, grounded in sexism and the adult/child, grounded in childism. Major reservations to the CRC could illustrate in several ways how the adult community regards children's rights as potential threats to their own privilege and power.

2.6 *Major Reservations to Children's Rights: The Need for Intersectional Analysis*

Although the CRC has received 197 ratifications since its adoption in 1989, major reservations to the CRC dilute its international protection for children and lower the intended ambitions of its articles. However, reservations to the CRC alone will not provide an overall picture of children's marginalization in the human rights discourse. Children as a heterogenous group actualize the framework of international rights examined through reservations to the CEDAW, CERD, and the UN Convention on the Rights of Persons with Disabilities CRPD, as well as the conventions on migrants' rights and indigenous peoples' rights.

By drawing on parallels with racism, sexism, and ableism, we may gain knowledge about how discrimination against children encompasses several intersecting systems of oppression. Children and youth, due to the interlocking systems of neo-colonialism, racism, sexism, ableism, and childism, are the first to experience how the subordination of race, class, gender, and abilities intersect. They are among the first to feel the effects of cuts in social services, healthcare, education, and other welfare provisions in a society that is supposed to provide the most vulnerable groups with an economic and social safety net.[51] Thus, only a plurality of children's voices on social injustice will adequately indicate where interventions are most relevant, and where human rights, on both societal and family levels, have not been realized.

50 For further discussions on patriarchal violence against children, see Adami and Dineen, 'Discourses of Childism: How COVID-19 has Unveiled Prejudice, Discrimination and Social Injustice against Children in the Everyday' *The International Journal of Children's Rights* 29, no.2 (2021): 353–370.

51 See Hill Collins, P., and Bilge, S., *Intersectionality* (Cambridge: Polity Press, 2016).

An intersectional analysis of public budgeting could provide us with preventive and positive measures to ensure the realization of the rights of children from the most marginalized groups in society (children living in poverty, housing segregation etc). Intersectional budget analysis asks key and overlooked questions such as: how are children with perceived disabilities and with minority religious and ethnic backgrounds affected by allocations of resources? Intersectional budget analysis raises questions about social inequality, power, relationality, social context, complexity, and social injustice for children from marginalized groups.[52]

3 Concluding Remarks

In this chapter, I have argued that 1) in order to challenge existing views about children, we need to be aware that anti-sexist and anti-racist lenses on human rights do not necessarily harmonize with anti-childist lenses on human rights that confront adultist norms; 2) cooperation between institutions for children's rights is not helped by a formal notion of age equality that disregards the difference between children and adults, whereas child equity questions how adultism as a power structure is maintained through adult and ableist normativity; 3) the right to participation requires changes in how social, legal, and political processes that affect children have been handled thus far in order to accommodate differences and enable children's decision-making capacity; 4) addressing the barriers faced by children in education require age-based harassment, assault, and discrimination against children in school to be named and faced; 5) patriarchal hierarchies that have denied women political agency by premising laws supporting political freedoms and autonomy on men alone can be analysed to shed light on discriminatory discourses of patriarchal structures that today deny children civil rights through paternalistic attitudes toward children's voices; and 6) resistance against the rights of the child in the form of reservations to the CRC indicate that, due to childism children are not regarded as rights subjects. Studies on racism, sexism, and ableism have shown how biased use of language serves to perpetuate the idea that not all human beings are equal or regarded as legal subjects with rights and freedoms.

A conceptual move from formal equality to child equity will enable analysis of the extent to which 'child friendly', 'child adapted', and 'best interests' initiatives and standards conceal more than paternalistic perspectives. Child

52 See for example https://wbg.org.uk/analysis/intersecting-inequalities/.

equity, as noted, is a structural concept that encapsulates the process towards equality and thus enables analysis of the unfairness in how, for example, the best-interest principle might be interpreted by adults through their own interests. As there is no single 'child perspective', this definition of child equity is called for to address the structure behind age discrimination against children.

This normative conceptualization needs to be tested through future empirical studies on instances of age discrimination against children, and statistics are needed on crimes targeting children (for example, crimes in the home, where we might encounter the problem of hidden statistics, and unfair treatment by social services of children that could be labelled as discrimination). Further studies into systemic childism would also provide us with a framework for understanding poverty and other social inequalities among children.

References

Adami, Rebecca, and Katy Dineen. 2021. "Discourses of Childism: How COVID-19 Has Unveiled Prejudice, Discrimination and Social Injustice against Children in the Everyday", *The International Journal of Children's Rights* 29: 1–17.

Aitken, Stuart, Ragnhild Lund, and Anne Trine Kjornholt. 2007. "Why Children? Why Now?", *Children's Geographies* 1–2(3): 3–14.

Bach, Michael, and Lana Kerzner. 2010. "A New Paradigm for Protecting Autonomy and the Right to Legal Capacity: Advancing Substantive Equality for Persons with Disabilities through Law, Policy and Practice", *Law Commission of Ontario*, October.

Bessell, Sharon. 2017. "Rights-Based Research with Children: Principles and Practice", in Tracey Skelton, Ruth Evans, and Louise Holt (Eds.), *Methodological Approaches Geographies of Children and Young People*, 223–40. Singapore: Springer.

Bülow, William. 2014. "The Harms Beyond Imprisonment: Do We Have Special Moral Obligations towards the Families and Children of Prisoners?", *Ethical Theory and Moral Practice* 17(4): 775–89.

Christensen, Pia, and Alison Prout. 2002. "Working with Ethical Symmetry in Social Research with Children", *Childhood* 9: 477–97.

Daly, Aoife, Rebecca Thorburn Stern, & Pernilla Leviner. 2022. "UN Convention on the Rights of the Child, Article 2 and Discrimination on the basis of Childhood: The CRC Paradox?", *Nordic Journal of International Law* 91: 419–452.

David, Paulo. 2002. "Implementing the Rights of the Child: Six Reasons Why the Human Rights of Children Remain a Constant Challenge", *International Review of Education* 48(3–4): 259–63.

Dolk, Klara. 2013. *Bångstyriga Barn: Makt, Normer Och Delaktighet i Förskolan* [Unruly Children: Power, Norms and Participation in the Preeschool]. Stockholm: Ordfront.

Federle, Katherine. 1993. "On the Road to Reconceiving Rights for Children: A Postfeminist Analysis of the Capacity Principle", *DePaul Law Review* 42(3): 983–1028.

Freeman, Michael. 2004. *Children's Rights. Vol. I.* 2 vols. Wiltshire: Ashgate Darmouth.

Hanson, Karl, and Noam Peleg. 2020. "Waiting for Children's Rights Theory", *The International Journal of Children's Rights* 28(1): 15–35.

Isenström, Lisa. 2020. "Children as Growing Rights Subjects – The Significance of Teachers' Actions", *The International Journal of Children's Rights* 28(2): 258–87.

Kaldal, Anna. 2020. "Barnets Bästa Vid Våld Mot Barn – Kan Eller Bör En Förälder Ges Behandling i Stället För Straff?", in Karin Åhman, Pernilla Leviner, and Kavot Zillén (Eds.), *Barnkonventionen i Praktiken: Rättsliga Utmaningar Och Möjligheter*, 331–56. Nordstedts Juridik.

Lindblad, Frank, and Katrin Lainpelto. 2011. "Sexual Abuse Allegations by Children with Neuropsychiatric Disorders", *Journal of Child Sexual Abuse* 20: 182–95.

Lundy, Laura. 2019. Editorial: "A Lexicon for Research on International Children's Rights in Troubled Times", *International Journal of Children's Rights* 27: 595–601.

Moller Okin, Susan. 1999. *Is Multiculturalism Bad for Women?* Princeton: Princeton University Press.

Punch, Samantha. 2002. "Research with Children: The Same or Different From Research with Adults?", *Childhood* 9(3): 321–41.

Reynolds, Pamela, Olga Nieuwenhuys, and Karl Hanson. 2006. "Refractions of Children's Rights in Development Practice: A View From Anthropology", *Childhood* 13(3): 291–302.

Sköld, Johanna, Bengt Sandin, and Johanna Schiratzki. 2020. "Historical Justice through Redress Schemes?", *Scandinavian Journal of History* 45(2): 178–201.

Stern, Rebecca. 2017. *Implementing Article 12 of the UN Convention on the Rights of the Child: Participation, Power and Attitudes*. Vol. 2. Stockholm Studies in Child Law and Children's Rights. Leiden: Brill.

Tisdall, Kay, and Samantha Punch. 2012. "Not so New? Looking Critically at Childhood Studies", *Children's Geographies* 10(3): 249–64.

Tobin, John. 2013. "Justifying Children's Rights", *The International Journal of Children's Rights* 21(3): 395–441.

Vedananda, Natasha S. 2019. "Learning to Heal: Integrating Restorative Justice into Legal Education", *New York Law School Law Review* 64: 95–114.

Wald, Michael. 2004. "Children's Rights: A Framework for Analysis", in Michael Freeman (Ed.), *Children's Rights*, I: 113–40. USA: Ashgate Darmouth.

Wall, John. 2019. "From Childhood Studies to Childism: Reconstructing the Scholarly and Social Imaginations", *Children's Geographies* 20(3): 257–270.

Young Equals. 2009. "Making the Case: Why Children Should Be Protected from Age Discrimination and How It Can Be Done, Proposals for the Equality Bill". UK: Children's Rights Alliance for England.

Young-Bruehl, Elisabeth. 2012. *Childism: Confronting Prejudice against Children*. New Haven: Yale University Press.

Young-Bruehl, Elisabeth. (1996). *The Anatomy of Prejudices*. Cambridge, Mass.: Harvard University Press.

United Nations Committee on the Elimination of Discrimination against Women (CEDAW) and the UN Committee on the Rights of the Child (CRC). *Joint general comment No.31 of the Committee on the Elimination of Discrimination against Women and No. 18 of the Committee on the Rights of the Child on harmful practices*. CEDAW/C/GC/31-CRC/C/GC/18 (4 November 2014).

United Nations Convention on the Elimination of Racial Discrimination CERD.

United Nations Committee on the Rights of the Child. *General comment No. 12 (2009). The right of the child to be heard*. CRC/C/GC/12 (20 July 2009).

A Response to Rebecca Adami

Katrin Lainpelto

In the chapter 'Childism – on adult resistance to children's rights', Adami discusses childism as barrier to the realization of children's rights. This question is highly relevant in the context of criminal proceedings. For young offenders, criminal proceedings expose how several, sometimes conflicting, interests need to be taken into account and balanced within a single legal context. Examples of such considerations include the need for an effective law enforcement, the function of retribution, general and individual preventive aspirations, victim reparations, and the particular vulnerability and protection needs of young offenders.

In the handling of criminal proceedings concerning young offenders, therefore, a multifaceted and complicated legal figure emerges: the child as an undeveloped adult, in need of support and protection; the child as an immature and therefore 'dangerous criminal' with a high risk for relapse; and the child as a mouldable lump of clay who can be reintegrated into society. In the context of criminal proceedings, these aspects mean that in some parts of the criminal proceedings, children should be treated as adults, while in other parts of the process children should be protected against being treated as adults. The latter position is possible because the juvenile justice system contains accepted deviations from the right to equality before the law. This differential treatment is justified with reference to the immaturity of children and young adults and their underdeveloped capacity to understand rules and societal norms, in addition to a great need for protection against the negative consequences of a legal penalty.

The legal reasoning behind the general characterization of the child as a multifaceted and complex legal figure seems to be based on a conflict between the equal-treatment argument and the protection argument. Critiques of the protection argument argue that acknowledgement of the child's vulnerability and need for protection is based on a child-adult classification and a negative stereotyping of children as a group. Through such an adult-centric perspective, childhood is viewed as an unavoidable stage – 'a necessary evil' – through which children need to pass to develop into competent and capable adults. Furthermore, differential treatment of young offenders can reinforce already existing negative stereotypes of children: deviations from the equal-treatment principle can evoke and strengthen beliefs about the inferiority of children in relation to adults. Therefore, in a worst-case scenario, differential treatment of children and young people can lead to stigmatization and even discrimination. Furthermore, a view of children as a homogeneous group can lead to the negation of an individually tailored treatment of children in legal proceedings, where the possibility to adapt and adjust measures can determine the success of such measures and the possibilities for the child's reintegration in society.

From a legal procedural perspective, the opposition between the equal-treatment argument and the protection argument can lead to factual consequences for a child accused of a crime. The conflict between these arguments can be found in the Convention on the Rights of the Child (CRC) and in the General Comments of the Committee on the Rights of the Child concerning children in conflict with the law. An example to be mentioned is Article 40 of the CRC, which in turn is based on the right to a fair trial as the right is stated in the ECHR, through which children are assured the same procedural safeguards as those given to adult offenders. A conclusion that could be drawn in relation to the CRC, at least to a certain degree, is that the Convention advocates equal treatment from a rights perspective.

On the other hand, both the CRC and the Committee on the Rights of the Child allow exceptions from the equal-treatment principle, and these exceptions are justified by the need for protection of children in the legal context of criminal proceedings. However, these exceptions – such as measures that aim to steer the child away from the ordinary criminal proceedings or limit the child's participation – can lead to a child not being granted the due-process protection stated in Article 40 of the CRC.

In other words, the legal handling of young offenders, which is considered to promote the best interests of the child, can *de facto* lead to a child not being able to enjoy his or her procedural rights to the same extent as an adult offender. Conversely, an emphasis on the rights perspective and procedural formality could hinder both a child-adopted treatment and fulfilment of the need for individually tailored diversion measures. Assigning adult due process-protection to children can also lead to adult liability principles, which stand in stark contrast to the child's need for protection as well as the importance of the reintegration of the child in society.

Overall, the conflicts of interest in the child-penalty process pose a risk that young offenders will be placed in procedural vacuum of sorts, where the attempts to achieve balance between the fairness of the process and the child's need for protection could lead to a child being ensured neither his or her procedural rights nor due access to a child-adapted criminal proceeding. The slightest imbalance between a rights perspective and a protection perspective will lead to noticeable procedural after-effects for the child – effects for the child *as* a rights holder or for the child *as* being just a child. The question, however, is whether one perspective or the other needs to be excluded, or whether the one perspective could paralyze the other. If we consider the objectives of the CRC, assuring the possibilities to reintegrate the child into society seems to be the desirable goal. Achieving this goal requires increased implementation of child-adapted and individually designed diversion measures. At the same time, such an arrangement highlights the urgency of a rights perspective.

The chapter by Adami on childism seems to introduce a third position, which might provide a solution to the conflict between a protection perspective and equal-treatment perspective within the juvenile justice system. An anti-childist analysis and theory might help us determine when either benevolent or hostile prejudices about children influence adult arguments against a strengthening of children's rights. This approach is in line with my argument: what is needed is a restructuring of the processes as such, so they do not reflect solely an adult perspective in courts, and assurance of necessary support that is sensitive to children's unique conditions, in order to ensure child equity instead of mere formal equality for children.

CHAPTER 7

Five Problems with Children's Participation Rights

Linde Lindkvist

1 Introduction

One of the perennial tensions in human rights scholarship is that between critique and activism. Many of us working on questions of human rights have been drawn to these out of personal conviction. Much like scholars of theology, we find the strength and motivation to engage with the endless stream of UN documents, court cases, empirical case studies, juridical doctrine, and conceptual analyses in hopes for a more just and humane world. Still, as scholars, we cannot let our critical mind go to rest, even when it comes to fundamental values. Although it is pointless to strive for objectivity, we are nonetheless called to engage critically with our chosen topics and to question even the most self-evident truths guiding our fields of study.

In the case of children's rights, this means – at the very least – to constantly remind ourselves and our readers of the most basic questions at play: What is a child? Why do we find it meaningful to speak of children as a special class of human beings? Why is the distinction between childhood and adulthood of moral, legal, and political relevance? Do children have rights? If so, is it for the same reason as other humans have rights?

I also think that the position of a student or scholar is one where we are called to be mindful of the fact that all attempts to codify the proper meaning of a concept like children's rights, including the UN Convention on the Rights of the Child (CRC), are conditioned by factors such as time, place, rules of procedure, power arrangements, expertise, and ideologies. The CRC was composed of fragments of earlier international instruments on children's rights, as well as bits and pieces of human rights law, humanitarian law, refugee law, labour law, and development policy, along with some novel ideas (such as the right to play) that surfaced in the course of the drafting process between 1978–1989. The Convention was not, in other words, a set of divine principles carved into stone by an impersonal world conscience. It was a work of political negotiation.

In his dissertation on children's rights in Swedish asylum procedures, Jonathan Josefsson notes that there is a tendency among child rights scholars to think of the CRC not just as a historically specific statement on what

DOI:10.1163/9789004511163_016

children's rights could be about, but as a self-evident, analytical framework of what children's rights essentially are. At worst, this creates a deafening feedback loop as child rights scholars attempt to shed light on norms and practices that stem from the CRC, using the Convention itself as their analytical lens.[1]

Breaking that feedback loop and taking more external – to some extent more detached – viewpoints on children's rights is one of the main challenges facing students and scholars of children's rights today.[2] This is not just for the sake of child rights studies as a sub-field of interdisciplinary human rights and childhood studies. The reason we need to let go of the CRC as our analytical framework is not just that doing so will likely improve the quality of our scholarly output. It is also likely to make that output more relevant outside academia. Child rights studies can never be cutting edge if the field merely echoes the way that children's rights are discussed among politicians, lawyers, activists, and practitioners. I do not think that our primary responsibility as scholars is to offer expertise and advice to decision-makers – even if I think that we should be free to do so as well. Rather, I think our job is to stimulate new ways of thinking, sometimes just by pointing to the limits and perplexities of rights activism and how this sometimes reinforces (or at least fails) to challenge wider social, economic, and political conjectures.[3]

As we attempt to stimulate this new thinking, however, we must first dare to become critics of ideas in which believe very deeply. Here, I think we have much to learn from theologians and scholars of religion, at least those of whom have come to see their scholarship as a struggle with their own traditions – as a struggle with the exclusionary aspects and troublesome effectual history of ideas and texts that they nonetheless may regard on a personal level as sacred.[4]

In this chapter, my struggle is what has become a particularly sacred aspect of contemporary child rights discourse: the rights of participation. Participation rights are frequently cited as being among the most innovative aspects that the CRC brought to the field of children's rights. Especially Article 12 – which concern's the child's right to have a say in matters of his or her concern – is frequently held forth as a symbol of an enlightened understanding of the child as an active social agent, not just in future days when he or she reaches the

1 Josefsson, J., *Children at the Borders* (Linköping University, 2016).

2 See also Holzscheiter, A., Josefsson, J., and Sandin, B., 'Child Rights Governance: An Introduction', *Childhood* 26, no. 3 (2019): 271–88.

3 In this respect, my perspective is similar to that of Moyn, S., 'A Powerless Companion: Human Rights in the Age of Neoliberalism', *Law & Contemp. Probs.* 77 (2014): 147–169.

4 See, for instance, Svartvik, J., *Bibeltolkningens bakgator: Synen på slavar, judar och homosexuella i historia och nutid* (Jönköping: Verbum, 2006).

age of majority, but in the here and now. Children's participation rights in general, and Article 12 in particular, have given rise since the mid-1990s to a whole corpus of material, from practical handbooks and workshops to serious scholarship. While this literature escapes an easy overview, it is made up to a large degree by works that offer practical advice on how to implement and monitor these rights in various social, political, and juridical settings, from schools to courtrooms.[5]

Let me first be clear that I think there are good reasons for holding that children should have rights that are typically associated with the concept of participation. After all, children are human beings. To the extent that rights such as freedom of expression, freedom of religion, freedom of assembly, freedom of information, and the right to a fair trial can be defended as human rights, they ought to apply to young people as well. It is also evident that initiatives aimed at advancing children's participation rights can be valuable in making public and private institutions more child-focused and child-inclusive. Children's participation rights can serve as reminders that even very young children are often more capable of expressing their own needs and interests than is commonly assumed, and that we must always meet children with at least the same amount of dignity and respect that we owe to other human beings.[6]

That said, the topic of children's participation rights also gives rise to a set of conceptual and practical issues that child rights scholars and activists need to bear in mind and grapple with in their work. The challenges ahead are not just about improving implementation, enforcement, and evaluation of these ideals. We must think about the relationship between children's rights and the broader social, economic, and political conditions in which such rights are articulated and institutionalized. Moreover, I think we have reason to be wary of the more fundamental conceptual issues that either comprise attempts to advance children's participation rights or arise as unintended consequences of such attempts.

I have structured this chapter as a list of five such problems or issues that I think are attached to the idea and practice of children's participation rights. This list is not exhaustive; nor do I think that the list itself reflects a coherent,

5 Lansdown, G., 'The Realisation of Children's Participation Rights'. In Percy-Smith, B. and Thomas, N., (Eds.), *A Handbook of Children and Young People's Participation* (London: Routledge, 2010): 11–23.

6 Alderson, P., *Young Children's Rights: Exploring Beliefs, Principles and Practice*, (2nd ed.). (Philadelphia: Jessica Kingsley Publishers, 2008); Leviner, P., 'Barns rätt till delaktighet'. In Åhman, K., Leviner, P., and Zillén, K. (Eds.), *Barnkonventionen i praktiken: rättsliga utmaningar och möjligheter* (Stockholm: Norstedts Juridik, 2020): 102–114.

alternative idea of children's rights. These problems are not visible when we use only one specific, theoretical standpoint. Rather, they involve both the idea of child participation as it is generally articulated, as well as the unintended consequences of trying to move from idea to practice.

2 Children's Participation Rights Are Often Confused with Participation as Such

A common way of describing the concept of a 'right' in moral and political philosophy is to say that it refers to claims that persons have *to* certain rights objects (e.g. bodily integrity, due process, the right to vote) and *against* a certain duty bearer (e.g. the state). When we say that children have a right to participation, participation becomes the object of that right. However, participation is only one component of the equation. We must also pin down the identity of the rights-bearing subject, this subject's claims (e.g. moral, political, or legal), and against whom such claims can legitimately be addressed. When we talk about rights, the idea at work is not just the quality or the character of the rights object, but the general status of the rights-bearing subject in society.[7]

Another crucial aspect is that the rights bearer does not have to make use of his/her right in order to have it realized. I can have a right to vote in an election, for instance, but may choose not to make use of that right. This means that if you want to know whether I have a right to vote, you cannot take my actual voting – or not voting – as your indicator. The same goes for the right to freedom of expression, which includes a right to speak up, but also a right to be silent. You might also think of the right to freedom of religion, which includes a right to worship in private or public, but also a right to keep one's beliefs to oneself.

These may seem like rather obvious points. Nonetheless, I think the distinction between participation rights and participation as such is often over overlooked by child rights scholars and practitioners. We tend to think that any instance where children successfully take part in decision-making is a sign that their rights are being realized.

A telling example is Roger Hart's 1992 essay on children's participation in community projects. Hart's text counts as one of the founding texts for the post-1989 child rights movement, especially because it contains what has

7 Feinberg, J., 'The Nature and Value of Rights', *The Journal of Value Inquiry* 4, no. 4 (1970): 615–625.

become a tremendously influential model for evaluating the extent and quality of children's participation: the so-called children's participation ladder.[8]

If we take a close look at Hart's essay, we see that he begins by citing the CRC and its Article 12 on the right to be heard. This is one of the few occasions in his text, however, where the concept of rights appears. The remainder is devoted to descriptions of more or less successful attempts of getting children involved in cooperative projects with adults, which Hart views as essential for assuring not only children's status as social agents in the present moment but their development towards becoming active and responsible citizens in the future.[9] The goal is not to create a right to participation, but to get children to participate.

What is lacking, therefore, not just in Hart's analysis but in so much of the related literature on children's participation rights, is an analysis of the institutional framework that is needed to make participation into a right rather than a mere act of goodwill that state representatives, community organizers, social workers, and parents can withdraw at will. I am aware of how much has been written in criticism of Hart's participation ladder, including by Hart himself, who recently declared that the participation ladder was obsolete. Still, I think the point is of broader relevance. Just getting children involved in particular processes does not mean that we have actually realized their *rights*.

3 There Is No Clear Definition of What Counts as Participation

The concept of participation rarely appeared in the drafting of the CRC. It is mentioned in only a few passages of the final text, such as in Article 23 on the rights of children with disabilities. Indeed, the word *participation* does not feature in Article 12, although this article subsequently came to be viewed as the Convention's most central statement on precisely this topic.

From a historical standpoint, it is curious that Article 12 has become so significant to child rights scholars and activists. Article 12 was one of the earliest articles to be adopted by the Working Group that drafted the CRC. It emerged from a series of debates in the early 1980s that principally revolved around the responsibility of the state vis-à-vis the child and his or her family. Whereas state-socialist delegates like Poland and the Soviet Union argued that states had a far-reaching responsibility for the child's welfare, a group of Western

8 Hart, Roger A., *Children's Participation: From Tokenism to Citizenship* (Florence: UNICEF, 1992).

9 Hart, R. (1992).

delegates (headed by the United States) insisted that the state mainly had a negative responsibility to respect basic liberties of speech, assembly, and religion. From the Western standpoint, the principal concern was not to advance a particular understanding of childhood, but to make sure that the Convention would not compromise already existing international standards on civil and political rights. It was through these Cold War-infected tensions around the relationship between the state's positive and negative duties and the relationship of economic, social, and cultural rights on the one hand, and civil and political rights on the other that Articles 12–16 of the CRC emerged.[10]

According to Nigel Cantwell, who followed the debates up close as a representative of Defence for Children International, Article 12 was crafted to address individual cases which involved some kind of formal decision that was of immediate relevance to a particular child, for instance in court or administrative proceedings or with regards to medical treatments. It was an article with a very specific area of application. It was not intended as a means of recognizing children as political subjects.[11]

It was only in the late 1980s that a group of NGOs and UNICEF officials began to speak of Article 12 and the ensuing clauses on civil rights in reference to the concept of participation. The aim at that time was simply to develop a heuristic device that would explain the Convention's principal message to international development experts, especially within UNICEF and the World Health Organization. The decision to group Article 12 with the other 'participation rights' of Articles 13–16 did not, in other words, represent a coherent philosophy of children's human rights, but merely a haphazard attempt to explain the Convention to a very specific audience.[12]

Therefore, the extent to which the concept of participation provides a fair description of the normative content in CRC Articles 12–16 is not clear. Article 12(1) evidently lends itself to a broad range of interpretations, but still seems to indicate that children's participation rights are mainly relevant to situations that involve some form of choice or decision by an adult or public institution on behalf of the child. It assumes the presence of an adult who is capable

10 Lindkvist, L., 'The Child Subject of Human Rights'. In Celermajer, D. and Lefebvre, A., (Eds.), *The Subject of Human Rights* (Stanford: Stanford University Press, 2020): 211–227.

11 Cantwell, N., 'Are Children's Rights Still Human?'. In Invernizzi, A. and Williams, J., (Eds.), *Human Rights of Children: From Visions to Implementation* (London: Routledge, 2011): 37–59.

12 Cantwell, N. (2011); Quennerstedt, A., 'Children, But Not Really Humans? Critical Reflections on the Hampering Effect of the "3 P's"', *The International Journal of Children's Rights* 18, no. 4 (2010): 619–635.

of 1) hearing the child and 2) making and implementing decisions that are informed by the child's views. In short, Article 12 is a list of conditions that must be fulfilled when adults intervene in children's lives.

The literature on children's participation rights has been overly concerned with a view of child participation as being involved in decisions made by adults, insisting that many children and adolescents have the capacity to influence the process and outcome of such decisions. The most radical view then becomes that children sometimes have the right and capacity to make such decisions for themselves.[13]

If we also consider the other rights that are usually categorized as participation rights – such as freedom of expression and freedom of assembly – we see that they also apply to situations where children occupy a place in public life, without necessarily being heard and without becoming subjected to adult action. These rights do not require the presence of adults who actively create safe spaces, act as an audience, or take action.[14] Instead, they mainly require that adults do not arbitrarily interfere when children express themselves. The problem, however, is that these rights do not fit with models of 'genuine participation', which are usually based on interpretations of Article 12.

4 Participation Indicates Peaceful Collaboration Rather than Protest

In a fascinating book on child participation in Swedish preschools, Klara Dolk highlights cases of non-participation and more or less outspoken protests of young children in organized activities as examples of social agency and rights-claiming. I think this is an excellent example of how children's participation rights can serve a critical purpose of challenging an established order and create space for children to develop their own sense of agency and selfhood.[15]

Nonetheless, this is not the standard view in the literature on children's participation rights, which instead tends to focus on examples when children act in ways that adults register as a constructive role in collaborative projects with

---

13 See Archard, D., *Children: Rights and Childhood*, (2nd ed.) (London: Routledge, 2004): 65–70.

14 These reflect Laura Lundy's criteria for adequate child participation, see further Lundy, L., 'United Nations Convention on the Rights of the Child and Child Well-Being'. In Ben-Arieh, A., Casas, F., Frønes, I., and Korbin, J. E., (Eds.), *Handbook of Child Well-Being Theories, Methods and Policies in Global Perspective* (Dordrecht: Springer, 2014): 2439–2462.

15 Dolk, K., *Bångstyriga barn: makt, normer och delaktighet i förskolan* (Stockholm: Ordfront, 2013).

adults, such as the building of a new playground or the successful organizing of some event.

Ann Quennerstedt has shown how one problem with the so-called '3 P's' model (provision, protection and participation) is that it is not clear how it aligns with the typical categories in human rights law: civil and political on the one hand, and economic and social and cultural rights on the other. Quennerstedt claims that by using concepts such as participation instead of civil and political rights, child rights scholars and activists inadvertently help to sharpen the distinction between children's rights and the wider framework of human rights. This in turn risks creating situations where children are offered weaker protection than other human beings and are given only 'light' versions of adult rights.[16]

Such differences are obvious if we look at the CRC text; for instance, Article 14 is substantially weaker than corresponding articles on religious freedom in international human rights law. However, the concept of participation is also problematic because it gives rights such as the freedom of expression and religious freedom an almost serene character. Following Hart, the 'genuine' exercise of such rights becomes those moments when children collaborate with adults in a spirit of mutual respect and understanding. This completely strips the rights in Articles 13–16 of their revolutionary and democratic origins. Freedom of expression, religious freedom, and freedom of assembly have traditionally been rights of dissent and resistance, not rights of participation.

From a wider human rights perspective, the only true rights of participation are precisely those that are typically denied to children: the right to take part in the governing of one's polity through elections or holding of public office. This is not the place to argue that children and adolescents should have such rights, but when considered in a broader perspective, it is misleading to say that children are entitled to participate in democratic life if they do not have the right to vote.[17]

5 Children's Participation Rights Privilege Certain Forms of Subjectivity

That Article 12 of the CRC speaks of the child's right to have a say in decisions pertaining to his or her life as conditioned by 'age and maturity'. This is a

16 Quennerstedt, A. (2010).

17 Wall, J., *Give Children the Vote: On Democratizing Democracy* (New York: Bloomsbury Academic, 2021).

troubling addition to international human rights law, which before 1989 had made no explicit link between the person's capacity and enjoyment of rights. It is true that the Universal Declaration of Human Rights (1948) conjures up a notion of an idealized rights-bearer as a person of 'reason and conscience' and that when children are mentioned in earlier documents, it is usually in reference to their 'physical and mental immaturity'. Still, general human rights law includes nothing to indicate that one's personal capacity is relevant when assessing the degree of rights protection.[18] As far as I can tell, this focus on natural competence (maturity) is unique to the CRC, and becomes all the more troubling when compared to an instrument such as the Convention on the Rights of Persons with Disabilities CRPD, which sees human capabilities as arising from an interaction between the person and his or her surroundings.[19]

E. Kay M. Tisdall and others working on child participation in court proceedings and other administrative processes have shown that the degree to which children are able to have an impact in individual cases greatly depends on their ability to adapt to outside expectations on behaviour and style of argumentation. Sometimes this means presenting oneself as adult-like in terms of composure, factual accuracy, and reasoning. On other occasions, the key is to come across as more infantile and vulnerable. In other words, in cases where the child's right to have a say and be heard are put to the test, the children who tend to be privileged that succeed in adapting to outside circumstances, those who successfully play the parts assigned to them.[20]

This issue is, of course, not exclusive to children. But children's rights are the only field where the question of natural capacity is spelled out as a criterion that courts and administrative bodies should take into account when assessing the weight to be given to the subject's personal views.

18 Brandstedt, E., 'I kraft av att vara människa: Om begreppet mänskliga rättigheter'. In Arvidsson, M., Sturfelt, L., and Halldenius, L., (Eds.), *Mänskliga rättigheter i samhället* (Malmö: Bokbox, 2018): 17–34.

19 See Ralph Sandland on the relation between children's rights and the rights of persons with disabilities: Sandland, R.,. 'A Clash of Conventions? Participation, Power and the Rights of Disabled Chidlren', *Social Inclusion* 5, no 3 (2017): 93–103.

20 Tisdall, E. K. M., 'Children and Young People's Participation: A Critical Consideration of Article 12'. In Vandenhole, W., et al., (Eds.), *Routledge International Handbook of Children's Rights Studies* (London: Routledge, 2015): 185–200.

6 Children's Participation Rights Can Distract from Wider, More Pressing Issues

In a recent piece on the principle of non-discrimination in the CRC, Rebecca Stern notes how the scholarship and practice on children's rights, at least in a Swedish context, have focused on two of CRC's so-called guiding principles: the best interest of the child and the rights of participation. An unintended consequence of this, Stern notes, is that child rights scholars and practitioners often overlook other aspects of children's rights, most notably the right to life and development and the principle of non-discrimination, which have also been included among the CRC's guiding principles.[21]

In a broader sense, I think it is essential to avoid thinking of children's rights as an isolated issue. We cannot fully safeguard the rights of children unless we also safeguard the rights of other persons in the communities to which they belong. For instance, we cannot address the child's right to adequate housing without simultaneously addressing the social and economic rights of their caregivers. The same goes for the rights that we associate with participation. If we are serious about seeking to promote children's rights of participation, we must also think hard about such general challenges to democratic life as shrinking civil space, the normalization of disinformation and hate speech, structural racism, and so on. In addition, if we are serious about trying to improve the opportunities for children's participation in society, we must also be alert to the general decline in areas such as party membership and the dwindling faith in democratic institutions in many liberal democracies.

It is difficult to see how developing more sophisticated theories and assessment models for children's participation rights could provide any solution of value. Rather, such models generally crystallize the view that children's participation rights form a separate issue, requiring specific techniques of implementation and that children must be approached differently from other human beings. A crucial challenge for child rights scholars and activists alike, in other words, is to link their pursuits to wider struggles for social and economic justice and inclusion, and thus dare to make children's rights into a matter not only of law and ethics, but of politics as well.

21 Thorburn Stern, R. 'Skydd mot diskriminering'. In Åhman, K., Leviner, P., Zillén, K. (Eds.), *Barnkonventionen i praktiken: rättsliga utmaningar och möjligheter* (Stockholm: Norstedts juridik, 2020): 51–71.

7 Conclusion

In this chapter, I have suggested that the topic of children's participation rights gives rise to a host of conceptual and practical problems concerning the relationship between children's rights and the wider fields of human rights and democracy. Again, my point is not to suggest that we ought to abandon the rights laid down in the CRC. As several of the chapters in this volume confirm, the Convention – including its enigmatic Article 12 on the right to be heard – can sometimes serve as potent tools for challenging situations when children are stereotyped and excluded from processes and decisions of their concern. Nevertheless, I also think there are strong reasons to look beyond the CRC and its commentary, if we are serious about the truism that children's rights are human rights. This looking beyond involves becoming acquainted with other parts of international human rights law and policy, such as the CRPD, which in sharp contrast to the CRC rejects the very idea that one's perceived maturity and mental capacity should determine the degree to which one is allowed to exercise fundamental rights. I also think this looking beyond can involve becoming more aware of the social and political conditions under which rights are either realized or compromised. Personally, I have become increasingly convinced that the most pressing challenges to children's active participation in society today are not just the prevailing negative attitudes toward children and their capacities. The more existential challenges to children's rights, I think, are tied to the much wider crises of human rights and democratic life that have become manifest in recent years, and which have been fuelled by right-wing populism, increased surveillance, shrinking civil space, and rising social and economic inequality. In taking such a broader view, we see how children's rights cannot be addressed in isolation. Only in a just and democratic society can children's rights become real and meaningful.

References

Alderson, Priscilla. 2008. *Young Children's Rights: Exploring Beliefs, Principles and Practice*. Philadelphia: Jessica Kingsley Publishers.

Archard, David. 2004. *Children: Rights and Childhood*. London: Routledge.

Brandstedt, Eric. 2018. "I kraft av att vara människa: Om begreppet mänskliga rättigheter", in Malin Arvidsson, Lina Sturfelt, and Lena Halldenius (Eds.), *Mänskliga rättigheter i samhället*, 17–34. Malmö: Bokbox.

Cantwell, Nigel. 2011. "Are Children's Rights Still Human?", in Antonella Invernizzi, and Jane Williams (Eds.), *Human Rights of Children: From Visions to Implementation*, 51–70. London: Routledge.

Dolk, Klara. 2013. *Bångstyriga barn: makt, normer och delaktighet i förskolan*. Stockholm: Ordfront.

Feinberg, Joel. 1970. "The Nature and Value of Rights", *The Journal of Value Inquiry* 4(4): 615–625.

Hart, Roger A. 1992. *Children's Participation: From Tokenism to Citizenship*. Florence: UNICEF.

Holzscheiter, Anna, Jonathan Josefsson, and Bengt Sandin. 2019. "Child Rights Governance: An Introduction", *Childhood* 26(3): 271–288.

Josefsson, Jonathan. 2016. *Children at the Borders*. Linköping University Press.

Lansdown, Gerison. 2010. "The Realisation of Children's Participation Rights", in Barry Percy-Smith and Nigel Thomas (Eds.), *A Handbook of Children and Young People's Participation*, 11–23. London: Routledge.

Leviner, Pernilla. 2020. "Barns rätt till delaktighet", in Karin Åhman, Pernilla Leviner, and Kavot Zillén (Eds.), *Barnkonventionen i praktiken: rättsliga utmaningar och möjligheter*, 102–114. Stockholm: Norstedts Juridik.

Lindkvist, Linde. 2020. "The Child Subject of Human Rights", in Danielle Celermajer, and Alexandre Lefebvre (Eds.), *The Subject of Human Rights*, 211–227. Stanford: Stanford University Press.

Lundy, Laura. 2014. "United Nations Convention on the Rights of the Child and Child Well-Being", in Asher Ben-Arieh, Ferran Casas, Ivar Frønes, and Jill E. Korbin (Eds.), *Handbook of Child Well-Being Theories, Methods and Policies in Global Perspective*, 2439–2462. Dordrecht: Springer.

Moyn, Samuel. 2014. "A powerless companion: Human rights in the age of neoliberalism", *Law & Contemp. Probs.* 77(4): 147–169.

Quennerstedt, Ann. 2010. "Children, But Not Really Humans? Critical Reflections on the Hampering Effect of the '3 p's'", *The International Journal of Children's Rights* 18(4): 619–635.

Sandland, Ralph. 2017. "A Clash of Conventions? Participation, Power and the Rights of Disabled Chidlren", *Social Inclusion* 5(3): 93–103.

Svartvik, Jesper. 2006. *Bibeltolkningens bakgator: Synen på slavar, judar och homosexuella i historia och nutid*. Jönköping: Verbum.

Thorburn Stern, Rebecca. 2020. "Skydd mot diskriminering", in Karin Åhman, Pernilla Leviner, and Kavot Zillén. (Eds.), *Barnkonventionen i praktiken: rättsliga utmaningar och möjligheter* (Stockholm: Norstedts juridik): 51–71.

Tisdall, E. Kay M. 2015. "Children and Young People's Participation: A Critical Consideration of Article 12", in Wouter Vandenhole, Ellen Desmet, Didier Reynaert, and Sara Lembrechts (Eds.), *International Handbook of Children's Rights Studies*, 185–200. London: Routledge.

Wall, John. 2021. *Give Children the Vote: On Democratizing Democracy*. New York: Bloomsbury Academic.

A Response to Linde Lindkvist

Anna Kaldal

In his chapter, Lindkvist challenges the principle of participation in Article 12 of the CRC as a statement of what children's rights essentially are. He encourages an alternative viewpoint in analysing the principle of participation in Article 12, by taking a more external and detached approach to children's rights. He asserts that several external viewpoints and theoretical standpoints are motivated because the challenges to children's participation rights involve two aspects: the idea of child participation as it is generally articulated in theory, and the unintended consequences of attempting to move from ideal to practice. He argues that letting go of the CRC as an analytical framework of children's participation rights will likely improve the quality of our scholarly output, while also making this output more relevant outside of academia.

In his analysis, Lindkvist applies five issues as external analytical viewpoints that are attached to children's participation rights: 1) the right-bearer status as a child in relation to the adult holding the power over realizing the child's rights; 2) participation being a light version of adults participation rights, e.g. not including freedom of speech, assembly, and the right to vote; 3) participation as realized through a peaceful dialogue between the adult (the power holder) and the child – and not a right to protest; 4) participation conditioned by the child's capacity (age and maturity); and 5) the risk that a narrow focus on Article 12 CRC poses of drawing attention from broader, more pressing concerns.

Lindkvist's analysis of children's right to participation thus goes beyond the wording of Article 12, the UN Committee on the Rights of the Child in its General Comments on the meaning of the article, and what he describes as child participation as it is generally articulated in theory. As a legal scholar and especially as a researcher of procedural law, my approach to children's right to participation has focused on the child's right to be heard and to have a say in decisions in legal proceedings. In these cases, the child's right to participate can be – and often is – limited by the child's capacity, motivated by the power-holder's assertion that limitation is in the best interest of the child. These two aspects – legal proceedings and influence in accordance with the child's capacity – are in line with Article 12 and the traditional interpretation of the article. Furthermore, legal doctrine traditionally does not problematize the law from an external viewpoint; it uses the law itself to analyse the law.

 | DOI:10.1163/9789004511163_017

Sweden has a rather long tradition of legislation on children's right to participate in administrative and legal proceedings. The last decades this development is related to Article 12 CRC, and because not all legal doctrine problematize the law from an external perspective, the discussion on children's participation rights has been limited in many ways to the approach that Lindkvist calls into question. His warning against using the norm itself as an analytical framework to analyse children's participation rights is therefore an important reminder to the legislator and legal scholar: loyalty to the established law itself risks standing in the way for a critical approach and therefore risks limiting a strengthening of children's rights instead of the opposite. Indeed, Lindkvist asserts, Article 12 could instead cement the view on children's participation rights presented in Article 12 being e.g. limited to court and administrative proceedings and not the child as an political subject, thus preventing further development of children's participation rights.

Having said that, we may need to ask ourselves this: Is the wording of Article 12 – the wording that narrows children's participation rights to administrative and court proceedings and gives scope for interpretation as to the child's impact on the decision – as far as the States Parties and the power holders are willing to go when it comes to children's rights? Is striving for even more change a radical political stand, or even a utopia?

In line with this, Lindqvist points to a politically sensitive issue that goes beyond the question of whether the child's right to participate according to Article 12 is limited in relation to other participation human rights. He argues that child-rights scholars and activists should pursue wider struggles for social and economic justice and inclusion, and that children's rights are not merely a question of realizing rights of children or even the rights of other persons in their respective communities. Ultimately, this is about allocation of resources and power. Bluntly put, this is in itself a political standpoint, but a standpoint that presents a less paternalistic view on children's rights, were the rights are given from the power holder to the powerless?

CHAPTER 8

Distributive Justice for Children

Lars Lindblom

1 Introduction

The debate on justice in philosophy revolves around two different problems. Roughly, the issue of retributive justice concerns the justification of punishment for crimes, whereas the problem of distributive justice has to do with who should get what goods. Large parts of the UN Convention of the Rights of the Child (CRC) can be read as spelling out what rights, resources and support children should have access to. This chapter, then, concerns distributive justice.

However, the problem of distributive justice tends to be conceptualized as a problem concerning adults. The social contract tradition in political philosophy is a case in point.[1] It takes the problem of politics to be about a group of people who gather to come to an agreement about how they should live together. They set down the principles for this in a contract to which they all agree. Underlying this approach to justice are ideas of autonomy and, especially, responsibility. To be autonomous is to be self-governing.

Usually, this ideal is set out in three assumptions. An autonomous agent is rational, informed, and not coerced.[2] If the parties to the agreement were not autonomous and hence not able to govern themselves, then it would be difficult to see the point of the contract exercise. Such assumptions of autonomy run deep in political philosophy.

One way of explaining what it is to be a child is to say that it is to be a person who has yet to develop autonomy.[3] This is also what justifies giving children education. They have a need to become informed and to develop their capacity

1 Hobbes, T., *Leviathan* (New Haven: Yale University Press, 2010); Rousseau, J., *The Essential Rousseau* (New York: Meridian Books, 1975); Rawls, J., *A Theory of Justice* (Cambridge: Harvard University Press, 1971).

2 Hannan, S., 'Childhood and Autonomy'. In Gheaus, A., Calder, G., and De Wispelaere, J., (Eds.), *The Routledge Handbook of the Philosophy of Childhood and Children* (London: Routledge, 2018): 112–122.

3 Schapiro, T., 'What is a Child?', *Ethics* 109, no. 4 (1999): 715–738. For a problematization of childhood responsibility, see Burroughs, M.D., 'Navigating the Penumbra: Children and Moral Responsibility', *The Southern Journal of Philosophy* 58, no. 1 (2020): 77–101.

for rationality. Another way of thinking about childhood is that it is a period of vulnerability.[4] If the autonomy of children is vulnerable, then it would be wrong to hold them accountable in the same way as autonomous adults.

Both ideas of childhood point in the same direction: we should not hold children responsible the same way we do adults, and perhaps we should not hold children responsible at all in this regard. This is not because children would be in some sense worse off than adults, but because they are different in a morally relevant way.[5] In this chapter, I will investigate what happens to theories of justice if children and related ideas of responsibility are taken seriously.[6] In particular, I will look at issues of equality of education through this lens.

In order to have an account of distributive justice, one needs to define both a principle of distribution and a metric of justice.[7] A principle of distributive justice specifies how things should be distributed. One example is the principle of strict equality – that each person should have an equal amount of what is valuable – but, somewhat surprisingly, equality has been understood in several different ways in recent literature.

Some have suggested that justice is about each person having a sufficient but not necessarily equal amount of what is valuable.[8] Others have proposed that equality should be understood as responsibility-catering, so that a just distribution tracks responsibility where appropriate.[9] Another approach starts from the observation that we could care about equality either because we find it important that each person gets an equal share or because we care about the situation of those who are worst off.[10] A prioritarian principle of justice then says that justice demands the distribution that is most beneficial to the least fortunate, even if this distribution is unequal. In this chapter, however, we will

4 Schweiger, G. and Graf, G., *A Philosophical Examination of Social Justice and Child Poverty* (Houndmills: Palgrave Macmillan, 2015).

5 Cf. Adami, R., Chapter 6 in this volume.

6 Cf. Leviner, P., and Holappa, T., Chapter 2 in this volume.

7 Anderson, E., 'Justifying the Capabilities Approach to Justice'. In Brighouse, H. and Robeyns, I., (Eds.), *Measuring Justice: Primary Goods and Capabilities* (Cambridge: Cambridge University Press, 2010): 81–100.

8 Frankfurt, H., 'Equality as a Moral Ideal', *Ethics* 98, no. 1 (1987): 21–43; Satz, D., 'Equality, Adequacy, and Education for Citizenship', *Ethics* 117, no. 4 (2007): 623–648.

9 Cohen, G. A., 'On the Currency of Egalitarian Justice', *Ethics* 99, no. 4 (1989): 906–944; Arneson, R., 'Equality and Equal Opportunity for Welfare', *Philosophical Studies* 56, no. 1 (1989): 77–93; Dworkin, R., *Sovereign Virtue* (Cambridge: Harvard University Press, 2000).

10 Parfit, D., 'Equality or Priority?' In Clayton, M. and Williams, A., (Eds.), *The Ideal of Equality* (London: Macmillan, 2000): 81–125.

not focus on this question,[11] but will instead investigate a set of topics that are more directly connected to how childhood may affect an account of justice.

In particular, we will focus on the metric of justice. This is an account of the goods with which the theory of justice is concerned. If we say e.g. that justice has to do with equality, then we must ask: equality of what? In the next section, we investigate how the assumption of responsibility and taking childhood seriously affect what this metric might be. Our answers there will have impact on other aspects of the theory of justice. Section three addresses the topic of time and justice; if the metric of justice involves goods that are only or especially valuable in childhood, then it seems that some costs in terms of such a metric cannot be compensated for in adulthood. Section 4 applies a distinction regarding approaches to justice – usually found in debates about economic policy – to the issue of education. Redistribution is where resources are redeployed to help out people who find themselves in a problematic situation, whereas pre-distribution is the idea that we should ensure that people have sufficient resources to avoid problematic situations.

The final section investigates whether there might be several different problems of justice, so that, for instance, one principle might be appropriate for the sphere of healthcare while some other rule may be more to the point for education. The chapter also sums up an account of distributive justice which takes children seriously by saying that the fundamental problem of justice is how to organize the main social institutions so that they cohere into a single, just system of social cooperation. This means, importantly, that e.g. the education system should be understood as working together with other important institutions like the family and the labour market. It means also that the institution of education may run on one principle of justice, but that the appropriate principle of justice for teachers may be another.

2 The Metric of Justice

If justice is about the distribution of some good, it of course becomes very important to figure out exactly what that good is. No one who has argued for equality has claimed that justice means that each person should get to watch an equal number of badminton games, or have the same number of hairs on their heads. A metric of justice should be something that is important for how

11 Cf., however, Scanlon, T. M., *Why Does Inequality Matter?* (Oxford: Oxford University Press, 2018).

one's life goes but abstract enough to avoid the specificity of amounts of badminton games. A salient idea is that justice is about welfare.

In this context, welfare usually means either happiness – to be in mental states that are inherently rewarding – or preferences satisfaction, i.e. getting what one prefers.[12] Note that this use of the term 'welfare' is distinct from the one used when we talk about the welfare state. The idea is that justice is achieved when everyone is equally happy. However, this idea is less popular than one might think; to understand why, we can turn to a much-discussed example that illustrates two things: the striking focus on the issues of adults in scholarship on the theory of justice, and the important role in this debate of the value of personal responsibility.

Assume that we have achieved equality of welfare and that there is a person – usually known as Louis – who finds that he wants to try a new approach to life.[13] In particular, he wants to be an expert on wine. He sets out to develop a very refined sense for fine wine and succeeds. However, this has a drawback: because fine wine is very expensive, he can seldom afford to have it, and this means that he will be less happy than people in general most of the time. Now, if our goal is equality of welfare and Louis is less happy than other people, then the straightforward implication is that other people should subsidize Louis's new expensive hobby. This, however, seems unfair since the inequality in welfare is the result of Louis's own choices. He is an autonomous agent and as such responsible for his actions.

Such arguments have led many political philosophers to turn instead to resourcism.[14] This is the view that the metric of justice should be a set of important resources. Views differ on exactly what these resources are, but they can include such things as money, education, and liberties. However, there is agreement on the idea that giving people resources retains the value of personal responsibility. This can be seen in the Louis case. If we start out from equality of resources, then the ideal remains satisfied – even if Louis develops an expensive taste. If justice is about resources, Louis is accountable for the tastes he develops. He will still have e.g. the same amount of money as other people, and if he had made other choices, he could have avoided the frustration he experiences.

Moreover, resourcism is neutral about the content of the good life. Autonomous persons in free societies will disagree about what the good life

---

12 Cf. Griffin, J., *Well-Being: Its Meaning, Measurement, and Moral Importance* (Oxford: Oxford University Press, 1986).

13 Dworkin, R. (2000).

14 Rawls, J. (1971); Dworkin, R. (2000).

consists of; some will decide to be religious, others will be hedonists, and yet others will think that Immanuel Kant figured it all out.[15] It would be unfair of the state to favour one of these views above the others. For reasons of both responsibility and neutrality, the metric of justice should be resources.

This line of argument seems to make good sense until one starts taking children into account. This is not only because we have discussed an example concerning wine, but rather because if children are persons who have yet to develop autonomy, they seem to fall outside the scope of justice.[16] The same holds true if we have reasons not to hold children responsible due to vulnerability.

Therefore, holding children responsible through resourcism seems unfair, and neutrality for persons who have yet to form a conception of the good life seems uncalled for. Moreover, the counterargument from expensive tastes to welfare as the metric of justice does not hold for children. The reason we moved from welfare to resources was that Louis was responsible for his choices, but if children are not yet fully autonomous, the conditions for holding them morally responsible are not satisfied. If Louis were a child that decided to take up sport fishing, there would be no reason in terms of justice to say that he should be personally responsible for the incurred costs. The argument for welfare still stands for the case of children.

This seems to create a problem for formulating a theory of the metric of justice. The reasons from adulthood do not apply to childhood and vice versa. The solution, of course, is to go for a pluralist metric of justice.[17] We could then say that what we owe as a matter of justice to adults are resources, but what we owe to children is welfare. There is one complication to this simple pluralism: children will become adults, and as future adults they need some resources in childhood, irrespective of whether these resources improve their welfare as children. Let us call such resources preparatory goods. One such paramount preparatory good is education.

However, there are other alternatives for determining the metric, the most important of which is what has come to be known as the capabilities approach.[18] This metric is concerned with what people can do and be. This is a

---

15 Rawls, J., *Justice as Fairness: A Restatement* (Cambridge: Harvard University Press, 2001).

16 Lindblom, L., 'Equality of What for Children'. In Drerup, J. et al., (Eds.), *Justice, Education and the Politics of Childhood* (Dordrecht: Springer, 2016): 89–100.

17 Cf. Cohen, G.A. (1989).

18 Nussbaum, M., *Creating Capabilities: The Human Development Approach* (Cambridge: The Belknap Press of Harvard University Press, 2011); Sen, A., *Development as Freedom* (New York: Knopf, 1999).

quite common approach to children and justice.[19] However, at first glance, the capabilities approach shares a problem with resourcism. To have a capability is to have the ability to choose a good, such as health or being able to read and write. Children, however, should have health and reading comprehension, and not just the opportunity to acquire and benefit from such functionings.

So why not just say, then, that children should have functionings and adults should have capabilities? Some may worry that a position that contains childhood welfare (or the functioning of happiness) cannot make sense in terms of justice for children. For instance, does it make sense to think of equality of education in terms of welfare, when schooling aims to prepare pupils for their future lives?

A very influential example in the literature on childhood can be used to illustrate that even education needs to concern itself with welfare. Compare two schools, one of which has a large programme for extra-curricular activities, and another that does not. However, each are equally good at providing the pupils with resources for their future lives, as measured by e.g. grades. Are the schools equally good in a way that allows us to say that equality of education is satisfied? Intuitively, we might view one school – the fun one – as better than the other. But could that amount to an injustice? Colin Macleod argues that it does: '[s]urely the difference is one that is salient from the point of view of justice since it is unreasonable to hold the children responsible for the significant differences in the quality of their childhoods'.[20] Children are owed both preparatory goods and welfare.

3 Timeframes

For the sake of argument, assume that we have agreed on thinking about distributive justice as the notion that each person should have equal resources. Now, how should we think of a situation where Bill gives Ted a birthday present? In one way, this creates an inequality in terms of resources, and seems to

---

19 Biggeri, M., and Mehrotra, S., 'Child Poverty as Capability Deprivation: How to Choose Domains of Child Well-being and Poverty'. In Biggeri, M., Ballet, J., and Comim, F., (Eds.), *Children and the Capability Approach* (Houndsmills: Palgrave Macmillan, 2011): 46–75; Domínguez-Serrano, M., del Moral-Espín, L., and Gálvez Muñoz, L., 'A Well-being of Their Own: Children's Perspectives of Well-being from the Capabilities Approach', *Childhood* 26, no. 1 (2019): 22–38; Schweiger, G. and Graf, G. (2015).

20 Macleod, C., 'Primary Goods, Capabilities, and Children'. In Robeyns, I. and Brighouse, H. (Eds.), *Measuring Justice. Primary Goods and Capabilities* (Cambridge: Cambridge University Press, 2010): 182–183.

imply that Ted should give the present back to Bill, but that would be an odd application of a theory of justice. What this example illustrates is that when developing a theory of justice, one must think about the timeframe over which justice ranges.

Two timeframes are salient here. In the example above, the timeframe was instantaneous, but a more common approach to time is to think of justice over whole lives. The standard approach in theories of justice is arguably to take the whole life into account. However, to avoid the perception that this is a very easy choice, we should note that choosing one or the other timeframe probably also depends on one's own view of the principle of justice.

Modern egalitarianism started with Rousseau, who conceived of equality as having to do with a floor of resources below which no one should fall and a ceiling above which no one should be able to go, because exceeding the ceiling would give people too much power over others.[21] If this is what we mean by equality, then we might want to say that every time someone becomes so poor that he or she falls below the threshold, or becomes wealthy enough to be too powerful, it is a problem of justice.

Nevertheless, we have some reason to focus on the whole-life view: we tend to be concerned with how whole lives go, and particularly so for children. We care about their futures. However, there is reason to think that the seemingly plausible whole-life view must be specified in more detail. We can see why this is so when we turn to the idea of how to conceive of children's welfare.

We said above that welfare is usually understood as either preference satisfaction or as being in pleasurable mental states. Now, for persons who have yet to achieve autonomy, getting their wishes fulfilled does not seem necessarily valuable, so let us focus on the mental-state view. In particular, let us look closer at an account of welfare for children, developed by Anthony Skelton, which says that such welfare 'consists in being happy in what is worthy of happiness'.[22]

Here is one reason to take such a view seriously; there is something of particular value with childhood. Specifically, it is a part of life where one has special access to what has been called the intrinsic goods of childhood.[23] Examples of

---

21 Rousseau, J. (1975).

22 Skelton, A., 'Utilitarianism, Welfare, Children'. In Bagattini, A. and Macleod, C., (Eds.), *The Nature of Children's Well-Being* (Dordrecht: Springer, 2015): 85–103, 98.

23 Brennan, S., 'The Goods of Childhood, Children's Rights, and the Role of Parents as Advocates and Interpreters'. In Baylis, F. and McLeod, C. (Eds.), *Family-making: Contemporary Ethical Challenges*. Oxford: Oxford University Press, 2014) 29–45. Cf. Brighouse, H. and Swift, A., *Family Values: The Ethics of Parent-Child Relationships* (Princeton: Princeton University Press, 2014). Cf. Aspán, M., Chapter 9 in this volume.

such goods are learning, play, discovery of the world at one's own pace, carefreeness, and unstructured time to developing capacities not related to work.[24] If it is true that we owe children a good childhood, where goodness is given by intrinsic goods of childhood, and a happy childhood, then we could combine these ideas and say that child welfare is being happy in virtue of the intrinsic goods of childhood.

If this position is true, it creates two potential problems. First, this view of welfare amounts to a form of restricted perfectionism; it combines perfectionism for children with neutrality for adults.[25] If neutrality is an important value, would this account of children's welfare conflict with justice for adults? There is reason to think that the combination of perfectionism for children with neutrality for adults can be successful. Goods like free play, learning, or carefreeness do not constrain one to become Kantian or religious as an adult. Moreover, these goods are to be complemented with neutral preparatory goods in terms of the pluralist metric we have been investigating here.

The second problem, however, will force us to revise our timeframe account. If intrinsic goods of childhood are particularly or specifically accessible in childhood, then it seems that a lack of such welfare cannot be fully compensated for in adulthood.[26] Free and carefree play seems valuable in a much more fundamental way for children than for the middle aged, so that childhood spent only studying and preparing for adulthood seems to lack something important that could not be compensated by any amount of opportunities to play at the age of 49. In terms of Macleod's school example, even if the school with the fun extra-curricular activities would provide at least a little worse preparation for adulthood, it may be the better school because it would take children's welfare interests into account.

Summing up, we have now reached the following position. The metric of justice for adults should be resources, but for children it is a combination of preparatory goods and welfare. Childhood welfare should be conceived of as happiness based on the experience of intrinsic goods of childhood. The timeframe for the adult part of the metric can be whole lives, but for childhood

---

For an overview of recent arguments regarding the value of childhood, see Gheaus, A., 'Childhood: Value and Duties', *Philosophy Compass* 16, no. 12 (2021): 1–11.

24 Gheaus, A., 'The "Intrinsic Goods of Childhood" and the Just Society'. In Bagattini, A. and Macleod, C., (Eds.), *The Nature of Children's Well-Being* (Dordrecht: Springer, 2015): 35–52.

25 Fowler, T., 'Perfectionism for Children, Anti-Perfectionism for Adults', *Canadian Journal of Philosophy* 44, nos. 3–4 (2014): 305–323.

26 Lindblom, L., 'Goods, Principles, and Values in the Brighouse, Ladd, Loeb and Swift Framework for Educational Policy-making', *Studies in Philosophy and Education* 37, no. 6 (2018): 631–645.

welfare it must be for the period during which intrinsic goods of childhood are accessible. That means that the timeframe for childhood welfare must be the period of childhood. If this is true, then justice demands that each child should have a just level of welfare.

4 Re- and Pre-distribution

Here are two ways of conceiving of policies for achieving distributive justice: helping people out of poverty or ensuring that people do not fall into poverty.[27] In the first case, we talk of redistribution and the second case we call pre-distribution. One can see the difference in perspective play out in general economic policy. A redistributive policy would be unemployment insurance – if you become unemployed you will get economic support – whereas a pre-distributive policy would be to ensure that property rights are defined so that unemployment does not entail a potential economic disaster for the person involved. For instance, if each person has sufficient funds – e.g. through a universal basic income – to be able to handle a period of unemployment, then the labour market as an institution will be designed so that there is less or little potential for people to fall into destitution.

Unemployment insurance may seem to have little bearing on justice for children, so here is an example from the educational sphere. Dyslexic pupils can get access to technical solutions such as reading and speech-to-text software. Should such aid be available to all pupils ahead of time or given out on a need basis? In other words, should we take a pre- or redistributive approach to this issue? It might be an open question as to which approach is more suitable for adults, but there seems to be a strong case for thinking about justice for children in a pre-distributive manner.

A reason to prefer redistribution is that it assumes responsibility in distributive justice. As we have seen, however, we have reason to think differently about holding children responsible. That seems a *prima facie* reason for taking a pre-distributive approach to educational equality. There may also be positive reasons for doing so. Pre-distribution seems to fit better with ideals of relational equality. If it is a goal of justice to ensure that people should see themselves as equal and act accordingly, then this goal would be better served in a society where peoples' needs are not consistently assessed, and assistance doled out after such assessments.[28] Developing a school system where some

27 Rawls, J. (2001).

28 Anderson, E., 'What is the Point of Equality?', *Ethics* 109, no. 2 (1999): 287–337.

pupils are not singled out needlessly as requiring special assistance seems preferable from this perspective.

An important upshot of this debate is that thinking about justice can mean thinking about institutions and how they should be designed, not just about who should get which resources here and now. This is also a lesson from the dyslexia example. For policy regarding children, a pre-distributive approach seems especially suitable.

5 Spheres of Justice

However, perhaps the search for *a* theory of justice is misguided. Michael Walzer suggests that we should conceive of society as consisting of a set of spheres of justice.[29] Justice in healthcare may concern medical needs, whereas just wages could be understood in terms of reward. Indeed, sometimes this is how we think about education; an equal education might be one that gives each pupil equal grades or sufficient knowledge to handle society as a citizen and employee. But in that case, what might be the correct principle for this sphere?

We can investigate this by turning to Christopher Jenck's useful example of Ms. Higgins.[30] She is thinking about how, as a teacher, she should go about making sure that she is treating the pupils in her classroom fairly. She starts from the assumption that she ought to spend an equal amount of time on each pupil, but then starts to wonder whether this is really fair when some pupils work harder than others. The harder-working students seem to deserve more attention – but then again, motivation seems to be a function of social background, which is a matter of luck, not choice. Therefore, it seems to Ms. Higgins that justice demands that she compensates for such luck of the draw.

However, if the result of nurture is the consequence of a kind of lottery, it seems that the outcome of nature is also the consequence of a lottery. Ms. Higgins decides to compensate for both lotteries, but soon finds that this is a practically impossible task, not the least for informational reasons. Therefore, she turns to the more practical approach of rewarding effort and indirectly punishing lack of effort. Finding the proper balance, however, turns out to be as complicated here as with the natural and social lottery. In the end, Ms.

29 Walzer, M., *Spheres of Justice: A Defense of Pluralism and Equality* (New York: Basic Books, 1983).

30 Jencks, C., 'Whom Must We Treat Equally for Educational Opportunity to be Equal?', *Ethics* 98, no. 3 (1988): 518–533.

Higgins decides to share her time equally between all pupils, but that just brings us back where we started.

Justice in the sphere of education is difficult, but perhaps we can make headway if we return to a point made above. Was not justice supposed to be about how institutions are organized? Here is one way to think about different kinds of problems of justice. We can make distinctions between global, domestic, and local justice.[31] Global justice as the name indicates, is about what a just world would be. Oftentimes, when we think about justice in general, we tend to think of how individual countries should be organized to be considered just. This would be a question of domestic justice.

If one takes this approach, then the fundamental problem of justice is how to organize the main social institutions so that they cohere into a single, just system of social cooperation. This means that the education system should be understood as working together with other important institutions such as the family and the labour market. Ms. Higgins is trying to handle the third kind of justice problem: that of local justice. This is the problem of how to act justly within institutions. Now, one can choose from several ways to create coherence between these levels. For instance, one could take the global level as fundamental and try to derive justice on the other levels from the demands of global justice. Here, however, let us take the following approach. Because the world is organized through countries and the way the country that we live in has a fundamental, comprehensive effect on how our lives turn out, we can take domestic justice as our starting point.

What would that mean for the account of justice we have sketched? It would mean that justice is about how we organize the institutions of society into one coherent whole, based on principles of justice that concern resources for adults and preparatory goods and welfare for children, while taking a pre-distributive perspective on policy. Importantly, we use a whole life timeframe for resources, but apply a childhood timeframe for children's welfare. This, then, sets the institutional background for Ms. Higgins's problem.

The educational system and the classroom are part of a larger system of institutions that should be organized so that justice in society prevails. The question is now how Ms. Higgins should act in the classroom according to a principle of local justice, given a just intuitional framework. One approach would be that the same principle of justice should guide both institutional design and local justice, but perhaps how Ms. Higgins should act as a teacher

31 Rawls, J. (2001).

is distinct from the question of how the institution of the educational system should be designed.

Assume that family law, the tax system, housing, and schools are organized to ensure that each child achieves a sufficient level of resources and welfare. For the educational system, this would mean that the curriculum, potential school choice systems, provision of course materials, quality of school premises, school lunches, access to educational aids, etc. all are provided with this goal in mind.[32] What, then, would be the best conception of the teacher's role?

There seem to be two conditions on such a principle of local justice: 1) it should work in tandem with the principles of domestic justice, and 2) it should express equal concern and respect for each person. The first condition is motivated by the importance of not undermining domestic justice. The second condition expresses the common idea that whatever justice is, it must be understood as assessing each life as equally important.[33]

These conditions suggest that a principle not considered by Ms. Higgins in the scenario described above, namely the prioritarian principle of helping the pupil who most needs help, might be an appropriate principle of local justice for education. Such a principle would support domestic justice in that it would help achieve the goal, on the domestic level, of assuring that each pupil is brought above the threshold of resources and welfare. It would express respect by providing help to each person who needs it and concern by taking their needs as a basis for giving help. Moreover, it seems an appropriate principle for children because it is not responsibility-sensitive. Children are not responsible for their need of help. In other words, if this account is correct, Ms. Higgins should devote her time, on the basis of a principle of local justice, to helping the children who need the most help.

Distributive justice for children asks different questions than justice for adults. Taking children seriously when developing an account of justice means that we must rethink our assumptions of autonomy and responsibility, reform our accounts of the metric of justice and of timeframes, and take a second look at our approaches to re- and pre-distribution as well as the spheres of justice.

References

Anderson, Elizabeth. 1999. "What is the Point of Equality?", *Ethics* 109(2): 287–337.

32 See Lindkvist, L., Chapter 7 in this volume.

33 Cf. Dworkin, R. (2000).

Anderson, Elizabeth. 2010. "Justifying the Capabilities Approach to Justice", in Harry Brighouse, and Ingrid Robeyns (Eds.), *Measuring Justice: Primary Goods and Capabilities* 81–100. Cambridge: Cambridge University Press.

Arneson, Richard. 1989. "Equality and Equal Opportunity for Welfare", *Philosophical Studies* 56(1): 77–93.

Biggeri, Mario, and Santosh Mehrotra. 2011. "Child Poverty as Capability Deprivation: How to Choose Domains of Child Well-being and Poverty", in Mario Biggeri, Jérôme Ballet, and Flavio Comim (Eds.), *Children and the Capability Approach,* 46–75. Houndmills: Palgrave Macmillan.

Brennan, Samantha. 2014. "The Goods of Childhood, Children's Rights, and the Role of Parents as Advocates and Interpreters", in Françoise Baylis, and Carolyn McLeod (Eds.), *Family-making: Contemporary Ethical Challenges*. Oxford: Oxford University Press.

Brighouse, Harry, and Adam Swift. 2014. *Family Values: The Ethics of Parent-Child Relationships*. Princeton: Princeton University Press.

Burroughs, Michael D. 2020. "Navigating the Penumbra: Children and Moral Responsibility", *The Southern Journal of Philosophy* 58(1): 77–101.

Cohen, G.A. 1989. "On the Currency of Egalitarian Justice", *Ethics* 99(4): 906–944.

Domínguez-Serrano, Monica, Lucia del Moral-Espín, and Lina Gálvez Muñoz. 2019. "A Well-being of Their Own: Children's Perspectives of Well-being from the Capabilities Approach", *Childhood* 26(1): 22–38.

Dworkin, Ronald. 2000. *Sovereign Virtue*. Cambridge: Harvard University Press.

Fowler, Timothy. 2014. "Perfectionism for Children, Anti-Perfectionism for Adults", *Canadian Journal of Philosophy* 44(3–4): 305–323.

Frankfurt, Harry. 1987. "Equality as a Moral Ideal", *Ethics* 98(1): 21–43.

Gheaus, Anca. 2015. "The Intrinsic Goods of Childhood' and the Just Society", in Alexander Bagattini, and Colin Macleod (Eds.), *The Nature of Children's Well-Being,* 35–52. Dordrecht: Springer.

Gheaus, Anca. 2021. "Childhood: Value and Duties", *Philosophy Compass* 16(12): 1–11.

Griffin, James. 1986. *Well-Being: Its Meaning, Measurement, and Moral Importance*. Oxford: Oxford University Press.

Hannan, Sarah. 2018. "Childhood and Autonomy", in Anca Gheaus, Gideon Calder, and Jurgen De Wispelaere (Eds.), *The Routledge Handbook of the Philosophy of Childhood and Children,* 112–122. London: Routledge.

Hobbes, Thomas. 2010. *Leviathan*. New Haven: Yale University Press.

Jencks, Christopher. 1988. "Whom Must We Treat Equally for Educational Opportunity to be Equal?", *Ethics* 98(3): 518–533.

Lindblom, Lars. 2016. "Equality of What for Children", in Johannes Drerup, Gunter Graf, Christoph Schickhardt, and Gottfried Schweiger (Eds.), *Justice, Education and the Politics of Childhood,* 89–100. Dordrecht: Springer.

Lindblom, Lars. 2018. "Goods, Principles, and Values in the Brighouse, Ladd, Loeb and Swift Framework for Educational Policy-making", *Studies in Philosophy and Education* 37(6): 631–645.

Macleod, Colin. 2010. "Primary Goods, Capabilities, and Children", in Ingrid Robeyns, and Harry Brighouse (Eds.), *Measuring Justice. Primary Goods and Capabilities*, 174–192. Cambridge: Cambridge University Press.

Nussbaum, Martha. 2011. *Creating Capabilities: The Human Development Approach*. Cambridge: The Belknap Press of Harvard University Press.

Parfit, Derek. 2002. "Equality or Priority?", in Matthew Clayton, and Andrew Williams (Eds.), *The Ideal of Equality*, 81–125. London: Macmillan.

Rawls, John. 1971. *A Theory of Justice*. Cambridge: Harvard University Press.

Rawls, John. 2001. *Justice as Fairness: A Restatement*. Cambridge: Harvard University Press.

Robeyns, Ingrid. 2003. *The Capability Approach: An Interdisciplinary Introduction*. Amsterdam: Mimeo.

Rousseau, Jean-Jacques. 1975. *The Essential Rousseau*. New York: Meridian Books.

Satz, Debra. 2007. "Equality, Adequacy, and Education for Citizenship", *Ethics* 117(4): 623–648.

Scanlon, Thomas M. 2018. *Why Does Inequality Matter?* Oxford: Oxford University Press.

Schapiro, Tamar. 1999. "What is a Child?", *Ethics* 109(4): 715–738.

Schweiger, Gottfried and Gunter Graf. 2015. *A Philosophical Examination of Social Justice and Child Poverty*. Houndmills: Palgrave Macmillan.

Sen, Amartya. 1999. *Development as Freedom*. New York: Knopf.

Skelton, Anthony. 2015. "Utilitarianism, Welfare, Children", in Alexander Bagattini, and Colin Macleod (Eds.), *The Nature of Children's Well-Being*, 85–103. Dordrecht: Springer.

Walzer, Michael. 1983. *Spheres of Justice: A Defense of Pluralism and Equality*. New York: Basic Books.

A Response to Lars Lindblom

Pernilla Leviner and Tim Holappa

In the chapter 'Distributive Justice for Children', Lars Lindblom challenges theories of justice from a child perspective. This is significant, as issues of distributive justice tend to be conceptualized as involving only adults and not children. Lindblom poses the question of what happens with such theories if children are taken seriously. The educational setting is used to highlight broader issues of equality for children. Against the backdrop of various principles and approaches to justice, Lindblom investigates how a child-focused view could affect our account of justice.

Four aspects of justice are investigated in the chapter: 1) the metrics of justice, i.e. the goods with which the theory of justice is concerned; 2) the timeframe taken into account, in which the 'whole-life perspective' is contrasted with a view of childhood as an important period in itself; 3) re- and predistribution as ways of differentiating between helping people up or preventing people from falling; and 4) the different spheres of justice in which society is divided.

Lindblom concludes that in order to take justice for children seriously, the prioritarian principle would be an appropriate perspective on justice. In the education setting, this would entail teachers helping students who most need help as the best means of achieving the goal: to bring each pupil above the threshold. In a broader sense, need is thereby the basis for providing help, and the strength of this approach to justice is that it also acknowledges that children are not responsible for their need for help.

From a legal, not the least a welfare law, perspective, Lindblom's analysis is very interesting. It challenges the 'go-to' notion of formal justice in public administrative law as it is found in the Swedish setting – namely of justice being achieved through legal certainty in the exercise of public power. The basis for this notion of justice specified in our constitution, the Instrument of Government (Section 1:9), is that everyone is equal before the law and that courts and public authorities are to observe objectivity and impartiality.[1] In other words, justice within the sphere of the exercise of public authority is achieved when like cases are treated alike; this notion, at least, is what is most

1 Bull, T. 'Objektivitetsprincipen'. In Marcusson, L. (Ed.), *Offentligrättsliga principer* (4th ed.). (Uppsala: Iustus förlag, 2020).

DOI:10.1163/9789004511163_019

often discussed in the Swedish legal literature.[2] Less discussed, but very central in welfare law and highlighted in Lindblom's chapter, is whether the administration and decisions by public authorities, from the perspective of the legal system and legislation, provide equal opportunities and the prerequisites for a good life. Indeed, ethical and legal principles do exist in certain areas of the legal system concerning welfare, for example, within healthcare, principles demand that those who are most sick receive care first (Section 3:1 Healthcare Act, *hälso- och sjukvårdslagen*). This can be seen as giving an expression for justice.[3] Another example can be found in the discussions regarding priorities during the Covid-19 pandemic; it was considered obvious that those who were most vulnerable were to be vaccinated first, etc.

It can be noted here that Lindblom's analysis of justice underscores new aspects in the discussion of how we view children and childhood during the pandemic. For example, it has been reported that child healthcare needed to take a back seat to allow its resources to be used in the care of adult Covid-19 patients. This can be questioned from the perspective of childhood as a particularly important (and brief) period. A child who must wait three months for an operation can experience a significantly greater negative effect than an adult with this same waiting period, as the wait could greatly delay a child's development.[4]

Relating to the Swedish legal view of justice, the concept of substantive justice within the field of welfare law can be discussed in contrast to the overarching focus on formal legal certainty that arguably dominates Swedish public-law discussions. In addition to living up to the formal requirements that are typically given as important principles for legal certainty, a decision in welfare law must be compatible with ethical requirements. It has been argued that for the exercise of public power by government authorities to be considered as substantively legally certain, the welfare state ought to focus on and protect the needs and interests of individuals, and that economic support is to be given based on substantive equality.[5] As legal support for this claim, reference

2 Marcusson, L. 'Förvaltningsrättens rättssäkerhetstänkande', *Förvaltningsrättslig tidskrift* 3 (2010): 141–154.

3 Legislative Bill 1996/97:60.

4 Dahlqvist, J., and Leviner, P., 'Barns rätt till liv, överlevnad och utveckling'. In Åhman, K., Leviner, P., and Zillén, K. (Eds.) *Barnkonventionen i praktiken – utmaningar och möjligheter* (Stockholm: Norstedts juridik, 2020): 91–101.

5 Gustafsson, H., *Rättens polyvalens, en rättsvetenskaplig studie av sociala rättigheter och rättssäkerhet* (Gothenburg: Göteborgs universitet, 2003); Bäckman, T., *Gynnande besluts negativa rättskraft och rättssäkerhet: för människor med funktionsnedsättning inom rättsområdena SoL och LSS* (Gothenburg: Göteborgs universitet, 2013).

is often made to Section 1:2 of the Instrument of Government, which prescribes that public power is to be exercised with respect to the equal worth of all and the liberty and dignity of the individual.[6] With respect to the right to support according to the Social Services Act (*socialtjänstlagen*) that we discuss in our chapter in this anthology, the starting premise for the decision-maker must be the needs of the individual. Support is in turn to be structured so that the individual achieves an adequate standard of living – something that can be seen as an expression for a form of substantive justice.[7]

In the Swedish welfare law discussion on substantive legal certainty in the welfare state, the child perspective is noted to a great degree by its very absence. In our chapter, we attempt to problematize the regulations and application of social economic support in connection to children. Based on Lindblom's analysis of children's rights and distributive justice, we also find that when it comes to adequate living conditions, additional questions can be raised when justice for children is taken to its limits, as opposed to when it is a question of justice for adults. As we point out in our chapter, requirements that can appear reasonable when imposed on adults are neither reasonable nor proportional when assessed from a child perspective.

It is important to note that as children cannot be held responsible for their needs in school, they cannot be held responsible for their needs for economic support; they have the right to be supported by their parents and, ultimately, by society. Depending upon the perspective of justice that is taken into account, the legal formation of the child's right to support can be discussed with different approaches; if one takes a starting point in the prioritarian principle, particular attention and support should be given to the most vulnerable children first. Children's rights clearly challenge our welfare system, but they also challenge our legal view of justice – something that Lindblom illustrates very well indeed.

References

Bull, Thomas. 2020. "Objektivitetsprincipen", in Lena Marcusson (Ed.), *Offentligrättsliga principer* (4th ed.). Uppsala: Iustus förlag.

6 Peczenik, A. *Vad är rätt?: om demokrati, rättssäkerhet, etik och juridisk argumentation*, (1st ed.). (Fritze, 1995), 92 and 97; Vahlne Westerhäll, L. *Den starka statens fall? En rättsvetenskaplig studie av svensk social trygghet 1950–2000* (Stockholm: Norstedts juridik, 2002), 51.

7 Vahlne Westerhäll, L. *Den starka statens fall? En rättsvetenskaplig studie av svensk social trygghet 1950–2000* (Stockholm: Norstedts juridik, 2002), 56–58.

Bäckman, Therese. 2013. *Gynnande besluts negativa rättskraft och rättssäkerhet: för människor med funktionsnedsättning inom rättsområdena SoL och LSS*. Gothenburg: Göteborgs universitet.

Dahlqvist, Julia, and Pernilla Leviner. 2020. "Barns rätt till liv, överlevnad och utveckling", in Karin Åhman, Pernilla Leviner, and Kavot Zillén (Eds.), *Barnkonventionen i praktiken – utmaningar och möjligheter*, 91–101. Stockholm: Norstedts juridik.

Gustafsson, Håkan. 2003. *Rättens polyvalens, en rättsvetenskaplig studie av sociala rättigheter och rättssäkerhet*. Gothenburg: Göteborgs universitet.

Legislative Bill 1996/97:60. *Prioriteringar inom hälso- och sjukvården* (Prop. 1996/97:60).

Marcusson, Lena. 2010. "Förvaltningsrättens rättssäkerhetstänkande", *Förvaltningsrättslig tidskrift* 3: 241–254.

Peczenik, Aleksander. 1995. *Vad är rätt?: om demokrati, rättssäkerhet, etik och juridisk argumentation* (1st ed.). Stockholm: Fritze.

Vahlne Westerhäll, Lotta. 2002. *Den starka statens fall? En rättsvetenskaplig studie av svensk social trygghet 1950–2000*. Stockholm: Norstedts juridik.

CHAPTER 9

Article 31 – the Forgotten Right to Cultural Life and the Arts

Margareta Aspán

1 Introduction

The imperative of Article 31 of the UN Convention on the Rights of the Child (CRC) is all but simple to grasp. It might be seen as a counterpoint to exploiting work and an excessively harsh and disciplining approach to a child's life. The formulations embrace the freedom of the child, and its engagement in play and participation in the surrounding world. Through Article 31, the ratifying states have agreed to *recognize* the child's right to rest and leisure, play and recreation, and free participation in cultural life and the arts, and also to *respect* and *promote* opportunities for the child to engage in cultural and artistic life. States Parties shall also 'encourage the provision of appropriate and equal opportunities for cultural, artistic, recreational and leisure activity'. How or even whether these different areas of provisions and opportunities are related to each other is not declared.

The child's activities described in Article 31 can be seen as signified by the contrasts to adulthood, with its connectedness to work, instrumentality, and obligations, as suggested by Daniel Thomas Cook.[1] The 'childness' is defined by the negations to adult activities, and accordingly established by pleasure, non-productivity, and freedom from obligations. In Cook's words, this interpretation of Article 31 reifies 'long and uncritically held associations between play and work, and child and adult, as the simple difference between /…/ obliged and unobliged activity'.[2] Is it at all possible to disentangle the confusion that has arisen in terms of play, culture, and arts in Article 31, which Cook sees in both the practices and the conceptual use of (stereotypically valued) child activities?[3]

1 Cook, D. T., 'Panaceas of Play: Stepping Past the Creative Child'. In Spyrou, S., Rosen, R., and Cook, D. T., (Eds.), *Reimagining Childhood Studies* (London: Bloomsbury Publishing Plc, 2018): 123–136.

2 Cook, D.T. (2018), 132.

3 See also Lundy, L., introduction in this volume, on the importance of children's own perspectives.

DOI:10.1163/9789004511163_020

In this chapter, I will problematize the rights to which Article 31 refers and how children are considered to be rights bearers, with a primary focus on the rights to culture and arts. Children's rights policies, such as the CRC, can of course be seen as important approaches for improving children's living conditions, as such agreements remind and urge us to take children seriously.[4] But as the CRC is the result of years of political negotiations,[5] it is equally important, as my aim is here, to scrutinize and trace the intentions behind it, as well as possible (or impossible) interpretations. This will be done by utilizing an interdisciplinary approach within studies in children's culture. Studies in children's culture embrace all the places and spaces that children inhabit and act within,[6] and are based both on social studies of childhood, such as sociological and pedagogical theorizing, and the traditions within humanities relating to aesthetics and culture politics. Studies in children's culture often include (as childhood studies) children's own perspectives on their lives, their meaning-making, and their *lived rights*,[7] or ways of *living rights*.[8] In this chapter and by contrast, I discuss adult views on childhood, that play a part in children's comprehensions of their possible positions. I do so by drawing on the concepts of *epistemic equality*, *enchantment*, and *encounters* from educational and philosophical research, as well as cultural geography. Herein, childhood is not defined as the counterpoint to adulthood. I suggest a reframing of the interpretation of Article 31 that is instead based on the similarities between adults and children in their shared and equal curiosity and creativity. Nevertheless, in this argument children's lack of experiences will not be overlooked or considered a deficiency. The child's potential lack of experience, as Manfred Liebel notes, merely 'imposes another way of thinking'.[9]

---

4 A discussion on children's rights-based approaches to policy is found in Bronagh, B., & Lundy, B., 'Children's rights-based childhood policy: a six-P framework', *The International Journal of Human Rights* 23, no. 3 (2019): 357–373. See also Freeman, M., 'Why It Remains Important to Take Children's Rights Seriously'. In Freeman, M. (Ed.) *Children's Rights: Progress and Perspectives: Essays from the International Journal of Children's Rights* (Brill, 2011).

5 See Lindkvist, L., Chapter 7 in this volume.

6 Johanson, K., 'Culture for or by the child? "Children's culture" and cultural policy', *Poetics* 38 (2010): 386–401.

7 See Karlsson, S., Chapter 10 in this volume.

8 Liebel, M., *Decolonizing childhoods: from exclusion to dignity* (Bristol: Policy Press, 2020).

9 Ibid., 167.

2 Culture and Arts: To What Child Is Article 31 Addressed?

The first draft of the CRC in 1978 did not consider all aspects that were subsequently included in Article 31, and addressed only the right to play and recreation. The suggestion to add the rights to 'freely participate in cultural life' came from Canada in 1983; this suggestion was accepted to the final draft, adopted in 1989. The addition of the right to participate freely in the arts is drawn from the UN Declaration of Human Rights. Paulo David, former Secretary of the UN Committee on the Rights of the Child, stresses that the chosen wording in the CRC of the child's *freedom* to participate in this domain points to a certain kind of child autonomy.[10]

David highlights three different meanings of the concept of culture, described as 1) culture as art, literature, music, theatre, etc. – 'the classical highbrow sense' and linked to the concept of '*cultivation*'; 2) culture as man-made *products and manifestations*, such as folk music, sports, and mass media; and 3) culture as patterns of thoughts in an *anthropological* sense.[11] Article 31 could be addressing all three, but as Article 30 explicitly concerns the child's right to enjoy culture in the sense of minority and indigenous culture, religion, and language, Article 31 supposedly denotes the other aspects. The concept of culture in Article 31, according to Rachel Hodgkin and Peter Newell, 'appears to be used in its artistic sense', whereas culture in other articles refer to customs and traditions.[12] Johan Fornäs adds another interpretation of the concept of culture as a meaning-making process, in a *hermeneutical* sense, with a connotation of culture closely linked to the anthropological concept as it, in a similar way, offers 'interpretive methods to read natural, social and cultural phenomena as meaningful "texts"'.[13]

In its General comment No. 17, the UN Committee on the Rights of the Child described in detail why the content of Article 31 is of importance in children's lives. The concept of culture seems to refer here to both the anthropological aspect of meaning-making and arts-making. The anthropological strand is shown, I would argue, when the Committee states that 'As [children] gain understanding of the cultural and artistic life around them from adult and

10 David, P., *A Commentary on the United Nations Convention on the Rights of the Child, Article 31: The Right to Leisure, Play and Culture* (Nijhoff: Brill, 2006), 28.

11 Ibid. 29–30.

12 Hodgkin, R. and Newell, P., *Implementation Handbook of the Convention of the Rights of the Child*, (3rd ed.). (Unicef, 2007), 469.

13 Fornäs, J., *Defending culture. Conceptual Foundations and Contemporary Debate* (London: Palgrave Macmillan, 2017), 52.

peer relationships, they translate and adapt its meaning through their own generational experience' and also: '[t]rough engagement with their peers, children create and transmit their own language, games, secret worlds, fantasies and other cultural knowledge'.[14] The meaning of culture as in arts is instead seen in the following:

> Participation in cultural and artistic activities are necessary for building children's understanding, not only of their own culture, but other cultures, as it provides opportunities to broaden their horizons and learn from other cultural and artistic traditions.[15]

Culture as an understanding of oneself and of others, with their own different cultures, is here seen to be reachable through one's participation in art traditions.

Through this participation, children are supposed to broaden their horizons, primarily as a distinct social category having particular (even secret) child culture and language, significantly different from those of other groups. The Committee in this comment also links Article 31 to the child's belonging to society, and to their own identity formation:

> Involvement in a community's cultural life is an important element of children's sense of belonging. Children inherit and experience the cultural and artistic life of their family, community and society, and through that process, they discover and forge their own sense of identity and, in turn, contribute to the stimulation and sustainability of cultural life and traditional arts.[16]

The Committee thus stresses the value of children's contribution to the reformulation of, and their participation in, the community into which they are born, but still presumably with a socially *different* identity.

Later in General Comment 17, there is one (1) formulation about children's own expressiveness through arts. The Committee suggests that the 'cultural and artistic expressions are articulated and enjoyed'[17] in children's everyday

14 UN Committee on the Rights of the Child. *General comment No. 17 (2013) The right of the child to rest, leisure, play, recreational activities, cultural life and the arts (art. 31)*. CRC/C/GC/17, para. 2.

15 Ibid., 5.

16 Ibid., 5.

17 Ibid., 6.

arenas, such as home, school, and public spaces; this formulation vaguely points out an approach to arts as engaging when made together with others, and not only as materials used for designated learning objectives.

Overall, the Committee's comment indicates that arts and cultural life bring children into several kinds of meaning-making processes. The children are described as contributors in their own right and in their own ongoing lives, not just for their future lives. However, General Comment 17 can also be interpreted in terms of what is missing, as in Cook's suggestion for how to understand Article 31. Nothing suggests that the *art in itself* can be seen as the very starting point for pleasure or experiencing or encountering the world. Instead, in this context it is the group of children, their demarcated and secret peer culture, that constitutes the joint reference for engagement. Play and recreation – wherein culture and arts are implicitly included – are distinctly associated with health, well-being, development, and learning.[18]

Arts according to General Comment 17, are not afforded to children as arts for arts' sake, or as enchantment, but as a platform for socialization, and primarily for predetermined learning and understanding. Cook concludes his reading of the General Comment 17 by stating that it 'reaffirms vague, oft-repeated connections between spontaneous play, creativity, learning, development, and pro-social activity'.[19] Adults are the ones defining *what* playing, learning, and development are, and *what is not* child-adequate. Through such generational ordering, the romanticized and essentialist child image persists.

To summarize, Article 31 leans at least partly on a view of childhood with specific outcomes in mind. Childhood is easily made into 'something which is to have an objective, a goal',[20] and children are still assumed to be distinctly different from other human beings, i.e. adults. However, there are ways to relate to children and childhood wherein their curiosity and being in the world are accounted for. Nigel Cantwell has suggested the need to link Article 31 (with its characteristics of fundamental freedoms) to a human-rights context.[21] Such a link was not made, I would argue, in the Committee's General Comment 17 referred to above.

After a brief look below into the concept of play and the focus on the child's development in Article 31, I will turn once again to the arts and the possibilities

18 Ibid., 4.

19 Cook, D.T. (2018), 132.

20 Ibid., 133.

21 Cantwell, N., 'Are Children's Rights Still Human?' In Invernizzi, A., and Williams, J. M., (Eds.), *The Human rights of children. From visions to implementation* (Farnham: Ashgate Publishing, 2011): 37–59.

of seeing children's and adults' experiencing and enchantment as shared in a curious encountering of the world.

3 Play as a Prioritized Activity for the Developing Child

Much has been said about the notion of play, one of the 'child-appropriate' activities mentioned in Article 31. Research from various disciplines has explored the meanings of children's play.[22] Research concerning children and arts is far from being equally as broad or profound as the work on children's play.

Article 31 has been mentioned in earlier research as an overlooked article in the CRC.[23] Nevertheless, the importance of culture and art seem to be sidelined in such debates by undue focus on the right to play.[24] To understand the reason behind the oblivion of the child's right to culture and arts, we need to problematize (in line with Cook) the prevailing conceptualizations of children as not yet social or expressive human beings. Eugeen Verhellen labelled children 'future performers' in this view, wherein children are *not yets*: 'not yet

---

22 See Andreu-Cabrera, E. et al., 'Play and childhood in ancient Greece', *Journal of Human Sport and Exercise* 5, no. 3 (2010): 339–347. Martin includes a research overview on initiatives for the right to play, see Martin, M. C., 'The state of play: historical perspectives', *International Journal of Play* 5, no. 3 (2016): 329–339. See also Colucci, E. and Wright, L., 'Moving Children's Participation Forward Through Article 31 – the Right to Play', *Canadian Journal of Children's Rights/Revue Canadienne des droits des enfants* 2, no. 1 (2015): 94–110.

23 The article 'Article 31 of the CRC. The Right to Play, Rest and Leisure: A Forgotten Right for Children?' (McNeill, 2020) only touches on the three rights objectives mentioned in the title, whereas culture and arts seem to be overlooked even when Article 31 is not. See McNeill, S., 'Article 31 of the CRC. The Right to Play, Rest and Leisure: A Forgotten Right for Children?', *The Kings Student Law Review* 10, no. 2 (2020): 1–17. Another recent study on Article 31 similarly emphasizes that it is forgotten, showing the frequently neglected importance of play – but not culture or arts – in early childhood education and care: Colliver, Y. and Doel-Mackaway, H., 'Article 31, 31 Years On: Choice and Autonomy as a Framework for Implementing Children's Right to Play in Early Childhood Services', *Human Rights Law Review* 21 (2021): 566–587.

24 McKendrick, Loebach, and Casey discuss the implementation of the right to play, drawing on the UN Committee on the Rights of the Child's General Comment No. 17 on Article 31 from 2013, relating this right to initiatives such as the International Play Association (IPA). See McKendrick, J. H., Loebach, J., and Casey, T., 'Realizing Article 31 through General Comment No. 17: Overcoming Challenges and the Quest for an Optimum Play Environment', *Children, Youth and Environments* 28, no. 2 (2018): 1–11.

knowing, not yet competent, not yet being'.[25] Such a discourse constructs children as primarily *different* but at the same time, they are *also* often expected to be 'active participants in society'.[26] The possible agency of children thus depends on how childhood is constituted in different situations, by expectations, and through narratives. The meaning of a child's agency in activities such as those mentioned in Article 31 is not a static phenomenon, as Susanne C. Ylönen shows. Agency must be contextualized, and what is considered to be *appropriate to the age of the child*, as conveyed in Article 31, is 'under constant negotiation in day-to-day interactions between children and their caretakers'.[27] If and when a child is seen as an agentic subject differs from one situation to another. In every situation the adult responsibility as duty-bearer[28] requests an awareness about conceptions of the child's maturity and capability: who do we consider capable, or mature enough, to have an opinion.[29]

4 Arts as a Possible Activity for the Creative Child

As childhood overall is unambiguously institutionalized and controlled, the school has thus come to be seen as the primary arena for children concerning experiences and expressions of the arts.[30] Another area of focus in research on

25 Verhellen, E., 'Facilitating Children's Rights in Education: Expectations and Demands on Teachers and Parents', *Prospects*, XXIX, no. 2 (1999): 223–231, 223.

26 Kjørholt, A. T., '"Imagined communities". The local community as a place for "children's culture" and social participation in Norway'. In Fog, O. K. and Gullov, E., (Eds.), *Children's places: Cross-cultural perspectives* (Milton Park: Taylor & Francis Group, 2003): 197–216, 203.

27 Ylönen, S., '"Childish" beyond Age: Reconceptualising the Aesthetics of Resistance'. In Eriksen Ødegaard, E. and Spord Borgen, J., (Eds.), *Childhood Cultures in Transformation 30 Years of the UN Convention on the Rights of the Child in Action towards Sustainability* (Leiden: Brill, 2021): 197–213, 198.

28 For a discussion about the concepts *duty-bearer* and *right-holder*, see Lundy, L., and McEvoy, L., 'Childhood, the United Nations Convention on the Rights of the Child, and Research: What Constitutes a 'Rights-Based' Approach?' In Freeman, M. (Ed.), *Law and Childhood Studies: Current Legal Issues Volume 14*, 75–91 (Oxford Univ. Press, 2012).

29 Bergström, Y., 'The Universal Right to Education: Freedom, Equality and Fraternity', *Studies in Philosophy of Education*, 29 (2010): 167–182; Lundy, L., '"Voice" is not enough: conceptualising Article 12 of the United Nations Convention on the Rights of the Child', *British Educational Research Journal* 33, no. 6 (2007): 927–942. See also Zillén, K., Chapter 5 in this volume.

30 Barton, G., (Ed.), *Literacy in the Arts: Retheorising Learning and Teaching* (New York: Springer International Publishing, 2014). See also Bresler, L., (Ed.), *Knowing bodies, moving minds: towards embodied teaching and learning. Serie:* Landscapes: The arts, aesthetics, and education; 3 (Dordrecht: Kluwer Academic, 2004); Bresler, L., (Ed.),

arts and childhood is the presumed relation between art and children's wellbeing. In such work, the concepts of *children's rights* and *children's wellbeing* have been 'twinned', according to Laura Lundy, despite the differences in both 'rationales and purposes'.[31] These concepts, notes Kay M. Tisdall, have been 'paired together' by both academics and policymakers, even if the different frameworks do not always overlap.[32]

In Sweden, as in other societies, the academic interest in children's right to arts and cultural life has increased since the 1970s, a change corresponding to society's more profound overall interest in children. According to Karin Helander, the concept of the child in the CRC refers to a child with a disposition for creativity. Helander argues that from a Nordic perspective, the democratic aims of education have been emphasized since World War II, highlighting the importance of the period of childhood and where the child became an object of national interest, 'seen as the key to the future'.[33] Helander also states that the CRC has had an impact on culture politics for children, in both policymaking and practice.[34] Since the ratification of the CRC, concepts such as the *child's perspective, participation,* and *the best interest of the child* have been adopted in cultural initiatives for children and young people. Helander attributes in part this change to the emerging interdisciplinary field of childhood studies and a renewed interest in linking several different academic understandings of children and childhood, for instance within social, cultural, psychological, and historical research.

With a basis in new research, especially on new-borns, it has become unquestionable that children are innately social and not at all *not-yets*. Neurology and cognition research have confirmed the child's abilities, for example to understand other people's emotions. Child psychologist Colwyn Trevarthen among others has described the human disposition to participate in social and cultural

---

International handbook of research in arts education (New York: Springer, 2007). Examples from Australia are discussed in Lemon, N., Garvis, S., and Klopper, C., *Representations of Working in Arts Education: Stories of Learning and Teaching* (Bristol: Intellect Books Ltd, 2014).

31 Lundy, L., 'United Nations Convention on the Rights of the Child and Child Well-Being'. In Ben-Arieh, A. et al., (Eds.), *Handbook of Child Well-Being Theories, Methods and Policies in Global Perspective* (New York: Springer, 2014): 2439–2462, 2440.

32 Tisdall, E. K. M., 'Children's Rights and Children's Wellbeing: Equivalent Policy Concepts?', *Journal of Social Policy* 44, no. 4 (2015): 807–823, 807.

33 Helander, K., 'The Child's Right to Culture and the Arts'. In Simonyi, A. and Cagan, D. L., (Eds.), *Nordic Ways* (Washington, D. C.: Brookings Institution Press, 2016): 100–104, 103.

34 Helander, K. 'Barnets rätt till kultur och konst'. In Cederborg, A.-C. and Warnling-Nerep, W., (Eds.), *Barnrätt. En antologi* (Stockholm: Norstedts Juridik, 2014): 186–198.

life as concerning everyone, from new-born to old. Trevarthen and Delafield-Butt assert that the child is born with 'the spirit of an inquisitive and creative human being, seeking understanding of what to do with body and mind in a world of invented possibilities'.[35]

It might be possible to read Article 31 of the CRC as founded – at least in part – in such a theoretical approach to children's innate capacities. Children can be seen in the CRC, according to Mai and Gibson, as 'cultural citizens'.[36] In General Comment No. 12, the UN Committee on the Rights of the Child draws a link between Article 31 and Article 12 on the child's right to participation, and the right to be heard. The General Comment establishes that 'children require play, recreation, physical and cultural activities for their development and socialization. These should be designed taking into account children's preferences and capacities'.[37] Worth noting is that arts, play, recreation, and culture constitute the basis for the child's *development* and – herein implied – the child's future, as *becoming* part of society in a socialization process. I would argue that these two main concepts – development and socialization – share an idea of a directed change. In this view, the desired outcome is always defined by adults, placing children in a position as objects for predetermined learning.

It would be reasonable to assume that any person's agency might be acknowledged in particular through experiencing and expressing art, as art according to Gert Biesta '*is* the dialogue of human beings with the world'.[38] Because culture can be interpreted as processes of collaborative meaning-making through communicative tools such as the arts, the differences between the adult and the child need not be over-emphasized.

35 Trevarthen, C. and Delafield-Butt, J., 'Intersubjectivity in the Imagination and Feelings of the Infant: Implications for Education in the Early Years'. In White, E. J. and Dalli, C., (Eds.), *Under-three Year Olds in Policy and Practice* (New York: Springer Link, 2017): 17–39, 37.

36 Mai, L. and Gibson, R., 'The rights of the putti: a review of the literature on children as cultural citizens in art museums', *Museum Management and Curatorship* 26, no. 4 (2011): 355–371.

37 UN Committee on the Rights of the Child. *General comment No. 12.* (2009) *The Right of the Child to be Heard.* CRC/C/GC/12, para. 25.

38 Biesta, G., 'What if? Art education beyond expression and creativity'. In Naughton, C., Biesta, G., and Cole, D. R., (Eds.), *Art, Artists and Pedagogy. Philosophy and the Arts in Education* (Abingdon: Routledge, 2018): 11–20, 18.

5 The Possibilities of Epistemic Justice: Encounters and Enchantments

The conventional hierarchical relationship between generations has been problematized by Karin Murris.[39] She has explored how the low status of children and childhood, in what she calls a *structural epistemic injustice,* affects all children. Her empirical study is grounded in the school arena, but the concepts are easily transferred into adult-child relations overall. Epistemic injustice corresponds here to the concept of *developmentality,*[40] ascribing irrationality to the child, and the state of being epistemically incomplete as a 'magical thinker'. For example, our commonly adopted approach to children's learning, which focuses on development, legitimizes a view of children's play in terms of how it can 'optimize' a child's improvements.[41] Murris suggests another view on the relation between the learner and the teacher, considering both as two learning subjects. Such joint meaning-making, as an open-minded approach to learning, is possible only when the participants are interrelated in a *symmetric* relation. This does not imply that they are all the same. The keyword of such a symmetry would instead be mutual respect. Research in which theories on children's development are complemented with theories on sociocultural surroundings and the child's agency might consequently turn the *developmentality approach* away from generalist theorizing to a view of children as subjects, involving their own 'stories, interests and views'.[42] This view also involves a turn to another learning theory. Learning as *change of one's perspective* points to an understanding of learning where we experience the world and see it in new ways by each *encounter* with it.[43] Such experiencing of new aspects of the world acts equally for the child and the adult. Structural epistemic injustice,

---

39 Murris, K., 'The Epistemic Challenge of Hearing Child's Voice'. *Studies in Philosophy and Education* 32, no. 3 (2013): 245–259.

40 Murris draws on the concept of epistemic injustice from philosopher Miranda Fricker. For elaboration on developmentality, see Fendler, L., 'Educating flexible souls: The construction of subjectivity through developmentality and interaction'. In Hultqvist, K. and Dahlberg, G., (Eds.), *Governing the Child in the New Millennium* (New York: RoutledgeFalmer, 2001): 119–142.

41 See also Kampmann, J., 'Children as Learners'. In Melton, G. B. et al., (Eds.), *The Sage Handbook of Child Research* (Thousand Oaks: Sage Publishing, 2013): 136–152, 140.

42 Murris cites Haynes, J., 'Listening to the voice of child in education'. In Gibson, S. and Haynes, J., (Eds.), *Perspectives on participation and inclusion: Engaging education* (London: Continuum, 2009): 27–43, in Murris, K. (2013), 254.

43 Wilson, H. F., 'On Geography and Encounter: Bodies, Borders, and Difference', *Progress in Human Geography* 41, no. 4 (2017): 451–471.

as I see it, would be maintained by excessive emphasis on a particular child culture, identity formation, and language.

Arts can give children, and indeed all of us, new experiences by shifting the experiencer's perspectives, and by challenging current understandings. Such *enchantments,* a concept from political theorist Jane Bennett, comprise a mood or a state of wonder, pointing to something meaningful and engaging.[44] It does not have to be joyful, as Pyyry stresses, and it might also be about experiencing 'a state of trouble, even fear'.[45] Even so, it refers to a feeling of 'wonder-at-the-world' or being spellbound.[46] Such moods are not age-specific, but can be stimulated in cross-generational exploration and meaning-making.

An important aspect of enchantment is that it can be encouraged intentionally, for example in school: it can 'be fostered through deliberate strategies'.[47] One main point is that the teacher must be open-minded and respond to what the children see, hear, feel, and express. Another main point is that even when we want to arrange opportunities for challenges, we never know what will happen, and that uncertainty is what makes every encounter unique. Still, adults can strive to offer children challenging or enchanting encounters. Research on children's experiences of culture and the arts can be informative far beyond children's actual encounters with drama, literature, film, or other aesthetic expressions. An interest in children's meaning-making together with adults who possess other experiences may constitute an opening to further recognition of how children use and construct knowledge about the society as a whole.

6 Conclusion: The Forgotten Rights?

David concludes in his commentary to Article 31 that the article 'may well be the most neglected provision by the CRC Committee since it started its monitoring work in 1991'.[48] If so, it is not surprising that the member states' compliance with the article has not been an important issue in any national jurisdiction. Although stated in 2006, David's critique against the CRC – that

44 Bennett, J., *The Enchantment of Modern Life: Attachments, Crossings, and Ethics* (Princeton: Princeton University Press, 2001).

45 Pyyry, N., 'Thinking with broken glass: making pedagogical spaces of enchantment in the city'. *Environmental Education Research* 23, no. 10 (2017): 1391–1401.

46 Bennett, J. (2005), 5.

47 Ibid., 4.

48 David, P. (2006), 17.

'the international jurisprudence of the CRC Committee is still very scarce and superficial' – still seems to be valid.[49] The reason that the Committee has, as David asserts, neglected Article 31, except for *General comment No. 17*, might not be due solely to lack of time or difficulties to collecting material for analysis. David points out that the matter of the right to art is considered 'a luxury', even though the importance of arts and cultural experiences, as well as play, cannot be disputed.[50]

Lundy has suggested that indicators for measuring implementation of rights must handle inequality on different levels:

> Child rights indicators must /…/ address issues of inequality and differential treatment in terms of state action, outcomes in practice and children's lived experiences.[51]

To this I also want to add Michael Freeman's insight that children's rights '[u]ltimately /…/ dissolve into questions of distributive justice'.[52] Here, we return to the matter of justice and the needed shift from the essentialist view on children and presuppositions about children's capabilities and maturity, and the need to question various forms of epistemic injustice – not least because Article 31 might be seen to embrace not only cultural rights but social and economic rights, which are underpinned by civil and political rights. In this volume, Linde Lindkvist suggests that withdrawing children's rights, as in the participation discourse, from adult's rights defined within political, social, and cultural domains, tends to maintain the distinction between generations and thus, presumably, a hierarchical positioning.

To be meaningful, children's rights must be co-constructed and handled by children themselves.[53] However, the opportunities for a child to be taken seriously and respected are not equal, but more or less dependent on personal interests of involved adults. Supposedly, if there were a profound interest in

49 Ibid., 17.

50 Ibid., 17. See further the education philosopher Maxine Greene for a discussion on why arts are of importance: Greene, M., *Releasing the imagination: essays on education, the arts, and social change* (San Francisco: Jossey-Bass, cop. 1995); Greene, M., 'Interlude 42: The arches of experience'. In Bresler, L. (Ed.), *International handbook of research in arts education* (Springer, 2007): 657–662.

51 Lundy, L. (2014), 2453.

52 Freeman, M., 'Limits of children's rights'. In Freeman, M. and Veerman, P., (Eds.), *The ideologies of children's rights* (Leiden: Martinus Nijhoff Publishers, 1992): 29–46, 41.

53 Liebel, M., 'Children's Rights as Living Rights: Why Human Rights Only Make Sense If They Are Connected to the Lives of Children', *Social Work Review* 11, no. 2 (2012): 13–26.

both research and organizations to truly understand children's views, lived experiences, and rights, the matter of culture and arts would not be so neglected.

References

Andreu-Cabrera, Eliseo, Mar Cepereo González, Fco. Javier Rojas Ruiz, and Juan J. Chinchilla-Mira. 2010. "Play and childhood in ancient Greece", *Journal of Human Sport and Exercise* 5(3): 339–347.

Barton, Georgina (Ed.) 2014. *Literacy in the Arts: Retheorising Learning and Teaching*. Cham: Springer International Publishing.

Bennett, Jane. 2001. *The Enchantment of Modern Life: Attachments, Crossings, and Ethics*. Princeton, N.J.: Princeton University Press.

Bergström, Ylva. 2010. "The Universal Right to Education: Freedom, Equality and Fraternity", *Studies in Philosophy of Education* 29: 167–182.

Biesta, Gert. 2018. "What if? Art education beyond expression and creativity", in Christopher Naughton, Gert Biesta, and David R. Cole (Eds.), *Art, Artists and Pedagogy. Philosophy and the Arts in Education*, 11–20. Oxon and N.Y.: Routledge.

Bresler, Liora (Ed.) 2004. *Knowing bodies, moving minds: towards embodied teaching and learning*. Dordrecht: Kluwer Academic.

Bresler, Liora (Ed.) 2007. *International handbook of research in arts education*. Dordrecht: Springer.

Bronagh, Byrne, and Laura Lundy. 2019. "Children's rights-based childhood policy: a six-P framework", *The International Journal of Human Rights* 23(3): 357–373.

Cantwell, Nigel. 2011. "Are Children's Rights Still Human?", in Antonella Invernizzi and Jane M. Williams (Eds.), *The Human rights of children: From visions to implementation*, 51–70. Farnham: Ashgate Pub, cop.

Colliver, Yeshe, and Holly Doel-Mackaway. 2021. "Article 31, 31 Years On: Choice and Autonomy as a Framework for Implementing Children's Right to Play in Early Childhood Services", *Human Rights Law Review* 21(3): 566–587.

Colucci, Emma, and Laura Wright. 2015. "Moving Children's Participation Forward Through Article 31 – the Right to Play", *Canadian Journal of Children's Rights/Revue Canadienne des droits des enfants* 2(1): 94–110.

Cook, Daniel Thomas. 2018. "Panaceas of Play: Stepping Past the Creative Child", in Spyros Spyrou, Rachel Rosen, and Daniel Thomas Cook. (Eds.), *Reimagining Childhood Studies*, 123–136. Bloomsbury Publishing.

David, Paulo. 2006. *A Commentary on the United Nations Convention on the Rights of the Child, Article 31: The Right to Leisure, Play and Culture*. Leiden: Martinus Nijhoff.

Fendler, Lynn. 2001. "Educating flexible souls: The construction of subjectivity through developmentality and interaction", in Kenneth Hulqvist, and Gunilla Dahlberg (Eds.), *Governing the Child in the New Millennium*, 119–142. N.Y. and London: Routledge Falmer.

Freeman, Michael D. A. 1992. "Limits of children's rights", in Michael Freeman and Philip Veerman (Eds.), *The ideologies of children's rights*, 29–46. Dordrecht: Martinus Nijhoff Publishers.

Freeman, Michael. 2011. "Why it Remains Important to Take Children's Rights Seriously", in Michael Freeman (Ed.), *Children's Rights: Progress and Perspectives: Essays from the International Journal of Children's Rights*, 5–25. Brill.

Fornäs, Johan. 2017. *Defending culture. Conceptual Foundations and Contemporary Debate.* Cham: Palgrave Macmillan.

Greene, Maxine. 1995. *Releasing the imagination: essays on education, the arts, and social change.* San Francisco: Jossey-Bass, cop.

Greene, Maxine. 2007. "Interlude 42: The arches of experience", in Liora Bresler (Ed.), *International handbook of research in arts education*, 657–662. Dordrecht: Springer.

Helander, Karin. 2014. "Barnets rätt till kultur och konst", in Ann-Christin Cederborg, and Wiweka Warnling-Nerep (Eds.), *Barnrätt. En antologi*, 86–198. Stockholm: Norstedts Juridik.

Helander, Karin. 2016. "The Child's Right to Culture and the Arts", in Andras Simonyi, and Debra L. Cagan (Eds.), *Nordic Ways*, 100–104. Washington DC.: Brookings Institution Press.

Hodgkin, Rachel, and Peter Newell. 2007. *Implementation Handbook of the Convention of the Rights of the Child.* New York: Unicef Press.

Johanson, Katya. 2010. "Culture for or by the child? 'Children's culture' and cultural policy", *Poetics* 38(4): 386–401.

Kampmann, Jan. 2013. "Children as Learners", in Gary B. Melton, Asher Ben-Arieh, Judith Cashmore, Gail S. Goodman, and Natalie K. Worley (Eds.), *The Sage Handbook of Child Research*, 136–152. Los Angeles: Sage Publication.

Kjørholt, Anne Trine. 2003. "'Imagined communities': The local community as a place for 'children's culture' and social participation in Norway", in Karen Fog Olwig, and Eva Gulløv (Eds.), *Children's places: Cross-cultural perspectives*, 197–216. London: Routledge.

Lemon, Narelle, Susanne Garvis, and Christopher Klopper. 2014. *Representations of Working in Arts Education: Stories of Learning and Teaching.* Bristol UK: Intellect Books Ltd.

Liebel, Manfred. 2012. "Children's Rights as Living Rights: Why Human Rights Only Make Sense if They Are Connected to the Lives of Children", *Social Work Review* 11(2): 13–26.

Liebel, Manfred. 2020. *Decolonizing childhoods: from exclusion to dignity*. Bristol: Policy Press.

Lundy, Laura. 2007. "'Voice' is not enough: conceptualising Article 12 of the United Nations Convention on the Rights of the Child", *British Educational Research Journal* 33(6): 927–942.

Lundy, Laura. 2014. "United Nations Convention on the Rights of the Child and Child Well-Being", in Asher Ben-Arieh, Ferran Casas, Ivar Frønes, and Jill E. Korbin (Eds.), *Handbook of Child Well-Being Theories, Methods and Policies in Global Perspective*, 2439–2462. Dordrecht: Springer.

Lundy, Laura, & Lesley McEvoy (2012). "Childhood, the United Nations Convention on the Rights of the Child, and Research: What Constitutes a 'Rights-Based' Approach?" In Michael Freeman (Ed.), *Law and Childhood Studies: Current Legal Issues Volume 14*, 75–91. Oxford Univ. Press.

Mai, Lea, and Robyn Gibson. 2011. "The rights of the putti: a review of the literature on children as cultural citizens in art museums", *Museum Management and Curatorship* 26(4): 355–371.

Martin, Mary Clare. 2016. "The state of play: historical perspectives", *International Journal of Play* 5(3): 329–339.

McKendrick, John H., Janet Loebach, and Theresa Casey. 2018. "Realizing Article 31 through General Comment No. 17: Overcoming Challenges and the Quest for an Optimum Play Environment", *Children, Youth and Environments* 28(2): 1–11.

McNeill, Sophie. 2020. "Article 31 of the CRC. The Right to Play, Rest and Leisure: A Forgotten Right for Children?", *The Kings Student Law Review* 10(2): 1–17.

Murris, Karin. 2013. "The Epistemic Challenge of Hearing Child's Voice", *Studies in Philosophy and Education* 32(3): 245–259.

Pyyry, Noora. 2017. "Thinking with broken glass: making pedagogical spaces of enchantment in the city", *Environmental Education Research* 23(10): 1391–1401.

Tisdall, E., Kay M. 2015. "Children's Rights and Children's Wellbeing: Equivalent Policy Concepts?", *Journal of Social Policy* 44(4): 807–823.

Trevarthen, Colwyn, and Jonathan Delafield-Butt. 2017. "Intersubjectivity in the Imagination and Feelings of the Infant: Implications for Education in the Early Years", in E. Jayne White, and Carmen Dalli (Eds.), *Under-three Year Olds in Policy and Practice*, 17–39. Singapore: Springer.

United Nations Committee on the Rights of the Child. *General Comment No. 12 (2009) The Right of the Child to be Heard*. CRC/C/GC/12 (20 July 2009).

United Nations Committee on the Rights of the Child. *General Comment No. 17 (2013) on The Right of the Child to Rest, Leisure, Play, Recreational activities, Cultural life and the Arts (art. 31)*. CRC/C/GC/17 (17 April 2013).

Verhellen, Eugeen. 1999. "Facilitating Children's Rights in Education: Expectations and Demands on Teachers and Parents", *Prospects* 209(2): 223–231.

Wilson, Helen F. 2017. "On Geography and Encounter: Bodies, Borders, and Difference", *Progress in Human Geography* 41(4): 451–471.

Ylönen, Susanne C. 2021. "'Childish' beyond Age: Reconceptualising the Aesthetics of Resistance", in Elin Eriksen Ødegaard, and Jorunn Spord Borgen (Eds.), *Childhood Cultures in Transformation 30 Years of the UN Convention on the Rights of the Child in Action towards Sustainability*, 197–213. Brill.

A Response to Margareta Aspán

Kavot Zillén

In 'Article 31: The forgotten right to cultural life and the arts', Margareta Aspán analyses the child's right to rest and leisure, to play and recreation, and to participate freely in cultural life and the arts, as well as the responsibilities of the state to respect and promote opportunities for the child to experience cultural and artistic life. The chapter challenges some of the stereotypical ideas and values about children's cultural activities being completely different from such activities for adults, by focusing on some of the similarities between adults and children in this regard and discussing various theoretical perspectives on the matter. As explained in Aspán's chapter, interest has grown recently regarding research on childhood and children's perspectives on their lives and the world.

However, as the author explains, these changes concerning children's own perspectives are not always recognized in the area of arts and culture, which to some degree rests on the prevailing conceptualization of children as passive human beings (or 'becomings') rather than independent right holders. These assumptions about children appear to be based on a prejudice: that children lack certain abilities and therefore are inferior to adults. This prejudice is sometimes referred to as childism.[1] To challenge these paternalistic ideas that promote stereotyping and disempowerment of children, Aspán's text illustrates how over-generalizations of children, entails a risk of undermining their possibilities to contribute and participate in the community and cultural life.

Presumptions that young people lack certain capacities or abilities can also be found not only in the judicial interpretation of law, but also in its creation. Such tendencies can even be found in the Preamble of the CRC, which stipulates that 'the child, by reason of his physical and mental immaturity, needs special safeguards and care (…)'. It could be argued that this line of reasoning is drawn from general assumptions about children's decision-making capacities – assumptions that oversimplify the truth, as individual variations in children's capacities must always be taken into consideration. Further, Aspán emphasizes the link between children's right to culture and art and their right to participation. Their opportunities to experience artistic life and be part of the construction of culture depends on their right to participation on their own terms.

1 See Adami, R., Chapter 6 in this volume.

From a child-rights perspective, it seems natural that children's right to art and culture includes genuine possibilities for children to participate in the cultural life of a society and express their own meanings through arts. Children's right to participation, set out in Article 12 CRC, is one of the core principles in the Convention and can be seen as an important prerequisite or foundation for several other children's human rights (such as the rights enshrined in Article 31). Accordingly, the realization of children's right to cultural life and arts depends on children having the right to freely express their views and facilitate their participation in all matters affecting their lives.

Unfortunately, as the chapter illustrates, there are barriers in implementing children's rights – such as the paternalistic view of children as distinctly different from other human beings. These ideas continue to influence the legal implications and interpretations of children's rights. As an example, children's legal position and their right to participation are dynamic and depend wholly on their age and increasing maturity. It can be argued that the concept of maturity and the different age standards restrict children's possibilities to participation because these concepts are constructed and interpreted from an adult perspective. As the author states in the chapter, adults are the ones who determine the definition of playing, learning, and development, and what is or is not child-adequate.

The chapter's conclusion is that children's right to culture and arts has been neglected and that the opportunities for a child being taken seriously and being respected are not equal; these opportunities are more or less dependent on the personal interest of the adult. From a legal point of view, the conclusion may be drawn that this sort of systematic stereotyping and disempowerment of children may constitute age-based discrimination, as this practice leads to different treatment in terms of the realization of the right to art and culture.

Article 2 of the CRC contains a general principle of equality and prohibition of certain forms of discrimination, including discrimination based on age. Although age limits can be lawful, the differentiation between children and adults illustrated in Aspán's article indicates fundamental challenges in balancing children's rights and needs. Since CRC entered into force 36 years ago, children's rights have gained increasing attention at international, regional, and national levels. Nevertheless, as has been stated many times before, a challenge remains: to find a proper balance between children's rights to protection and their right to participation as equal rights holders – not mere subjects of protection.

CHAPTER 10

Ethnography of Lived Rights – Methodological and Ethical Considerations When Researching Rights *with* Children

Sandra Karlsson

1 Introduction

In 2015, approximately 70,000 asylum-seeking children arrived in Sweden; some 35,000 of these children, aged mostly from infancy to 12 years, arrived with their families.[1] During this period, many families with children were housed in asylum centres. This chapter builds on a one-year ethnographic fieldwork project in 2015–2016, involving children (6–12 years old) living with their families in one of Sweden's largest asylum centres. These children arrived in Sweden during the so-called 'refugee crisis', when Swedish asylum politics moved swiftly from solidarity to enforced migration control.[2] In this political context, the human-rights perspective was abandoned, and asylum-seeking children were quite paradoxically denied their rights at a time when Sweden was planning to incorporate the UN Convention on the Rights of the Child (CRC) into its legislation.[3]

Research on children's rights has long tended to focus on CRC on a policy level instead of directing attention to the actual meanings of rights in children's everyday lives.[4] This chapter explores other perspectives, namely, ethnographic research with children and will, in particular, discuss methodological and ethical considerations when researching rights with children. The chapter discusses the following: a) the politics of ethnography with a marginalized

1 Swedish Migration Agency. *Statistik: Inkomna asylärenden* (2016).

2 Elsrud, T., Gruber, S., and Lundberg, A. (Eds.). *Rättssäkerheten och solidariteten: Vad hände? En antologi om mottagande av människor på flykt.* (Linköping: Linköping University Electronic Press, 2021).

3 Lundberg, A, 'Management of "the unaccompanied": In search of a rights-based approach in the context of Swedish "crisis politics"'. In Bhabha, J. Kanics, J and. Senovilla Hernàndez, D. (Eds.), *Research handbook on child migration* (Cheltenham: Edward Elgar Publishing, 2018): 260–278.

4 Quennerstedt, A., 'Children's rights research moving into the future: Challenges on the way forward', *International Journal of Children's Rights* 21 (2013): 233–247.

DOI:10.1163/9789004511163_022

group of children; b) research ethics as 'doing' children's rights; and d) ethnography as a tool for exploring children's lived rights. This chapter builds on my doctoral thesis where I further developed the concept children's *lived rights,*[5] and the discussion will here point to the potential of ethnographic fieldwork and participatory methods with children as fruitful approaches for conducting empirical explorations of rights as lived.

Scholars have argued that more attention should be given to explorations of children's experiences of their rights and have advocated empirical explorations of how rights are realized or denied in the political contexts where children lead their lives.[6] Interdisciplinary, child-centred explorations of children's rights could examine, for instance, how rights are understood through children's everyday concerns and everyday practices.[7] Childhood sociology is concerned with the conditions of childhood and the power relations in which children are entangled; both are important aspects to consider when examining how children's rights are respected in child-adult relations in various political contexts.[8]

Despite the advocacy for empirical explorations of children's rights, few studies have actually explored rights through children's perspectives. The research that does engage in empirical research on children's rights, and that has inspired my work, has relied on interviews.[9] While I have also taken inspiration from previous anthropological approaches to children's rights,[10] existing

5 Karlsson, S., *Children's lived rights: The everyday politics of asylum-seeking children* (Stockholm University, 2021).

6 Alanen, L., 'Taking children's rights seriously', *Childhood* 17, no. 1 (2010): 5–8; Mayall, B., 'The sociology of childhood in relation to children's rights', *The international journal of children's rights* 8, no. 3 (2000): 243–259.

7 Hanson, K., 'Killed by charity: Towards interdisciplinary children's rights studies', *Childhood* 21, no. 4 (2014): 441–446; Mayall, B. 'The sociology of childhood and children's rights'. In Vandenhole, W., Desmet, E., Reynaert, D. and Lembrechts, S. (Eds.) *Routledge international handbook of children's rights studies* (New York: Routledge, 2015): 77–93.

8 Alanen, L., 'Taking children's rights seriously', *Childhood* 17, no. 1 (2010): 5–8; Freeman, M., 'The sociology of childhood and children's rights', *The international journal of children's rights* 6, no. 4 (1998): 433–444. Mayall, B., 'The sociology of childhood and children's rights'. In Vandenhole, W., Desmet, E., Reynaert, D. and Lembrechts, S. (Eds.) *Routledge international handbook of children's rights studies* (New York: Routledge, 2015): 77–93; Reynaert, D., Bie, M.B. and Vandevelde, S., 'Between "believers" and "opponents": Critical discussions on children's rights', *International Journal of Children's Rights* 20, no. 1 (2012): 155–168.

9 C.f. Bhabha, J., 'Arendt's children: Do today's migrant children have a right to have rights?', *Human Rights Quarterly* 31, no. 2 (2009): 410–451; Lundberg, A., and Dahlquist, L., 'Unaccompanied children seeking asylum in Sweden: Living conditions from a child-centred perspective', *Refugee Survey Quarterly* 31, no. 2 (2012): 54–75.

10 Reynolds, P., Nieuwenhuys, O., and Hanson, K., 'Refractions of children's rights in development practice: A view from anthropology', *Childhood* 13, no. 3 (2006): 291–302.

research in this field of inquiry has tended to focus on childhoods in the majority world,[11] or a bottom-up approach to children's rights in the so-called 'developing world'.[12] This research field takes an interest in a child-centred approach to notions of rights and studies how international conventions may clash or coincide with local conceptions of rights. In particular, the question of child labour and objections to a Eurocentric understanding of rights has been discussed as a form of 'third-world resistance'.[13]

In this chapter, I respond to the call for a bottom-up and child-centred approach to research on children's rights, by exploring how rights are lived in an asylum context in a European society. The tension here lies between migration control and children's rights in a Swedish asylum context and how rights are lived from the perspectives of a particularly vulnerable group of children in Sweden. I argue that this approach is interesting owing to Sweden's expressions of pride in its protection of children's rights, despite that research has shown that Swedish asylum policies impinge on the rights of asylum-seeking children.[14]

11 Aitken, S.C., 'Children's rights: A critical geographic perspective'. In Vandenhole, W., Desmet, E., Reynaert, D. and Lembrechts, S., (Eds.), *Routledge international handbook of children's rights studies* (New York: Routledge, 2015): 131–146; Kallio, K.P., 'Desubjugating childhoods by listening to the child's voice and childhoods at play', *ACME* 11, no. 1 (2012): 81–109.; Kallio, K.P., Mills, S. and Skelton, T., (Eds.), *Politics, citizenship and rights* (Singapore: Springer Singapore, 2016): 189–205.

12 Hanson, K., and Nieuwenhuys, O., (Eds.) (2013); Liebel, M., *Children's rights from below: cross-cultural perspectives* (Basingstoke: Palgrave Macmillan, 2012); Reynaert, D., Bie, M.B. and Vandevelde, S. (2012).

13 Rajagopal, B., *International law from below: Development, social movements and Third World resistance* (Cambridge: Cambridge University Press, 2003); Hanson, K., and Nieuwenhuys, O., (Eds.) (2013); van Daalen, E., Hanson, K., and Nieuwenhuys, O., 'Children's Rights as Living Rights', *The International Journal of Children's Rights* 24, no. 4 (2016): 803–825; van Daalen, E., and Hanson, K., 'The ILO's Shifts in Child Labour Policy: Regulation and Abolition', *International Development Policy* 11 (2019):133–150; Reynolds, P., Nieuwenhuys, O., and Hanson, K., 'Refractions of children's rights in development practice: A view from anthropology', *Childhood* 13, no. 3 (2006): 291–302.

14 Lundberg, A., 'The best interests of the child principle in Swedish asylum cases: The marginalization of children's rights', *Journal of Human Rights Practice* 3, no. 1 (2011): 49–70; Ottosson, L., and Lundberg, A., '"People out of place"? Advocates negotiations on children's participation in the asylum application process in Sweden', *International Journal of Law, Policy and the Family* 27, no. 2 (2013): 266–287.

2 The Politics of Ethnography with a Marginalized Group of Children

Ethnography refers here to the study of children's everyday life through ethnographic fieldwork: 'being there' in the field with the children under study. It is also a theoretically informed methodology that analyses lived experiences on the basis of detailed observations.[15] Ethnography has been emphasized as a way to deepen the empirical insights into children's perspectives and understandings of their lived realities,[16] but the methods involved have rarely been used to explore children's rights.[17] Nonetheless, I argue that ethnographic fieldwork and child-centred methods developed in childhood studies are particularly useful for exploring children's rights. I argue moreover that critical or political ethnography is especially advantageous when exploring the life worlds of asylum-seeking children, as their rights must be understood in relation to their socio-legal position in the midst of asylum politics.[18] A political approach to ethnography entails a theoretically grounded analysis of the everyday politics that marginalized groups engage in and that do not necessarily take place openly in public spaces.[19] I have been particularly inspired by theoretical contributions to *children's everyday politics* and scholars who have advocated ethnographic research of children's *political matters of importance* in their everyday lives.[20] In line with other scholars in the field,[21] I argue that the research process cannot be understood as something located outside the relations of power that are built into the asylum system that regulates and controls children seeking asylum. In a similar vein, children's rights cannot be understood as located outside the relations and practices of research. My point here is that these implications

15 Fine, G. A., 'Towards a peopled ethnography: Developing theory from group life', *Ethnography* 4, no. 1 (2003): 41–60; Willis, P., and Trondman, M., 'Manifesto for ethnography', *Ethnography* 1, no. 1 (2000): 5–16.

16 James, A., 'Giving voice to children's voices: Practices and problems, pitfalls and potentials', *American Anthropologist* 109, no. 2 (2007): 261–272.

17 Brittle, R., and Desmet, E., 'Thirty Years of Research on Children's Rights in the Context of Migration', *The International Journal of Children's Rights* 28, no. 1 (2020): 36–65.

18 For a discussion on rights of children in vulnerability see Peleg, N., Introductory Note in this volume.

19 Schatz, E., 'Ethnographic immersions and the study of politics'. In Schatz, E. (Ed.), *Political ethnography: What immersion contributes to the study of power* (Chicago: University of Chicago Press, 2009).

20 Kallio, K.P. and Häkli, J., 'Are there politics in childhood?', *Space and Polity* 15, no. 1 (2011): 21–34.

21 White, A., and Bushin, N., 'More than methods: Learning from research with children seeking asylum in Ireland', *Population, Space and Place* 17, no. 4 (2011): 326–337.

necessitate the researcher's political commitment to the rights of the participating children throughout the research process.

3 Research Ethics as 'Doing' Children's Rights

My study has been informed by a rights-based approach to research with children.[22] In my view, adult researchers should acknowledge children as rights subjects because this has significant implications for the research process. Most importantly, it increases the likelihood that adult researchers will strive to respect children's rights in field relations and in the research process itself.[23] This approach also concerns children's participatory rights in research, aiming to give children more influence over the research process and the choice of methods.

I perceive an ethically informed research process as a very political project, which involves 'doing' children's rights relationally and not merely studying rights as a phenomenon outside the research process. Adult researchers engaging in research on children's rights should thus be committed to an ethically informed, rights-based methodology, where the researchers' view of and relational approach to children as rights subjects should permeate the whole research process.

My commitment to taking the children seriously as subjects with rights involved taking sides with the children. I argue that the political context in which the participating children were placed made it ethically problematic to take an objective stance to their rights. In my ethically informed interventions,[24] I chose for instance to defend and support the children when they were treated incorrectly or wrongfully accused by other adults in the field.

In my study, research *with* children as rights subjects also entailed being perceptive to the children's wishes regarding *when*, *where*, *how*, and *with whom* they wanted to share their experiences. Informed consent is a vital part of ethical guidelines for research involving children. In my study, both the parents

---

22 Bessell, S., 'Rights-Based Research with Children: Principles and Practice'. In Evans, R., and Holt, L., (Eds.), *Methodological approaches* (Singapore: Springer Singapore, 2017): 223–240; Lundy, L., and McEvoy L., 'Children's rights and research processes: Assisting children to (in)formed views', *Childhood* 19, no. 1 (2011): 129–144.

23 Skelton T., 'Research with children and young people: Exploring the tensions between ethics, competence and participation', *Children's Geographies* 6, no. 1 (2008): 21–36.

24 Cf. Dennis, B., 'What does it mean when an ethnographer intervenes?', *Ethnography and Education* 4, no. 2 (2009): 131–146.

and the children themselves 'signed' a consent form before participating in the research. The children were handed a piece of paper where they could write their name and specify whether they wanted to participate in the research by drawing a circle around 'yes' or 'no' or alternatively around a sad or happy smiley face. In addition, the children's consent was continually negotiated throughout the research process, even after the more formal consent at the outset of the study.

In comparison to formal consent, I perceive relationally negotiated consent as being intimately related to respecting the integrity of children. For my study, this entailed being particularly perceptive to the children's wishes expressed through their verbal communication, but also my attentiveness and responsiveness to their non-verbal communication when observing the children's body language or facial expressions. This meant that in the field, I chose not to intrude when a child did not greet me as they passed by or when a group of children turned their backs towards me; in addition, I always asked the children for permission before joining in activities or entering a room. Naturally, some children showed very clearly at times that they did not want to talk to me and, at one point, one child even ran away from me when I approached him. My ambition was thus to give the children influence over when, where, and how they wanted to interact with me, and I tried my best to respect their boundaries. My attentiveness to the children's non-verbal communication became even more crucial because at the start of the study as I did not share a common language with many of the children.

In addition to this relational approach to research ethics, a researcher is also obligated to follow certain ethical guideleines when engaging in research with children. However, the imperative to recognize children as rights subjects in research may be compromised at times by adultist research ethics.[25] In my research, my ambition was to respect children's participatory rights, but in the field, some of the children also made me pay attention to their means of claiming their right to participate on their own terms. For instance, my eagerness to follow the ethical guidelines sometimes meant that the children criticized me. One child in particular seemed to think that I was too anxious when trying to make sure I had received their informed consent. In the initial phase of the fieldwork, Enya protested against my overload of information and interrupted me: 'We've got it! This is the third time you've told us about your book!' Earlier, Enya had also criticized me for not giving her an information letter about the research project in her first language, as I had assumed (based on her skills in

25 For a further discussion on childism and adultism, see Adami, R., Chapter 6 in this volume.

Swedish) that a letter in Swedish would be sufficient. In the following days, she continously questioned me about the translation process and complained that it was taking too long. In this way, she claimed her right to participate and to be properly informed about the research project.

The children in my study claimed their right to participate in many ways that exceeded the adultist ethical guidelines. When I first informed the children about the research project, many of them shouted out, 'yes, you can talk to me!'; then they looked perplexed and some even protested loudly when I explained that I must first ask their parents before they could participate. The children clearly expressed their resistance to the notion that their desire to participate was not sufficient until their parents agreed to allow their participation.

In a way, this reveals how the recognition of children as rights subjects in research ethics can be compromised. This dilemma became even more evident when one child was very eager to participate in the research project, but his father did not consent to his son's participation. When this young child was excluded from engaging in the research methods together with the other children, he protested loudly and expressed his disappointment to me and to his father. I have chosen to interpret the children's critique and resistance as children's claims to their right to participation, but researchers sometimes fail to acknowledge children's participation when it is not performed as the researcher intended.[26]

In this section, I discussed matters involved in 'doing' children's rights as part of the research ethics process, and how children may claim their rights in relation to the researcher. In the next section, I introduce how I used ethnography as a tool for exploring children's lived rights in an asylum context.

4 Ethnography as a Tool for Exploring Children's Lived Rights

Over the course of my one-year ethnographic fieldwork project, I followed the children in their everyday spaces (the asylum centre and the school), spending three to four days a week, 8 am to 4 pm (and sometimes 6 pm) with them. I was with the children during all their school-day activities which meant playing with them in the schoolyard, eating with them in the canteen, and observing educational practices in the classrooms. I also accompanied the children during their physical education classes and other sports activities in the

26 Gallacher, L-A. and Gallagher, M., 'Methodological immaturity in childhood research?: Thinking through "participatory methods"', *Childhood* 15, no. 4 (2008): 499–516.

vicinity. At the asylum centre, I often visited the children and their families in their individual family rooms, but I spent most of my fieldwork time playing with the children in the asylum centre's communal areas and outside, mainly on the football pitch.

I thus explored children's perspectives by being present *with* the children – that is, by following them in their everyday spaces and engaging in their everyday practices. More specifically, I followed the children by playing, walking, and talking with them in their school and the asylum centre where they lived.

In my study, children's verbal 'voices' were elicited mainly through informal conversations and a variety of participatory methods.[27] These methods included visual methods, mappings, diaries, and worksheets with open-ended questions as well as open-ended sentence-starters. In these methods, the children could draw or write in a language of their choosing. In addition, a few children participated in somewhat semi-formal conversations, although this was generally not a preferred method for sharing their experiences with me. I also avoided formal interviews as they might remind children about the asylum interrogation at the Migration Agency.[28]

My questions in the task-based methods were sometimes inspired by certain themes on children's rights in the various UN General Comments. However, I avoided using formal rights language in my conversations with the children, as I deemed it unethical to introduce rights that these children were in fact denied; this sheds light on one of the ethical challenges in ethnographic research on the rights of marginalized children. In my study, therefore, I developed methods for studying rights, and ways of asking the children about the conditions for their rights as well as their expectations or aspirations, that could help me analyse their experiences from a child-rights perspective. This also meant that, as the children taught me which methods worked and which they preferred, I continually introduced and tried a range of methods throughout the project.

At the outset of the study, I introduced what I call a 'sun diagram' in which the children could fill in the sun's 'rays' with answers to the following question: 'What do you think children who have recently come to Sweden need to feel good?' I deliberately posed the question in a way that referred to newly

---

27 Christensen, P., and James, A., 'Researching children and childhood'. In Christensen, P. and James, A. (Eds.), *Research with children: Perspectives and practices* (London: Falmer Press, 2000): 1–9; Punch, S., 'Research with children: The same or different from research with adults?', *Childhood* 9, no. 3 (2002): 321–341.

28 Cf. Seeberg, M. L., Bagge, C., and Enger, T. A., 'No place: Small children in Norwegian asylum-seeker reception centre', *Childhood* 16, no. 3 (2009): 395–411.

arrived children in general, to avoid being too intrusive, while it also enabled me to identify what the children themselves considered to be important for their wellbeing. In this way, certain themes emerged that were important for the children, namely housing, play, and school. I perceive the arenas that the children identified as being closely linked to their social rights as stipulated by the CRC. In a similar method using a 'flower diagram', the children could write names on the leaves of a happy or a sad flower to identify how persons in their everyday spaces, mostly adults, treated them and made them feel.

The children's written material was also collected using various worksheet questionnaires with open-ended questions. The questionnaires enabled me to ask more detailed questions concerning the themes that I had previously identified as important for the children using task-based methods and field observations. Every questionnaire ended with an open section where the children could write more freely about what they saw as matters of importance. I adapted these methods depending on the children's literacy and, to allow inclusion of all the children, I developed questionnaires with open-ended sentence-starters, such as 'I feel good when …'. Later, I also used questionnaires where the youngest children could answer the questions by colouring smileys.

I also introduced diaries; for these, the children were given brief instructions, but the method was meant to enable the children to write more freely about their experiences. Each child was given a pencil and notebook, and these items were much appreciated, but they were used mainly for purposes other than those I had in mind. One child told me he had given the notebook to his father to use while studying Swedish, and two girls used the notebook for drawings. Children and adults in asylum contexts often have little access to pens and paper, which may explain why the materials that I provided for the research methods were used for other purposes.

Another method I used was mapping, which allowed me to explore the children's experiences of places and relations in them. The children were asked to attach smiley stickers with various colours, shapes, and facial expressions to the maps – showing a printed aerial photo of their local community – to indicate the places where they felt safe/unsafe; their favourite places; places they went during their free time; where their friends lived; and any 'no-go' places. The children were also asked to share their experiences of a particular place and explain why a certain place felt safe/unsafe. This method enabled analysis of children's access to different social spaces and relations from a rights perspective while also revealing the relational aspect of how their rights were realized in different spaces.

In addition to these task-based methods, I also engaged in walking tours when I accompanied the children from the school to the asylum centre. These walking tours created opportunities for talking with the children outside institutional settings; they were guided by the children themselves and enabled me to learn about the children's embodied attachments to and experiences of different places. During these walks, the children pointed out places that were important for their access or non-access to play in their local community. The walking tours also included the asylum centre where the children took me on tours through the indoor premises and the outdoor environment, and thus enabled me to learn from the children about the local politics at the asylum centre. For example, the children showed me prohibition signs at the centre and explained how the regulation worked. During these walking tours, I was also able to analyse the children's embodied affective reactions to different places and to adults that we encountered, such as reception staff members, the centre manager, and security guards.

Playing with the children turned out to be one of the most important ways of engaging in ethnographic participation in the children's lives. My participation in this activity was thus one of my primary ethnographic practices; it was also crucial to gaining the children's acceptance and learning from them about their lived worlds. This and all my other fieldwork methods generated data that helped me understand and analyse children's lived rights.

Ethnography entails an ongoing process of analysis while one is in the field and the interpretation of data allows the ethnographer to perform a more abstract analysis.[29] In my analytical work, I analysed the children's articulations and practices as well as their embodied affective expressions in relation to how I perceived the children's rights as embedded in the power relationships in their everyday spaces. My analysis thus considers how asylum-seeking children are positioned in the systems of power that are embedded in asylum politics and that create conditions for these children's rights, and how children navigate in these conditions.

My ethnography was theoretically informed by children's everyday politics,[30] and I specifically explore how, as revealed in children's voice and agency, rights become a political matter of importance for children in their everyday lives. I have analysed children's verbalizations as children's political articulations[31] and how these articulations revealed matters of rights. In this

29 Emerson, R. M., Fretz, R. I, and Shaw, L. L., *Writing ethnographic fieldnotes* (2nd edition). (Chicago: University of Chicago Press, 2011).

30 Kallio, K.P., and Häkli, J., (2011).

31 Mitchell, K., and Elwood, S., 'Mapping children's politics: The promise of articulation and the limits of nonrepresentational theory', *Environment and Planning D: Society and Space* 30, no. 5 (2012): 788–804.

way, I demonstrate how children's lived rights can be understood through children's critical articulations against being denied their rights.[32] In my analysis, these articulations revealed how the children identified and criticized conditions that denied them their rights. I was also able to analyse how their articulations revealed their expectations regarding conditions that would enhance their wellbeing. The children's articulations regarding wellbeing, for instance, revealed the importance of having a safe place to call home, having access to play, and having access to school.

When I asked the children about their experiences at the asylum centre, I could also identify the discrepancy between their expectations and their lived realities. I realized that the children's articulations revealed their ideas of right and wrong and noted with interest how their ideas coincided with their formal rights (e.g. the right to an adequate standard of living and housing;[33] the right to play; the right to school). The children would describe, for instance, how overcrowding limited their possibilities to find a place of their own in the family room where they could do homework or play without the intrusion of other family members or even other residents. Many children also talked about how they lacked opportunities for play or how their parents lacked access to facilities for cooking proper meals. Children's verbalizations also revealed how they were affected by not having access to school and the long wait to be assigned a school.

In their articulations, the children also described relational aspects of how their rights were respected – or violated – in adult-child relations. In particular, the children described the adult professionals at the asylum centre as 'very aggressive' or 'very scary' and said that the staff did not have a child-friendly attitude.[34] Children's lived rights claims concerned recognition – as revealed in their articulated critique against being treated in a non-child-friendly way by adults or being denied their rights when their treatment was based on their social position or legal status instead of their personhood.[35] Mohamed said:

32 Karlsson. S., '"You said 'home' but we don't have a house": Children's lived rights and politics in an asylum center in Sweden', *Children's Geographies* 17, no. 1 (2019a): 64–75.

33 For a discussion on children's right to an adequate standard of living, see Leviner, P. and Holappa, T., Chapter 2, this volume.

34 The children's experiences here relate to the discussion on childism and adultism by Adami, R., Chapter 6 in this volume.

35 Karlsson, S. (2021).

> I have been here one year and, so far, I've not gotten the rights I should have. The answer is always that we are too many. I thought I would have more rights in a land of freedom.

Mohamed's comment illustrates how people seeking asylum are sometimes talked about in terms of numbers instead of individuals. Many of the children also described experiences of disciplinary threats that entailed being relocated to less attractive housing or being sent away to 'the North', referring to the north of Sweden, which had been described to the children as a very cold, dark, and isolated place in Sweden.[36] I was also able to analyse the children's articulated emotions, such as their reports of being 'afraid' of the security guards at the asylum centre, as a way of understanding how the children were emotionally affected when their rights were denied in adult-child relations. Children's lived rights can thus be understood through the ways that children articulate emotions, which reveal how children are emotionally affected when their rights are restrained or denied.[37]

The children also criticized the prohibition on play at the asylum centre, and thus identified how their right to play was denied. However, despite prohibitions and fear of repurcussions, some children were innovative in seeking out hidden places to play. My engagement in their play enabled me to observe and analyse how, in their hidden practices, the children claimed spaces for play; I analysed these actions as children's spatial claims to their right to play.[38]

My participatory approach to ethnography with children also allowed me to gain an understanding of children's perspectives through their embodied and emotional experiences. In particular, my attention to children's *navigation*[39] in the asylum centre enabled firsthand observation of the children's experiences through their embodied and affective ways of expressing themselves. In this way, I could interpret the children's 'voices' through their affective reactions,

36 Karlsson. S., (2019a).

37 Karlsson, S., '"They cry, cry, they want to go to school": the micro-politics of articulated emotion and asylum-seeking children's sense of belonging in relation to the Swedish school', *Children and Society* 33, no. 5 (2019b): 429–442.

38 Karlsson, S., '"Do you know what we do when we want to play?": Children's hidden politics of resistance and struggle for play in a Swedish asylum center', *Childhood* 25, no. 3 (2018): 311–324.

39 Wood, B.E., 'Crafted within liminal spaces: Young people's everyday politics', *Political Geography* 31, no. 6 (2012): 337–346. De Certeau, M. *The practice of everyday life*. (University of California Press, 1984).

such as freezing, going silent, and changing their facial expressions, tone of voice, or bodily postures.[40]

It has been argued that children's non-verbal 'voices' and their silences can provide important insights into their experiences[41] and especially, perhaps, in asylum contexts.[42] In my analysis, the children's embodied and affective reactions became intrinsic for my understanding of their lived rights in this political context. I thus argue that one of the main advantages of an ethnography of children's lived rights is how it offers a way to observe and analyse children's affective and embodied reactions as entangled in the politics that restrain or deny them their rights.[43] When following the children as they navigated the asylum centre, I could observe their affective reactions when they encountered certain staff members and security guards, and how their embodied fear was revealed in bodily reactions such as freezing, turning silent, changing their facial expression, or shifting their gaze. My ethnography thus entailed emotional participation that prompted my attentiveness to the children's emotions.[44] My attention to the children's emotions and affect also increased my attentiveness to my own feelings in the field: in a way, *feeling with* the children and taking their fears seriously became an additional, important ethnographic research practice.

I have chosen to call the children's fears their *lived fears*[45] and I have analysed how both their articulations and these affective reactions may reveal that their rights were in fact denied in adult-child relations. In many ways, the children's feelings of fear involved not only their fear of deportation; indeed, these lived fears, entangled in their daily interactions, affected their everyday lives on many levels. I argue that this lived fear reveals how the children, in their uncertain positions as rights subjects, were deeply emotionally affected by relations and practices in a political context in which their rights were restricted or denied.

The children's fear of relocations as a result of threats from adults at the asylum centre was revealed in their play practices and shows how asylum

40 Cf. Kallio, K.P., 'Performative bodies, tactical agents and political selves: Rethinking the political geographies of childhood', *Space and Polity* 11, no. 2 (2007): 121–136.

41 Spyrou, S., 'Researching children's silences: Exploring the fullness of voice in childhood research', *Childhood* 23, no. 1 (2016): 7–21.

42 Kohli RKS., 'The sound of silence: Listening to what unaccompanied asylum-seeking children say and do not say', *British Journal of Social Work* 36, no. 5 (2006): 707–721.

43 Karlsson, S., (2019b).

44 Darling, J. 'Emotions, encounters and expectations: The uncertain ethics of "the field"', *Journal of Human Rights* 6, no. 2 (2014): 201–212.

45 Karlsson, S., (2021).

politics were entangled with the local politics at the centre. The children's uncertain position in these asylum politics weakened their possibility to claim their rights; this is exemplified by how one child expressed that she wanted better housing, but was scared she would be sent to even worse housing if she expressed such wishes. The children's fears meant that they engaged in hidden politics instead of confrontational politics with openly articulated rights claims.[46] The children instead channelled their critique or concerns through me, the researcher, behind the back of the institution that was denying them their rights.

Being with the children for a longer period of time helped me understand how asylum politics did indeed seep into their everyday lives and that these politics were entangled in the spatial politics of the asylum centre. It allowed me to explore the various ways that the children reacted to and criticized these conditions, and in some ways also claimed their rights. Children's lived rights were thus empirically understood through the politics that the children demonstrated in their articulations and acts of resistance, as well as the political aspects of their affect and emotion.[47] The children did not passively accept the asylum conditions for their rights. Instead, and in their own ways, they protested against discriminating practices and developed aspirations to have 'their right to have rights'.[48]

Ethnography became an important tool for understanding not only children's verbalized perspectives but also their emotional and affective experiences in this asylum context. My ethnographic fieldwork with children allowed me to perceive children's perspectives and experiences beyond children's verbalizations and introduced important ways of exploring children's rights without applying a formal rights language.

5 Conclusion

In this chapter, I introduce lived rights, as developed in my previous work, as an interdisciplinary approach for exploring children's rights in the political contexts where children lead their lives. I discuss methodological and ethical

46 Scott, J. *Domination and the Arts of Resistance: Hidden Transcripts.* (Yale University Press, 1992).

47 Ibid.

48 Arendt, H., *The origins of totalitarianism* (Schocken Books, 1951). For a discussion on children considered to have 'weak' relations to Sweden and their 'right to have rights', see Schiratzki, J., Chapter 1 in this volume.

considerations in explorations of children's rights when engaging in research with children, and in particular I discuss the ethical considerations involved in the process of 'doing' children's rights in fieldwork relations with marginalized children. I specifically argue for the necessity of respecting children's integrity and acknowledging children as rights subjects in fieldwork relations and the research process as a whole. I demonstrate, moreover, how children's agency and resistance in the research process can be particularly important to acknowledge in relation to their participatory rights. My reflections are based on how the children in my study repeatedly exercised their agency and claimed their right to information and participation on their own terms. The children recurrently questioned my approach when I followed the formal guidelines for research ethics; they constantly expressed their own ideas about their preferred methods, interrogated me about the questions I asked, and corrected me when I misunderstood something. Here, I mean that in a sense, the children claimed their participatory rights in the research process and questioned adultist research ethics.

My argument in this chapter builds on an advocacy for ethnography as a method for exploring children's rights as lived rights in the political contexts where children lead their lives. I have discussed in particular how ethnography became a tool for exploring asylum-seeking children's lived rights in a specific asylum context. I suggest that ethnography with children is a particularly fruitful method for exploring rights through children's lived experiences and that it may add important insights beyond policy-level research or even interview studies with children. In addition to describing children's verbalized critique of denial of rights, I have underscored the importance of listening to children's non-verbal, embodied expressions. In my work, this meant exploring children's navigation at an asylum centre to analyse how their voice and agency revealed the relational and spatial dimension of their rights. I have discussed in particular how ethnography enabled analytical attention to children's emotional and affective ways of expressing themselves and how, in my work, this became pivotal for understanding asylum-seeking children's embodied, lived fears as intrinsic to their lived rights. I argue that children's agency and voice – both verbal and non-verbal – are crucial for understanding the realization of children's rights in their lived forms. While this chapter focuses on children's lived rights in an asylum context, I argue that the theorization and methodology that I have developed as a way to understand rights as lived can also be fruitful in exploring the lived experiences of other marginalized groups from a rights perspective.

References

Ahmed, Sara. 2014. *The cultural politics of emotion* (2nd ed.). Edinburgh: Edinburgh University Press.

Aitken, Stuart. 2015. "Children's rights: A critical geographic perspective", in Wouter Vandenhole, Ellen Desmet, Dider Reynaert, and Sara Lembrechts (Eds.), *Routledge international handbook of children's rights studies*, 131–146. New York: Routledge.

Alanen, Leena. 2010. "Editorial: Taking children's rights seriously", *Childhood* 17(1): 5–8.

Arendt, Hannah. 1951. *The origins of totalitarianism*. Schocken Books.

Bessell, Sharon. 2017. "Rights-Based Research with Children: Principles and Practice", in Ruth Evans, and Louise Holt (Eds.), *Methodological approaches*, 223–240. Singapore: Springer Singapore.

Bhabha, Jaqueline. 2009. "Arendt's children: Do today's migrant children have a right to have rights?", *Human Rights Quarterly* 31(2): 410–451.

Brittle, Ruth, and Ellen Desmet. 2020. "Thirty Years of Research on Children's Rights in the Context of Migration", *The International Journal of Children's Rights* 28(1): 36–65.

Christensen, Pia, and Allison James. 2000. "Researching children and childhood", in Pia Christensen, and Allison James (Eds.) *Research with children: Perspectives and practices*, 1–9. London: Falmer Press.

Darling, Jonathan. 2014. "Emotions, encounters and expectations: The uncertain ethics of 'the field'", Journal of Human Rights 6(2): 201–212.

De Certeau, Michel. 1984. *The practice of everyday life*. California: University of California Press.

Dennis, Barbara. 2009. "What does it mean when an ethnographer intervenes?", *Ethnography and Education* 4(2): 131–146.

Elsrud, Torun, Sabine Gruber, and Anna Lundberg. (Eds.). 2021. *Rättssäkerheten och solidariteten: Vad hände? En antologi om mottagande av människor på flykt*. Linköping: Linköping University Electronic Press.

Emerson, Robert, Rachel Fretz, and Linda Shaw. 2011. *Writing ethnographic fieldnotes*. (2nd ed.). Chicago: University of Chicago Press.

Fine, Gary Alan. 2003. "Towards a peopled ethnography: Developing theory from group life", *Ethnography* 4(1): 41–60.

Freeman, Michael. 1998. "The sociology of childhood and children's rights", *The international journal of children's rights* 6(4): 433–444.

Gallacher, Leslie-Anne, and Michael Gallagher. 2008. "Methodological immaturity in childhood research?: Thinking through 'participatory methods'", *Childhood* 15(4): 499–516.

Hanson, Karl, and Olga Nieuwenhuys (Eds.). 2013. *Reconceptualizing children's rights in international development: Living rights, social justice, translations*. Cambridge: Cambridge University Press.

James, Allison. 2007. "Giving voice to children's voices: Practices and problems, pitfalls and potentials", *American Anthropologist* 109(2): 261–272.

Kallio, Kirsi Pauliina. 2007. "Performative bodies, tactical agents and political selves: Rethinking the political geographies of childhood", *Space and Polity,* 11(2): 121–136.

Kallio, Kirsi Pauliina. 2012. "Desubjugating childhoods by listening to the child's voice and childhoods at play", *ACME* 11(1): 81–109.

Kallio, Kirsi Pauliina, and Jouni Häkli. 2011. "Are there politics in childhood?", *Space and Polity* 15(1): 21–34.

Kallio, Kirsi Pauliina, and Sarah Mills. 2016. "Editorial: Geographies of children and young people's politics, citizenship and rights", in Kirsi Pauliina Kallio, Sarah Mills, and Tracey Skelton (Eds.), *Politics, citizenship and rights*, 189–205. Singapore: Springer Singapore.

Karlsson, Sandra. 2018. "'Do you know what we do when we want to play?': Children's hidden politics of resistance and struggle for play in a Swedish asylum centre", *Childhood* 25(3): 311–324.

Karlsson, Sandra. 2019a. "'You said 'home' but we don't have a house': Children's lived rights and politics in an asylum centre in Sweden", *Children's Geographies* 17(1): 64–75.

Karlsson, Sandra. 2019b. "'They cry, cry, they want to go to school': The micro-politics of articulated emotion and asylum-seeking children's sense of belonging in relation to the Swedish school", *Children and Society* 33(5): 429–442.

Karlsson, Sandra. 2021. *Children's lived rights: The everyday politics of asylum-seeking children*. PhD dissertation. Stockholm: Stockholm University Press.

Kohli, Ravi KS. 2006. "The sound of silence: Listening to what unaccompanied asylum-seeking children say and do not say", *British Journal of Social Work* 36(5): 707–721.

Liebel, Manfred. 2012. *Children's rights from below: Cross-cultural perspectives*. Basingstoke: Palgrave Macmillan.

Lundberg, Anna. 2011. "The best interests of the child principle in Swedish asylum cases: The marginalization of children's rights", *Journal of Human Rights Practice* 3(1): 49–70.

Lundberg, Anna. 2018. "Management of 'the unaccompanied': In search of a rights-based approach in the context of Swedish 'crisis politics'", in Jaqueline Bhabha, Jyothi Kanics, and Daniel Senovilla Hernàndez (Eds.), *Research handbook on child migration*, 260–278. Cheltenham: Edward Elgar Publishing.

Lundberg, Anna, and Lisa Dahlquist. 2012. "Unaccompanied children seeking asylum in Sweden: Living conditions from a child-centred perspective", *Refugee Survey Quarterly* 31(2): 54–75.

Lundy, Laura, and Lesley McEvoy. 2011. "Children's rights and research processes: Assisting children to (in)formed views", *Childhood* 19(1): 129–144.

Mayall, Berry. 2000. "The sociology of childhood in relation to children's rights", *The international journal of children's rights* 8(3): 243–259.

Mayall, Berry. 2015. "The sociology of childhood and children's rights", in Wouter Vandenhole, Ellen Desmet, Didier Reynaert, and Sara Lembrechts (Eds.), *Routledge international handbook of children's rights studies*, 77–93. New York: Routledge.

Mitchell, Katahryne, and Sarah Elwood. 2012. "Mapping children's politics: The promise of articulation and the limits of nonrepresentational theory", *Environment and Planning D: Society and Space* 30(5): 788–804.

Ottosson, Lisa, and Anna Lundberg. 2013. "'People out of place'? Advocates' negotiations on children's participation in the asylum application process in Sweden", *International Journal of Law, Policy and the Family* 27(2): 266–287.

Punch, Samantha. 2002. "Research with children: The same or different from research with adults?", *Childhood* 9(3): 321–341.

Quennerstedt, Ann. 2013. "Children's rights research moving into the future: Challenges on the way forward", *International Journal of Children's Rights* 21(2): 233–247.

Rajagopal, Balakrishnan. 2003. *International law from below: Development, social movements and Third World resistance*. Cambridge: Cambridge University Press.

Reynaert, Didier, Maria Bouverne-De Bie, and Stijn Vandevelde. 2012. "Between 'believers' and 'opponents': Critical discussions on children's rights", *International Journal of Children's Rights* 20(1): 155–168.

Reynolds, Pamela, Olga Nieuwenhuys, and Karl Hanson. 2006. "Refractions of children's rights in development practice: A view from anthropology – Introduction", *Childhood* 13(3): 291–302.

Schatz, Edward. 2009. "Ethnographic immersions and the study of politics", in Edward Schatz (Ed.), *Political ethnography: What immersion contributes to the study of power* (1–22). Chicago: University of Chicago Press.

Seeberg, Marie Louise, Cecilie Bagge, and Truls Andre Enger. 2009. "No place: Small children in Norwegian asylum-seeker reception centre", *Childhood* 16(3): 395–411.

Skelton, Tracey. 2008. "Research with children and young people: Exploring the tensions between ethics, competence and participation", *Children's Geographies* 6(1): 21–36.

Spyrou, Spyros. 2016. "Researching children's silences: Exploring the fullness of voice in childhood research", *Childhood* 23(1): 7–21.

Swedish Migration Agency. 2016. "Statistik: Inkomna asylärenden" https://www.migrationsverket.se/Om-Migrationsverket/Statistik.html.

van Daalen, Edward, and Karl Hanson. 2019. "The ILO's Shifts in Child Labour Policy: Regulation and Abolition", *International Development Policy* 11: 133–150.

van Daalen, Edward, Karl Hanson, and Olga Nieuwenhuys. 2016. "Children's Rights as Living Rights", *The International Journal of Children's Rights* 24(4): 803–825.

White, Allen, and Naomi Bushin. 2011. "More than methods: Learning from research with children seeking asylum in Ireland", *Population, Space and Place* 17(4): 326–337.

Willis, Paul, and Mats Trondman. 2000. "Manifesto for ethnography", *Ethnography* 1(1): 5–16.

Wood, Bronwyn. 2012. "Crafted within liminal spaces: Young peoples' everyday politics", *Political Geography* 31(6): 337–346.

A Response to Sandra Karlsson

Johanna Schiratzki

Research on children's rights within human sciences is rich in research perspectives and methods. Research methods include quantitative methods as well as qualitative and mixed methods. Within qualitative research, research methods on children's rights range from archive studies, legal science analysis and other document analysis to first-hand observations, interviews, and participatory approaches. Each method has its advantages and drawbacks, and a researcher's choice of method will depend on the discipline and the questions to be explored.

An issue common to all areas of human sciences is how to include the views of the research subjects – in this context, the children's own views – in research (and practice) while neither victimizing nor patronizing these children. This fundamental challenge is explored by Sandra Karlsson.

A starting point is the quest for empirical knowledge on children's rights on not only a policy level but in their everyday lives. Yet another point of departure (although this approach is not spelled out in Karlsson's chapter) is that the more vulnerable the child is, the more crucial the legal rights the child could invoke. For asylum-seeking children in Sweden, the CRC is important owing to its influence on legislation as well as its application in individual cases. Karlsson points to yet another aspect of children's rights: how to understand ways in which children identify themselves and claim their rights. She discusses the concept of children's '*lived* rights'.

In her ethnographic research on children's lived rights, Sandra Karlsson has chosen a participatory method. This choice is inspired by an ambition to give children more influence in the research process. During her year of fieldwork with asylum-seeking children aged six to twelve, Karlsson participated in the children's lives by walking, talking, and playing with them.

Through this method, she detects children's critical articulation of what is being denied them, their claims for recognition, and their critique of being treated according to social position instead of personhood. Her observations are focused on interpreting body language, affective reactions, facial expressions, and bodily postures as well as verbal expressions. The research method includes an analysis of what children express through their fears, children's perceived aggressiveness, and how Karlsson's notion of 'lived fear,' affects children's 'lived rights'.

 | DOI:10.1163/9789004511163_023

Among the challenges associated with participatory methods – and recognizable from other face-to-face research methods – are power asymmetries. Within Childhood Studies, the asymmetry in child-adult relations is added to the more generally recognized asymmetry between the researcher and the informants. One way to reduce this asymmetry and enhance research subjects' integrity is to ensure secrecy as to the identity of the research person and the provision of informed consent. In Karlsson's research on asylum-seeking children, participating children's verbal consent was continually renegotiated, in addition to the parents' written consent.

Sandra Karlsson continues by discussing how she made a 'decision to take sides with the children' as a way to respect their integrity during her fieldwork. As with all good intentions, it is interesting to explore possible drawbacks of this approach. One such drawback could be that the children might develop increased expectations on the researcher's ability to enhance their lived rights. Another (at least theoretical) downside could be the researcher's possible tendency to take sides not only with the child, but against key persons in the child's life, such as parents or siblings. Karlsson approaches some of these challenges in her description of how a child who was excluded from the research project, because his parent(s) did not provide consent, was eager to be included in a play-like phase of the fieldwork. As a result of the child's expressed wishes to be part of the research, he was included in the group of children that wrote and drew with the researcher, and the non-consenting parent was informed afterwards.

To me, this dilemma takes us back to the fundamental power asymmetry between researcher and research subjects – children and adults alike. I wonder how the integrity and vulnerability of the asylum-seeking child as well as the parents and the family as a whole should be regarded. This issue in turn mirrors the crucial question: who is best positioned to determine what is in the best interests of the child – the child, the parents, or the professional decision-maker or the researcher.

Index

www.ingramcontent.com/pod-product-compliance
Lightning Source LLC
Chambersburg PA
CBHW071226230926
51849CB00001B/40
* 9 7 8 9 0 0 4 5 1 1 1 5 6 *